Southern Africa

The Escalation of a Conflict

SIPRI
Stockholm International Peace Research Institute

SIPRI is an independent institute for research into problems of peace and conflict, with particular attention to disarmament and arms regulation. It was established in 1966 to commemorate Sweden's 150 years of unbroken peace.

The Institute is financed by the Swedish Parliament. The staff, the Governing Board and the Scientific Council are international. As a consultative body, the Scientific Council is not responsible for the views expressed in the publications of the Institute.

Governing board

SIPRI

Stockholm International Peace Research Institute

Sveavägen 166, S-113 46 Stockholm, Sweden
Cables: Peaceresearch, Stockholm
Telephone: 08-15 09 40

Southern Africa
The Escalation of a Conflict

A politico-military study

SIPRI

Stockholm International Peace Research Institute

Praeger Publishers
New York and
London

Almqvist & Wiksell
International
Stockholm

Copyright © 1976 by SIPRI
Sveavägen 166
S-113 46 Stockholm, Sweden

First published by the
Stockholm International Peace Research Institute
in cooperation with
Almqvist & Wiksell International
26 Gamla Brogatan, S-111 20 Stockholm
and
Praeger Publishers
111 Fourth Avenue
New York, NY 10003

ISBN 91-2200051-8

Library of Congress Catalog Card Number:
76-4518

Printed in Sweden by
Almqvist & Wiksell, Uppsala 1976

CONTENTS

TABLES, CHARTS AND PLATES

Preface

This study describes the conflict in Southern Africa between the black peoples and the white ruling class. It was carried out between the beginning of 1973 and February 1975. The military coup in Portugal in 1974 brought an end to Portuguese colonial rule in Africa and led to a situation in which Rhodesia, South Africa and South African-ruled Namibia remain the sole white-ruled states in the area—and also on the entire African continent, the sole exceptions being the two territories of Spanish Sahara and French Somaliland.

This study covers the former Portuguese colonies of Guinea-Bissau, Angola and Mozambique, Rhodesia, the Republic of South Africa and Namibia. The role of Portugal in Africa is discussed in connection with the changing balance of power in the area, brought about by the independence of the former Portuguese colonies.

The strategic importance to the West of the Republic of South Africa is investigated. This is related to the access to raw materials such as gold and uranium, important to the world economy, to the possible need to safeguard the sea-route around the Cape of Good Hope and to the possible future great power arms race in the Indian Ocean. The arms build-up in South Africa since 1960 is discussed in a separate section, which also deals with the country's achievements in the mastering of nuclear technology.

This is no conventional conflict study insofar as no attempts are made to provide "conflict solutions" or present a systematic collection of "future scenarios". The emphasis has been on providing a factual account of the prevailing social and political conditions, including the mobilisation of the black peoples that led to the wars in Portuguese Africa, and that are at work at present in the white-ruled South. The military capability of the countries involved, as well as the possibility of foreign interests in the future of these states are of utmost importance to an assessment of the outcome of the present struggle in Southern Africa.

This study attempts to illustrate that there is no single cause of war: the resort to armed warfare depends on a combination of many factors at work simultaneously. At one point in the historical development of a given conflict a limit is reached from where there is no return to reformist methods.

The escalation of the conflict has not yet reached this perceived point of no return in the remaining white-ruled states in Southern Africa. In Part IV the impact of the change of regime in Portugal on Rhodesia and South Africa is investigated, with the aim of seeing whether the new situation north of the Zambezi is likely to lead to concessions on the part of the white regimes or to an escalation of military and other measures to preserve the *status quo* in these countries.

To predict the future on a scientific basis is almost impossible in the social sciences. The coup in Portugal is a good illustration of this, catching as it did practically the entire world community unprepared. This study stops short of definite predictions, and merely outlines more or less likely developments.

One major question, to which there is no easy answer, remains whether a future war in Southern Africa—such as the current civil war in Angola— might escalate into an international war. For this reason, the situation in this area calls for international attention. The 30-year Viet-Nam War started as a minor civil war between the North and the French-occupied South of the country. The lessons of this experience should not be forgotten.

Many persons have been very helpful in commenting on the manuscript of this study, in particular: Ulrich Albrecht (Freie Universität Berlin), Zdenek Červenka (The Scandinavian Institute of African Studies, Uppsala), the British writer Basil Davidson, Asbjörn Eide (PRIO, Oslo), Peter Lock (Vereinigung Deutscher Wissenschaftler, Hamburg), Abdul Minty (The Anti-Apartheid Movement, London).

The book was written by Signe Landgren-Bäckström, a member of the SIPRI research staff.

January 1976

Frank Barnaby
Director

Introduction

Square-bracketed references, thus [1], *refer to the list of references on page 24.*

This study describes the political and military conflict taking place in Southern Africa between a majority of the African population and the white minority regimes, with particular reference to the arms build-up in the Republic of South Africa since 1960. The units of analysis are the six nations and territories directly involved: Namibia, the Republic of South Africa, and Rhodesia, the former Portuguese colonies of Angola and Mozambique in Southern Africa, and one country in West Africa—Guinea-Bissau—which has been included for political rather than geographical reasons. The remaining nations in Southern Africa—Botswana, Lesotho, Malawi, Swaziland, Tanzania, Zaire and Zambia—are discussed only in terms of their relations to the countries in conflict.

Because of its past importance as a colonial power in Africa and the implications of its relinquishment of this role, Portugal is also included. The change of regime in Portugal in April 1974 resulted in a dramatic shift in the balance of power in Southern Africa. Before that date the Portuguese armed forces in Africa supported and defended white supremacy in the area. But after the ousting of the Caetano regime it became apparent that Portugal would withdraw from Africa. Now that Angola and Mozambique are becoming independent nations under African regimes, Rhodesia and the Republic of South Africa will be the only white minority-ruled states left in the African continent.

The central issue examined in this survey is whether or not the conflict in Southern Africa is likely to escalate into a regional or global war involving external powers. The aim is to present the facts to enable an appraisal of this issue to be made. The approach is strictly empirical.

The purpose of the study is not to present solutions to the problems facing Southern Africa nor to create any conflict theory. The intention is rather to provide material relevant to an evaluation of *conflict determinants*—the combination of factors that may be decisive in a situation where a local or limited political and military conflict, such as that occurring in Southern Africa, threatens to escalate into general war.

An effort has been made to distinguish a common pattern of conflict in the countries concerned in order to provide the basis for predictions of possible future developments—with the proviso, of course, that the social sciences do not often lend themselves to prediction.

It is hoped that much of the information given here will be of value in future research. Many underdeveloped areas may experience a similar type of confrontation—between a majority of the population, living under subsistence economic conditions, and a ruling minority determined to maintain the *status quo*. A comparison of conflict determinants could also be made in these cases. Where a similar type of confrontation fails to occur, it may nevertheless be possible to distinguish the factors that have prevented it. No such comparison will be attempted here, however, because this study deals exclusively with Southern Africa.

In popular language, the struggle in Southern Africa could be described as a conflict between the "haves" and the "have-nots". It could also be cited as an example of what Dom Helder Camara, Archbishop of Recife in Brazil, has called the ongoing Third World War—the war between the rich and the poor. The unique feature of the essentially political conflict developing in Southern Africa, however, is the issue of *race*.[1] The white populations in all the countries concerned enjoy wide-ranging privileges that have been denied to Africans by law, as, for example, in the Republic of South Africa, or by custom in other areas. The Africans have become a deprived people, while the white populations have become the political and economic elite. This has not come about by historical accident, but as a definite result of expansion on the part of the European colonial powers which began several centuries ago. This does not mean that a similar pattern does *not* prevail in other areas of the world, but it is in Southern Africa that the white-black pattern corresponds in the most clear-cut way to the rich-poor situation.

I. *The framework of analysis*

An underlying assumption in this study is that the arms build-up in Southern Africa is a function of the growing conflict between the African population and the white minority regimes. The concept of an "arms race" implies a

---

[1] In the terminology relating to race, "white" is used for the white regimes and population. "African" refers to black African regimes or population and is employed alternatively with "black African" or "independent African".

Officially, South Africa divides its population into groups: Whites, Indians, Coloureds and Bantu. Coloureds refers to persons of mixed origin, sometimes also called Cape Africans—the majority live in the Cape Province. Persons of Asian descent other than Indian, such as those of Malay origin, are also classified as Coloured. Bantu refers to black Africans. (The word Bantu is actually the name of the largest African language group.)

It is fully recognized that the white South Africans or Mozambique-born Portuguese are *geographically* Africans and not Europeans, despite the fact that "European" is often used synonymously with "white" in the countries concerned. But this study focusses on race rather than on geographical origin.

The term "liberation movement" is used throughout for the militant, organized African opposition engaged in guerilla warfare against white rule in the countries concerned. The term "guerilla armies" refers to such movements. The movements concerned are listed in the area descriptions in section V.

The terms "Eastern" and "Western" powers are used synonymously with Communist and capitalist powers, reflecting the competing socioeconomic systems rather than geographic location.

2

certain balance of strength between the opponents in a conflict. No such balance exists in Southern Africa where, by any standards of measurement, the Republic of South Africa is the leading military power. Nevertheless, modern, sophisticated—and expensive—weapons are now also being acquired by underdeveloped and poor nations in the region, such as Zambia and Tanzania, and by the guerilla armies. It can, therefore, be said that an arms race has begun.

A number of basic ideas[2] have been investigated in this study.

The first is that the unresponsiveness of established political systems is one major determinant of the escalation of this type of confrontation. This has been illustrated by the history of armed revolution in Portuguese Africa and by present developments in Namibia, Rhodesia and South Africa. This idea appears to be supported by the history of armed revolutions in general, as well as by some non-revolutionary advances of the working classes —such as, for example, the labour movements in Scandinavia, where after World War I, the established systems proved to be responsive rather than intransigent.

The second is that the Republic of South Africa is not only the leading military power in the area, but is, in all respects, the decisive factor in the region. Such vital international issues as the question of non-African strategic interests in safeguarding the Cape Route—particularly for oil transportation to Europe—and great-power rivalry in the Indian Ocean are related to South Africa's key position. Foreign interests in the natural resources of the region will also influence future developments.

The third is that weapons are ultimately produced, bought or sold for use in war, with no guarantees that they will be used solely for defence against external aggression, even though every government, including that of the Republic of South Africa, claims that "defence" is the purpose of an arms build-up.

These issues raise some fundamental research questions: (a) What are the conflict determinants and can the same or similar factors be found in each country covered here? (b) Is a common pattern of conflict escalation discernible? (c) How has the coup in Portugal changed the balance of power in the area? and (d) Will there be in the future a more general war in Southern Africa, or is it possible to distinguish factors indicating a possible peaceful solution?

The concept of a "peaceful solution" as it is used here differs from that commonly applied in peace and conflict research. In this study "peaceful solution" is related to a "system response": namely, that the representatives of an established political system—for example, in Rhodesia—will indicate their willingness to consider the demands of the African population, thus allowing a *de facto* bargaining procedure, yielding some *de facto*

---

[2] The following ideas or assumptions are *not* to be regarded as *hypotheses* nor as theoretical assumptions that will be proved.

results. Obviously, the appearance of a system response in a given situation can divert or prevent a conflict from escalating into a war.

The question has also been examined of whether a future general war in Southern Africa would remain local or, as often claimed, develop into an international confrontation similar to the war in Viet-Nam.

The conclusions are summarized in Part IV as *assessments*—in terms of probabilities, not certainties.

In order to arrive at these assessments, an area survey covering both the conflict development and the structure of the military establishments, with particular reference to the Republic of South Africa, was found necessary. Such a survey has the advantage of presenting an overall picture based on something more than intuition and covering more than one aspect of the situation in Southern Africa. Many excellent studies have already been made, dealing exclusively with the military strength of one or several countries or with political developments in the individual countries or the area as a whole. The advantage of these studies lies in the richness of detail resulting from thorough historical research. An area survey of the kind undertaken in the present volume provides, on the other hand, a broad perspective and tends to stress similarities between nations rather than the unique features of any one nation.

II. *Sources and methods*

The sources used for this study are material from the world press, books, parliamentary reports and other official documents. The sources of military data for Portugal, Rhodesia and South Africa are the SIPRI arms trade and production registers. First published in the *SIPRI Yearbook of World Armaments and Disarmament 1968/69,* these registers are based on a wide variety of published material—including, for example, 30 daily newspapers and 250 technical journals and periodicals from different parts of the world. Specific sources of information for a given weapon transfer or production item will be supplied on request. The general method used in deciding whether or not to include a given weapon in the registers has been to evaluate the comparative reliability of—preferably—a large number of independent sources of the same information.

Many sources of information on Southern Africa are partisan, and many statements made by them cannot be taken at face value. However, even when using partisan sources, it is possible to uphold standards of objectivity. The arguments and actions of both sides can be carefully studied to ensure that no material is excluded, especially when such material runs contrary to the researchers' preferences. Further, without trying to prove an argument "right" in an absolute sense—an impossibility in any case in the field of political science—it is always possible to compare the statements in an argument with what takes place in reality. For example, if South African authorities claim that Chinese army engineers built the Tanzanian railway in order to prepare for a guerilla war in Africa, and if this idea cannot be corroborated from any other source, the argument is judged to be weak. Any argument can be investigated for logic, consistency and contradictions.

A large number of partisan sources can, in fact, be highly useful for evaluating information. If, for example, the Movimento Popular de Libertação de Angola (MPLA) claims to be the leading nationalist movement in that country, the statement alone hardly merits acceptance as a fact. But if a report also appears from the enemy (in this case, the Portuguese secret police) attributing most of the military activity in Angola to the MPLA, the statement can be regarded as having received some corroboration.

Objectivity in research is especially difficult to claim when a political conflict is being studied. Speaking on objectivity, Amilcar Cabral, the late leader of the PAIGC (Partido Africano da Independência da Guiné e Cabo Verde) in Guinea-Bissau, made the following observation about the efforts of the British writer Basil Davidson to awaken public and governmental opinion to what was happening in Portuguese Africa:

But Europe, Cartesian and overdeveloped, demands the most objective objectivity wherever there is war: the wounds and the corpses . . . How will he [Davidson] possibly convince his fellow countrymen, those phlegmatic British, that distrustful Europe, that so respectable *Times,* that so well-informed opinion, unless there are corpses duly named and noted, bombs with labels of origin, a napalm case with due degree of injury? Thanks, therefore, to those criminal airmen of Portugal who came in the time of your visit [1a].

The analysis in this study has been made at the level of political and military events, including, to a lesser degree, what may be called "verbal events" (official statements, statements by individuals and the like) in the countries concerned. Thus, inferences about intentions are drawn from conduct and less from programmatic statements. This means, for example, that the economic conditions in the Bantustans (black settlement areas) in South Africa are regarded as "hard facts"; but the government's statements about the viable future of the Bantustans are not necessarily accorded the same weight. More confidence is placed in arguments and statements which appear to be consistent with observable "hard facts".

Finally, it should be pointed out that certain value judgments underlie this as well as any other conflict study.[3] The main value judgment here is that the United Nations declaration of human rights provides a better and more viable ideal for a nation's internal policy than, for example, the ideology of

[3] For a discussion of objectivity in social science and the question of value-free social science research, see, for example, Gunnar Myrdal's *Asian Drama* [16]. Professor Myrdal concludes that there is no such thing as a value-free social science.

apartheid. Further, it is held that wealth should be distributed for the benefit of the majority in any given population, and political power shared on a majority basis. Integrity demands of the investigator that he strive to cover all kinds of information sources, to take all arguments seriously, and to analyse them all on an equal basis. This has been attempted here and must suffice to justify the claim of objectivity in this type of study.

III. *The choice of Southern Africa*

Since the Sharpeville massacre in South Africa in 1960, international attention has become increasingly focussed on Southern Africa. The wars in Portuguese Africa began in 1961. Guerilla attacks have occurred in Rhodesia since 1965 and in Namibia since 1966. During the height of the Viet-Nam War, world attention waned, but since 1970 the situation in Southern Africa has aroused increasing attention in international forums like the UN, in the mass media, among scholars[4] and the general public.

Before 1961, wars in Africa remained limited in time and scope, despite such international involvement as occurred in the Congo in the early 1960s. The Mau-Mau uprising in Kenya, the civil war in Nigeria and the Rwanda-Burundi confrontations were generally regarded as examples of tribalism or secessionism, lacking major interest or consequences for powers outside Africa.

But the outbreak of armed warfare in Angola, Guinea-Bissau and Mozambique brought a new type of war to Sub-Saharan Africa, with implications for the entire continent. A time of decision had arrived when choices had to be made for or against Portuguese colonial rule in the first place, and then for or against the white-minority regimes of Rhodesia and South Africa. The sole precedent for this type of war on the African continent was, in fact, the Algerian liberation war. The opposing parties in these hitherto separate struggles share one point of view: that this is essentially one and the same conflict, despite unique features in each territory. This is because what is ultimately at stake in all the countries concerned is the elimination of white supremacy. The "domino theory", virtually rejected in the context of the United States' commitments in South East Asia, seems to be accepted without question inside and outside Southern Africa: if Guinea-Bissau "falls", Mozambique will "fall"; if Mozambique "falls", Rhodesia will "fall", and so on. To the ruling whites, this is a frightening possibility; to the African, it presages hope.

---

[4] Paradoxically, the academic world has sometimes seen Africa as a continent with a region-wide low level of military expenditure, low-level great-power interest, and even as a continent suitable for some regional arms reduction measures. See, for example, reference [17].

IV. *International organizations and Southern Africa*

Before World War II, there were only three independent states in Africa: Ethiopia, Liberia and the Union of South Africa. In 1956 there were only nine independent states in Africa that were also members of the United Nations. By 1963 this number had increased to 35. Following the liberation of Algeria from French rule, the uprising in Angola and the civil war in the Congo, these newly independent states created a forum for African influence over African affairs, the *Organization of African Unity* (OAU). The OAU was established in 1963 for the purpose of freeing the entire African continent from colonialism and white rule. A Liberation Committee was simultaneously created to channel military and other material aid to African liberation movements in contested territories.

For a brief period, another African organization existed which had the more limited purpose of uniting the liberation movements in the Portuguese colonies. This was the *Conferência das Organizações Nacionalistas das Colónias Portuguêsas* (CONCP), which was established in Rabat, Morocco in 1961. Its Secretary-General was a Mozambican, Marcelinho dos Santos, one of the future leading members of the *Frente de Libertação de Moçambique* (FRELIMO). After a few years CONCP ceased to function. Although it was revived in Dar es Salaam in Tanzania in 1965, CONCP has never played a military role.

The *United Nations* has been concerned with various aspects of problems in Southern Africa since 1946, when India complained that South Africa had enacted discriminatory legislation against South Africans of Indian origin. The apartheid question was placed on the agenda of the UN General Assembly in 1952, where it has remained a smouldering issue. Since 1960, the question of racial conflict in Southern Africa has been before the UN Security Council, as can be seen from the following selection of resolutions:

1 April 1960: Resolution 134, stating that if the situation in South Africa following the Sharpeville massacre continues, international peace and security might be endangered.

31 July 1963: Resolution 180, calling upon UN member states to prevent the sale and supply of arms for use by Portugal in its African territories.

7 August 1963: Resolution 181, calling for an international arms embargo on South Africa.

4 December 1963: Resolution 182, extending the arms embargo on South Africa to cover military know-how and equipment for the manufacture of arms.

9 June 1964: Resolution 190, urging South Africa to renounce the death penalty for acts resulting from opposition to apartheid and from the Rivonia trial of the opposition leaders.

29 May 1968: Resolution 253, calling for mandatory economic sanctions on Rhodesia.

Several special UN committees dealing with Southern Africa were also set up during the 1960s, such as the Special Committee on Decolonization (1961), later known as "The Committee of 24"; the Special Committee on Apartheid (1963), and the Council for South West Africa (1967), subsequently renamed the Council for Namibia.

On 2 November 1973 the UN General Assembly adopted a resolution that 1973–83 be proclaimed as the "Decade for Action to Combat Racism and Racial Discrimination in all its Forms and Manifestations". On 2 April 1974, the General Assembly adopted a draft convention making apartheid a crime against international law, subject to punishment, but very few countries had ratified this convention by the end of that year.

After 1970, other international organizations also began to focus attention on Southern Africa. The International Court of Justice ruled in 1971 that South Africa's continued presence in Namibia was illegal. The World Council of Churches initiated and led boycott campaigns against certain Western companies active in Southern Africa. In 1974, the International Labour Organization (ILO) for the first time openly committed itself to assisting the liberation movements by providing administrative training for Africans from liberated areas in the Portuguese territories.

These international measures did not achieve the desired effects, which were, in short, to bring independence to Portuguese Africa and Namibia, and black majority rule to Rhodesia and South Africa. In other words, there was no *system response* to the UN demands from the powers concerned. If there had been, events in Africa could well have taken an entirely different course. In the absence of system response, the conflict in Portuguese Africa escalated from reformism to armed revolution, and the notion that armed warfare was the only solution spread to the other countries concerned.

One reason for the failure of these measures is the fact that UN General Assembly resolutions have the nature of *recommendations;* they are not automatically binding decisions for the member states. In fact, the economic sanctions on Rhodesia remain the sole mandatory embargo decision ever passed by the UN. Even if a nation that has agreed to abide by a Security Council resolution or has ratified a UN convention should subsequently break the agreement, the UN Security Council cannot automatically impose sanctions by force. International criticism is the most stringent punishment that can be expected for breaking an embargo decision.

Thus, despite UN resolutions, NATO member states continued to supply weapons and military equipment to Portugal, which then used them in Africa; many states went on providing South Africa with arms and military technology, and Rhodesia was enabled to survive the economic blockade because of the support it received from South Africa and because of the availability of trade outlets through Portuguese Mozambique. South Africa retained control over Namibia, to which its apartheid laws were extended and where security was maintained by its police and troops.

By 1974, the armed revolution in Portuguese Africa had resulted in a military stalemate. Neither side was able to bring about a final military solution. This prospect of war without victory led eventually to the change of leadership in Portugal and created a new situation for the remaining white regimes. The Organization of African Unity reverted to its pre-1969 militant stance of supporting armed struggle against those same minority governments. Anxiety that a future, large-scale war might develop began to be expressed by numerous outside observers, representatives of international organizations and African statesmen.

The following statement by a former US Ambassador to the United Nations, Charles Yost, illustrates this general apprehension of a coming showdown in Southern Africa:

The real focus of potential catastrophe is, however, Southern Africa where 35 million blacks are still anachronistically ruled and in some cases grievously oppressed by white minorities, ranging from 19 per cent of the population in South Africa to 5 per cent in Rhodesia. If this anomaly is not corrected gradually and peacefully, it will be corrected suddenly and hideously in years to come. Moreover, far from being bulwarks against Communism, as the white governments claim to be, it is their inflexible adherence to immobility and apartheid which offer the best opportunity for the establishment of eventually triumphant Communist movements in Africa ... Someday Southern Africa will be shockingly and hideously on the front pages of the world press. Then the Western powers will ask themselves why they did not, with all the nonmilitary resources at their command, push and drive South Africa, Rhodesia and Portugal into the modern world while there was still time [2].

V. *Area description*

Southern Africa

White-ruled Africa's frontier with the independent African-ruled states in the north is indicated on the map on the inside covers. Before the 1974 coup in Portugal, this frontier ran along Portuguese Angola's northeastern borders with Zaire and Zambia and followed the Zambezi river which marks off Rhodesia's northern border with Tanzania. The Republic of South Africa was cut off from direct contact with hostile African states through the existence of these vast, white-controlled territories, including Rhodesia, which served as buffer zones. The new frontier, after the coup in Portugal, is also indicated on the map. It shows that South Africa will have to accept a common border with independent Mozambique in the northeast, ruled by the Socialist-oriented FRELIMO government, and that it will also share a common border with Namibia in the northwest and with the future, independent, black-ruled state of Angola. Rhodesia's dwindling value to South Africa as a buffer zone is well illustrated by the new frontier line.

Considering the fact that practically the entire African continent was broken up into European colonies until well into the twentieth century, it is a truism to state that the present conflict between the African population and the whites of European origin is a remnant of the colonial past. But it may be helpful, all the same, to consider this aspect of history when dealing with the widespread accusation, often repeated by the regimes of South Africa and Rhodesia, that the African opposition and guerilla movements are in fact acting under the influence of a "foreign ideology". Such thinking is illustrated by the following statement by the South African Defence Minister, P. W. Botha:

Like the rest of the Free World, the RSA is a target for international communism and its cohorts—leftist activists, exaggerated humanism, permissiveness, materialism, and related ideologies. In addition the RSA has been singled out as a special target for the by-products of their ideologies, such as black racialism, exaggerated individual freedom, one-man-one-vote, and a host of other slogans employed against us on a basis of double standards [3a].

White settlement

South Africa

The first European settlers came to the Cape of Good Hope in South Africa in the seventeenth century. In 1652 the Dutch East India Company founded Cape Town, and Dutch settlers soon moved northwards and eastwards, outside the company-controlled territories, and brought in Africans from the east and west coasts to work on European farms. In their expansion they took land by force from the Africans, and, for more than 100 years, wars continued between the Bantu-speaking peoples and the Europeans. When Britain wrested control of the Cape from the Dutch in 1806, the Dutch settlers—the Boers, who opposed British rule—began to move north, occupying the present Orange Free State and the Transvaal in South Africa.

The Anglo-Boer war broke out in 1899, and the Boers were eventually defeated. The four provinces—the Cape, Natal, the Orange Free State and the Transvaal—became part of the British Empire and were amalgamated in the Union of South Africa in 1910.

In 1948, the National Party, under Prime Minister Malan came to power, and in 1961 South Africa left the Commonwealth and declared itself a republic.

Namibia

South West Africa, known after 1968 as Namibia, was a German colony from 1884 until 1914. Shortly after the beginning of World War I it was invaded by South African forces fighting on the side of the Allied Powers. By the middle of 1915, South West Africa was completely occupied. South Africa administered the territory under a League of Nations mandate which, after World War II, was transformed into a United Nations mandate. In 1966 the United Nations officially terminated this mandate, declaring that administration over the territory should be turned over to a UN body, the Council for Namibia, until an independent Namibian government could be established.

Rhodesia

The British colony of Rhodesia was settled largely on the initiative of Cecil Rhodes, founder of the British South Africa Company and Prime Minister of the Cape colony, who led a force of 600 men in 1890 into the territory that the Africans called Zimbabwe.[5] In 1922 the white inhabitants were allowed to decide whether Rhodesia should become a crown colony or a member of the Union of South Africa; the Africans, having no voting rights, could not influence this decision. In 1923 Rhodesia became a British colony, under the name of Southern Rhodesia.

In 1953 the country became a part of the Central African Federation of the British Empire, which included the colonies of Northern and Southern Rhodesia and Nyasaland (the present Zambia, Rhodesia and Malawi respectively). The Federation was dissolved in 1963 when Zambia and Malawi became independent. In 1965 the white-minority regime of Southern Rhodesia declared the colony independent of Britain—the so-called UDI declaration (Unilateral Declaration of Independence).

The Portuguese territories

In 1497, the Portuguese became the first Europeans to arrive in *Mozambique,* after rounding the Cape of Good Hope and sailing into the Indian Ocean. During that century they also arrived on the west coast of Africa. In 1575 the town of Luanda in Angola was founded as a trading settlement. In the seventeenth century, the slave trade became important and African slaves were taken from Bissau, Angola and Mozambique to the Portuguese plantations in Brazil.

By the end of the nineteenth century, Portugal had agreed on colonial boundaries with its colonial rivals, Britain and Germany, and had suppressed much of the African resistance. Portuguese Guinea was not entirely subjugated, however, until 1936. Prior to 1951, when the Portuguese constitution was revised, these African possessions were designated as colonies, subject to the 1933 Colonial Act. In 1951, they were classified as Overseas Territories, making up an integral part of Portugal. In 1972 the designation was again changed: Angola and Mozambique nominally became autonomous states, but still remained an integral part of Portugal.

---

[5] Zimbabwe was an ancient city which became the capital of a kingdom that arose during the fifteenth century. The word means "stone building" in the Shona language.

Population and geographical characteristics[6]

The *Republic of South Africa* has an area of about 1.2 million km². According to an estimate issued by the Department of Statistics in Pretoria in September 1974, the total population in June 1974 was 24.9 million. The black African population has increased faster than any of the other groups in the period since the June 1970 census—by 11.3 per cent, reaching a total of 17.7 million, and is expected to continue to grow rapidly. The number of Coloureds was 2.3 million and Indians 709000. The whites number approximately four million. The largest cohesive group of whites consists of more than two million Afrikaners mainly of Dutch descent who also make up the country's political majority and thus have great political power. Although their common interest in maintaining supremacy over the black majority has brought the Afrikaners and the whites of English origin closer together over the years, there is still a definite line of separation between the two groups within South African society. For example, the English and Afrikaners attend separate schools and universities, tend to live in separate areas and belong to different religious denominations. The two official languages in South Africa are Afrikaans, derived from Dutch, and English.

The administrative capital is Pretoria. South Africa shares borders with Mozambique, Rhodesia, the Republic of Botswana (formerly the British Bechuanaland Protectorate, a High Commission territory, independent since 1966), and with Namibia, which is under South African rule.

In the northeast, touching the Mozambican border, lies the independent Kingdom of Swaziland; and in the central part of the Drakensberg mountains, encircled by South Africa, is the independent Kingdom of Lesotho. These two countries, formerly British High Commission territories, became independent in 1967 and 1966 respectively.

Unlike the other countries included in this study, South Africa is highly developed and industrialized. It accounts for 40 per cent of the continent's total industrial production and, according to Prime Minister Vorster, its GNP (Gross National Product) increased by a factor of 10 between 1948 and 1973 [4].

The minerals of South Africa make it one of the richest countries in the world. For many years gold has been its most valuable mineral: in 1972, South Africa accounted for 77 per cent of total gold production in the Western world [5]. It is estimated that South Africa holds the major part of the Western world's known reserves of gold and diamonds, 70 per cent of the reserves of primary platinum, chromite and fluorspar, and 30 per cent of uranium oxide [6]. The increase in the price of gold in recent years, to more than $160 per ounce by early 1974, gave South Africa an unprecedented economic boost. The Republic also has large coal deposits. Oil prospecting

[6] Except when otherwise stated, the information on population statistics and geographical characteristics was taken from the *Statesman's Yearbook 1974/75* [5].

12

has been conducted for many years with the assistance of foreign companies. In December 1974, persistent speculations appeared in the South African press to the effect that a major oil strike had taken place, but no official confirmation or denial was issued.

Agriculture in South Africa is rich and highly developed. Plantation farms produce the principal export crops: tobacco, grapes and other fruits, sugar, maize and cotton.

Namibia has an area of about 825 000 km² but is sparsely populated. In the 1974 census the total population of 852 000 included 99 000 whites. Some 30 000 of the whites are still German nationals. The remainder of the population comprises 10 different African peoples and Coloureds. The main tribal grouping, the Ovambos, numbers 396 000.

In the north, Namibia shares borders with Angola and Zambia, in the east with Botswana, and in the west it faces the Atlantic Ocean. The capital is Windhoek.

In addition to being one of the world's greatest producers of diamonds, Namibia mines other valuable minerals, such as lead, copper and zinc ores and uranium. The country is essentially stock-raising, since the scarcity of water makes crop agriculture virtually impossible. The Cunene river scheme, an irrigation project undertaken jointly by Portugal and South Africa, for common use of this river along the Angolan border, will serve to develop agriculture in the north of Namibia. The Cunene Dam will also supply electricity for the Rossing uranium mine.

Rhodesia covers an area of about 390 000 km². It is situated between the northern border of the Transvaal in South Africa and the Zambezi river. Its neighbour in the north is Zambia, in the east, Mozambique, and in the west, Botswana. The capital is Salisbury.

The population in 1974 was 6.1 million, of which 5.8 million were Africans, 273 000 whites and 27 600 Asians and Coloureds.

Rhodesia has rich mineral resources of gold, copper, asbestos, chromium, nickel and tin. The commercial agricultural products are tobacco, maize, cotton, wheat, coffee, tea and citrus fruits. Timber is also produced. Most of Rhodesia's exports and imports after 1965 have passed through the ports of Beira and Lourenço Marques in Mozambique.

Mozambique occupies an area of about 785 000 km². In the east it is bounded by the Indian Ocean, and in the north it shares a border with Tanzania along the Ruvuma river. The border faces Malawi and Zambia in the northeast and Rhodesia in the west. To the south lie South Africa and Swaziland. The capital is Lourenço Marques. From Rhodesia, the Zambezi river runs through the Tete district in Mozambique to the Indian Ocean. The hydroelectric and irrigation project of the Cabora Bassa Dam has been set up on the Zambezi river in Tete.

13

Table 1. Population groups in Southern Africa

mn

	South Africa	Namibia	Rhodesia	Angola	Guinea-Bissau	Mozambique	Total
Blacks	18.0	0.7	5.8	5.4	0.7	8.8	**39.4**
Coloureds	2.3	–	–	–	–	–	**–**
Indians	0.7	–	0.03	–	–	0.05	**3.08**
Total non-whites	21.0	0.7	5.83	5.4	0.7	8.85	**42.5**
Whites	4.0	0.01	0.03	0.03	–	0.02	**4.1**

Source: Reference [5] and SIPRI worksheets.

The population, according to the census of 1970, was 8.2 million. In 1973 it was estimated to have reached 8.9 million, of whom 97.7 per cent were Africans and 1.7 per cent whites [7]. The Africans represent 19 ethnic peoples belonging to seven major groups and several minor tribes. Seventeen African languages are spoken in the country.

Mozambique has primarily been an agricultural country, plantation-grown sugar and cotton making up half of its exports by value. Other important cash crops are tea, coconuts and groundnuts. But the search for vital strategic raw materials has produced results since the mid-1960s which will lead to a restructuring of the agricultural economy. Surveys conducted by the Portuguese government and Western companies have revealed an immense economic potential; not only is there water wealth, essential for agriculture, but there are also deposits of minerals.

Mining will provide the basis for industrialization, and an iron and steel industry was already at the planning stage in 1973. Valuable seams of coal from which coke can be made have been discovered, and 35 million tons of reserves of titaniferous magnetites, copper, fluorspar, manganese, nickel, chromium and asbestos have been pinpointed, especially in a sector in and around the Tete district [8]. Oil prospecting has been conducted for some years by Western companies in Mozambique.

Angola, which has more than 1 000 miles of coastline, is bounded by the Atlantic Ocean in the west and Zaire in the north. The Angolan enclave territory of Cabinda is situated north of Angola and is physically separated from it by Zaire territory. Zambia is situated to the east, and Namibia, with the Caprivi Strip, lies to the south. The capital is Luanda. Angola has an area of about 1.25 million km². The population at the 1970 census was 5.7 million, including 300 000 whites. The African population is made up of over 80 ethnic peoples belonging to five major ethnic groups and several smaller tribes, and is divided into 11 African language groups.

Angola, the richest of Portugal's former African colonies, produces valuable mineral exports. Iron ore is mined at Cassinga, diamonds are said to abound in the Lunda district, and copper and manganese are also mined. Oil reserves have been discovered near the coast, and especially in Cabinda, although the exact volume of the oil finds is disputed. In 1972 a find of enormous size was reported in the Gulf company's journal, the *Orange Disc,* but other newspaper reports concerning seven unannounced discoveries, mainly offshore, were denied by Gulf officials. However, in connection with a campaign in the United States, directed against Gulf's activities in Angola and led by the US National Council of Churches, the Gulf Oil Corporation stated in 1974 that Angola accounted for 10 per cent of Gulf's proven resources and for 6 per cent of its total profits [9]. Cabindan oil production in 1973 was estimated at 7.5 million tons [10].

Angola's main cash and export crops are coffee, cotton, maize and palm oil products. Forestry and cattle-breeding are also important in the economy. The main food crops are cassava, groundnuts, maize and rice. One of the principal development projects is the Cunene Dam, mentioned above, designed to develop agriculture in the southwest and supply electricity to parts of Angola and Namibia. Until 1960, 50 per cent of Angola's exports were made up of coffee and diamonds; by 1970, however, oil had become the leading export. High-grade iron ore is expected to become another leading export item.

Guinea-Bissau, (the former Portuguese Guinea), with an area of 36 000 km², includes the Bolama island and the Bijagos archipelago. It is situated north of the Gulf of Guinea in West Africa, bounded in the north by Senegal and in the south by the Republic of Guinea. Its capital is Bissau. The ten islands known as the *Cape Verde islands* are situated in the Atlantic Ocean about 650 km off the coast of Senegal. Their total area is about 4 033 km². According to the 1970 census, the Cape Verde population numbered 272 000, including 4 000 whites.

No up-to-date information exists on the present population of Guinea-Bissau, but in the 1970 census it totalled 487 744.[7] According to an estimate made in 1974 by the PAIGC State Commission of Economy and Finance, 350 000 people were then living in the liberated zones in Guinea-Bissau and 300 000 more in the areas still controlled by the Portuguese. An additional 150 000 refugees, residing in Senegal, Guinea and Gambia, were expected to return to Guinea-Bissau after independence [11]. White settlement did not take place in Portuguese Guinea on the same scale as in Portugal's other African territories. In 1974 the white colony was made up of some 3 000 persons, mainly Portuguese civil servants and traders.

The African population in Guinea-Bissau comprises 17 different ethnic peoples belonging to five major ethnic and language groups. The Cape Verdians are descendants of Portuguese settlers and the African slaves who were brought to work on the plantations. A large number of these

---

[7] The 1970 census figures in the Portuguese colonies were little more than estimates, based on pre-war figures, as the authorities were unable to count most of the population.

people have moved to Guinea-Bissau, and the immigrant colony of Cape Verdian mulattos has come to play an important role in the country.

Guinea-Bissau and Cape Verde are poor agricultural areas. The main export crops from the mainland are rice, palm oil products and timber. The Cape Verde islands are essentially volcanic; exports are coffee, oil, beans and bananas.

The parties to the conflict

African liberation movements

The following presentation of African liberation movements includes only those which operate in a dual role, as political parties possessing a military wing in the form of a guerilla army. Other African political organizations opposing white minority rule will be discussed in Part II.[8]

The oldest African nationalist organization on the continent is the African National Congress of South Africa (ANC), established in 1912 in the *Republic of South Africa* to work for equal political and economic rights for the African population. It has cooperated to a certain extent with the South African Communist Party (SACP), which was founded later and which remains the sole white organization demanding the complete abolition of apartheid. In 1948, when the Nationalist Party took power, SACP went underground. The ANC was declared illegal in 1960 and now operates from Tanzania. The first ANC military group, set up in 1961, called itself *Umkhonto we Sizwe* (Spear of the Nation), but this particular name was not used after 1962. The declared aim of the ANC in 1974 was to create a democratic multiracial state through armed struggle against white minority rule.

In the 1950s the ANC was led by Albert Luthuli, who received the Nobel Peace Prize in 1960, returned to South Africa and remained virtually imprisoned until his death in 1967. Another well-known leader, Nelson Mandela, was sentenced to life imprisonment in 1963 and has been in jail on Robben island ever since. Following Mandela's detention, Oliver Tambo became the acting president and the secretary-general is Alfred Nzo. The ANC is not a Communist party, despite the presence of Communists among its members. It is better described as an African-led nationalist organization which is attempting to encompass the largest possible section of the radical opposition against the apartheid system. The relationship between the ANC and the South African Communist Party was clearly defined by Nelson Mandela in his defence speech at the famous Rivonia trial in 1964:

[8] No exclusive listing of African movements will be provided. It may be noted that Professor John Marcum, in his book *The Angolan Revolution* (1969), listed 36 nationalist movements, five "common fronts" and five labour movements in Angola alone; three nationalist movements in Guinea-Bissau; five in Mozambique, plus five international organizations opposing Portugal's presence in Africa.

The ANC has never at any period of its history advocated a revolutionary change in the economic structure of the country, nor has it, to the best of my recollection, ever condemned capitalist society . . . The ANC, unlike the Communist Party, admitted Africans only as members. Its chief goal was, and is, for the African people, to win unity and full political rights. The Communist Party's main aim, on the other hand, was to remove the capitalists and to replace them with a working-class government. The Communist Party sought to emphasize class distinctions whilst the ANC seeks to harmonise them. This is a vital distinction. It is true that there has often been close cooperation between the ANC and the Communist Party. But cooperation is merely proof of a common goal—in this case the removal of white supremacy—and is not proof of a complete community of interests [12].

The rival organization to the ANC, the Pan Africanist Congress of Azania,[9] was formally constituted in 1959. The PAC grew out of the ANC Youth League, a group of young activists who since 1943 had gathered around the charismatic figure of Anton Lembede in Johannesburg. Deeply dissatisfied with the ANC, the PAC accused it of collaborating with the white ruling class and of being strongly influenced by the white, Moscow-oriented SACP. The ideology of the PAC has presented a confusing pattern: although generally adopting an anti-Communist stance and criticizing the alleged SACP influence in the ANC, the organization was occasionally labelled pro-Chinese. At the same time, the PAC opposed the multiracialism of the ANC, an attitude which enabled the white regime in South Africa to accuse the organization of propagating a creed of black racial superiority. An examination of the aims of these rival organizations would indicate, however, that their differences were not so great as they have been made to appear.[10] The declared goal of the PAC remains that of creating a democratic state, based on African nationalism, after first destroying white supremacy through armed struggle. This coincides in essence, with ANC aims.

In 1960 a military wing of the PAC, called Poqo, appeared. Like the ANC, the PAC was also banned in 1960. Its members and leaders escaped to Lesotho, then a British territory. In 1963 the PAC headquarters there were raided by South African and British police and the leaders were again forced to flee. The new headquarters were established in Tanzania. A futile attempt was made in Tanzania to form a united front with the ANC, and the two organizations remain separate and hostile.

Active political activities within *Namibia* (South West Africa) began in 1958 and resulted in the creation of several tribal-based organizations, the largest of which was the Ovambo People's South West Africa People's Organization. The Ovambo People's Organization began using the name SWAPO around 1960 and eventually developed into a national liberation movement. Its first president, Sam Nujoma, is still in office.

---

[9] It has not been possible to establish any connection between the word Azania and South Africa. According to Basil Davidson, the word first occurred in a Greek text of about A.D. 150, applying very vaguely to the East African interior.
[10] For a detailed account of the development and ideology of the ANC and the PAC, see, for example, *African Liberation Movements* [18] and "Nelson Mandela Speaks" [12].

Military training abroad of SWAPO members started sometime after 1963. Three years later, in 1966, SWAPO announced for the first time its intention to launch an armed struggle to liberate the territory of Namibia from South African rule. At a special SWAPO planning and policy session in Tanzania at the end of 1969 it was declared that, from then on, primary emphasis would be on armed struggle. During this session the People's Liberation Army of Namibia (PLAN), which was to be based outside Namibia, was formally set up. As a political party, however, SWAPO is still allowed to function inside Namibia although the South African authorities insist that it is merely a tribal organization.

The initial aim of SWAPO was limited to working for the abolition of the contract labour system in Namibia (see page 34). Eventually it broadened its programme to include the total liberation of Namibia and the establishment of African majority rule. The overriding objective thus became national liberation, coupled with the abolition of the apartheid system which the South African regime had imposed upon Namibia. Ideologically, SWAPO advocated the creation of a democratic state which would offer social progress to Africans. This goal was articulated by the SWAPO leader Herman Toivo ja Toivo in his speech before the Pretoria court in 1968, when he said:

I have come to know that our people cannot expect progress as a gift from anyone, be it the United Nations or South Africa. Progress is something we shall have to struggle and work for. And I believe that the only way in which we shall be able and fit to secure that progress is to learn from our experience and mistakes. We do not expect that independence will end our troubles, but we do believe that our people are entitled—as are all peoples—to rule themselves. It is not really a question of whether South Africa treats us well or badly, but that South West Africa is our country and we wish to be our own masters [13].

In *Rhodesia,* African nationalism arose before World War II. In 1934 the African National Congress of Southern Rhodesia was established as a proto-nationalist organization of African elites who appealed to the white regime for reforms. The following year marked the formation of the Youth League of Salisbury, an all-African group which grew more militant with the passage of time. During the 1950s a succession of different political groups arose, only to be banned. In 1961 Joshua Nkomo formed the Zimbabwe African People's Union (ZAPU) and became its first president.[11] ZAPU was accorded the same treatment in 1963 that other militant organizations had received: it was outlawed and forced into exile. Nkomo himself was imprisoned at Gonakudzingwa in 1964 where he remained until 1975 without ever having been charged with any crime. His successor, James Chikerema, the acting president, directs operations from the new headquarters in Lusaka, Zambia.

[11] For a detailed account of the development of African political organizations in Rhodesia, see for example, *Rhodesia: The Struggle for a Birthright* [19].

Prior to Nkomo's imprisonment in 1963 the ZAPU executive split, and some former ZAPU members who rebelled against Nkomo's leadership established in the same year the Zimbabwe African National Union (ZANU). The president was the Rev. Ndabaningi Sithole. Sithole and many of the ZANU party leaders inside Rhodesia were detained even before the government banned ZANU in 1964 and they remained in prison until 1975. After their imprisonment, the actual direction of ZANU was in the hands of Herbert Chitepo, Rhodesia's first African lawyer, killed in 1975. ZANU's military commander by 1974 was Chisaya Tongarara, and its battle orders used the names of chiefs of the ancient Monomatapa empire, of which the Tete province in Mozambique as well as Zambia were once a part.

After Rhodesia's unilateral declaration of independence in 1965, both ZAPU and ZANU decided on armed struggle against the Ian Smith regime. ZANU's military wing, the Zimbabwe African National Liberation Army (ZANLA) launched its first attacks in 1966, the same year that ZAPU's military wing, the Zimbabwe Liberation Army, came into existence. Several attempts to unite the two movements failed; in 1974, ZAPU and ZANU were still operating as separate movements. An ideological debate intensified the original tribal and personality tensions, but the actual ideological positions of both movements in 1974 could better be described in terms of African nationalism than of any particular Socialist orientation.

The repeated failures of the ZAPU and ZANU leaders to unite led to the creation in 1971 of a third movement: the Front for the Liberation of Zimbabwe (FROLIZI), intended to serve as a united front for the previous two. But the merger envisaged at the time never took place, and FROLIZI also remained an independent movement. The only African political organization allowed to function prior to the merger in 1975 of all the Rhodesian nationalist movements was the African National Council (ANC), led by Bishop Abel Muzorewa. The ANC was set up in 1971 to influence Britain to accept the African demand for majority rule before granting independence to Rhodesia.

In *Angola* three rival liberation movements were competing in 1974 for influence and outside support. These were the Movimento Popular de Libertação de Angola (MPLA), headed by Dr Agostinho Neto; the Frente Nacional de Libertação de Angola (FNLA), led by Holden Roberto; and União Nacional para a Independência Total de Angola (UNITA), led by Jonas Savimbi.

The MPLA was founded in 1956 as a clandestine nationalist party, inspired by the newly formed Angolan Communist Party, which was an offshoot of the Portuguese Communist Party. The MPLA's immediate predecessor was a grouping of small radical organizations, and its first programme was very similar to that of the Angolan Communist Party. Subsequently, several other small anti-Portuguese groups joined the MPLA. At this early stage, the MPLA was active mainly in Luanda and other urban centres. Its leaders represented Angola's African intelligentsia. Its first secretary-general was the poet Viriato da Cruz. Others among the leadership were the poet Mario de Andrade and the physician and writer Agostinho Neto. In 1962, Dr Neto was elected president of the MPLA, a post which he still retained in 1974. The MPLA has headquarters in Zambia and the Congo Republic; its programme is clearly socialistic and envisages a future, multiracial, egalitarian society, based on a revolutionary change in the economic system.

The FNLA originated among the Bakongo people in northern Angola, from whom it still derives most of its support. Since 1954, several exile groups in what is now Zaire have been engaged in the struggle to revive the ancient Congo Kingdom.

In 1958 a movement of broader scope was set up by a merger of these groups. Called the União das Populações de Angola (UPA) and based in Zaire, it was led by Holden Roberto, who was the personal protégé of President Mobutu of Zaire. In 1962, the name FNLA was given to Holden Roberto's armed forces in the north. That same year, an exile government called the Govêrno Revolucionário de Angola no Exílio (GRAE) was set up in Kinshasa. This exiled government enjoyed the backing of President Mobutu but was never representative of the Angolan population. The role that Mobutu played initially in the founding of GRAE and the military movement FNLA, and his persistent efforts to present Holden Roberto as the future leader of Angola, can only be understood against the background of the way in which Mobutu himself assumed power. The Mobutu regime came to power in the Congo after the civil war with the assistance of the USA. This initial US-backing of the FNLA has subsequently been acknowledged by Roberto himself.

The leadership of the FNLA, as well as its supporters, were from the outset violently opposed to Communism, which in the Angolan context meant that they were committed to opposing the Socialist MPLA movement as well as the Portuguese. The MPLA tried from 1961 onwards to reach a common front with Holden Roberto but was always rejected. Instead, these two movements became engaged in an embryo civil war against each other.

Over the years, the controversy between the FNLA and MPLA continued, fomented by tribal tensions as well as by differences of political opinion. The ideology of the FNLA was, in addition to being anti-Communist, also strongly black-African nationalist—that is, resentful of the MPLA intellectuals who in the main were *assimilados,* of mixed European-African origin (see below, page 72).

UNITA was founded in 1966 for much the same reasons that FROLIZI had been in Rhodesia, ostensibly to try to unite the resistance. But UNITA was also a result of a split within the GRAE exile government and in reality became a splinter movement. Its leader, Jonas Savimbi, resigned from GRAE in 1964 to found UNITA, after having rejected an offer to join the MPLA. Savimbi and his associates remained based inside Angola, and declared the mobilization and organization of the peasants as two of their principal goals. They refused to use camps outside the country or to be led by big foreign powers. UNITA has often been denounced by the other movements, as being alternatively "Maoist" or "US-sponsored". It was, in fact, originally structured as a Communist party which followed Lenin's principle of democratic centralism and was led by a collective leadership. Its members were organized in party cells. After the coup in Portugal in 1974, UNITA emerged as the Angolan liberation movement most acceptable to the white community inside Angola. This led to the movement being called a "Portuguese stooge".

All three liberation movements established guerilla armies and captured certain territories.

In *Mozambique* the liberation struggle developed quite differently from that of Angola. The sole liberation movement became the Frente de Libertação de Moçambique (FRELIMO), which represented the Mozambican people in the interim government that was set up in 1974 to prepare for national independence.

FRELIMO was formed in June 1962 in Dar es Salaam, Tanzania, by three exile African nationalist movements. The first president was Dr Eduardo Mondlane, and the first vice-president was the Rev. Uria Simango, who was later to try, but without success, to form a rival movement. The well-known leftist poet Marcelino dos Santos became Secretary for External Relations. The leadership came from many parts of Mozambique and was thus not tribally-based. Several leaders represented the peasant cooperatives in the north. The aim of FRELIMO from its very creation was to liberate Mozambique from Portuguese rule and create a multiracial, Socialist state. In the words of Dr Mondlane: "Liberation is to us not simply a matter of expelling the Portuguese: it means reorganizing the life of the country and setting it on the road to sound national development" [14]. FRELIMO's guerilla army launched its first attacks in 1964.

FRELIMO experienced a severe leadership crisis after the assassination of Eduardo Mondlane in 1969, but it managed nevertheless to develop and consolidate its forces in both the political and military fields. The successor to Eduardo Mondlane was a military commander, Samora Machel, who became the first President of independent Mozambique in June 1975. In the interim government, set up in September 1974, the Prime Minister was another military commander, Joaquim Chissano.

For a limited period a rival movement to FRELIMO was also in existence. In 1965, the Comité Revolucionário de Moçambique (COREMO), was set up by several movements that opposed FRELIMO policy.

21

COREMO became the subject of some controversy and was accused alternatively of being "Maoist" or "CIA-led", but there was, in fact, little evidence of any foreign influence other than from Portugal at a later phase (see below, page 23). COREMO claimed to have a guerilla army operating in the Tete province, but by 1974 FRELIMO's advances had overshadowed COREMO's activities. After the coup in Portugal, COREMO claimed a share in the future nationalist government of Mozambique, but it did not win the recognition to which it aspired.

In *Guinea-Bissau*, which became independent in September 1974, the development of the liberation struggle was very similar to that in Mozambique. In 1956, six African intellectuals met in Bissau to organize the clandestine Partido Africano da Independência da Guiné e Cabo Verde (PAIGC), which became the major nationalist party and the ruler of Guinea-Bissau. One of the founders was Amilcar Cabral, who served as president of the PAIGC until his assassination by the Portuguese in January 1973. Apart from being a revolutionary and a political organizer, Amilcar Cabral was a theoretician in his own right: he avoided commitment to any foreign revolutionary model and was able as a consequence to secure aid from all possible donors. He once said:

However great the similarity between our various cases and however identical our enemies, national liberation and social revolution are not exportable commodities; they are . . . increasingly . . the outcome of local and national elaboration, more or less influenced by external factors . . . but essentially determined and formed by the historical reality of each people, and carried to success by the overcoming or correct solution of the internal contradiction between the various categories characterizing this reality [15].

The aim of the PAIGC was to create a one-party state, comprising Guinea-Bissau and the Cape Verde islands, with a Socialist development programme. This aim was being realized after independence, giving Guinea-Bissau a more radical profile than most other independent African nations possess.

The PAIGC also experienced internal conflict, resulting from tensions between mainland Africans and the mulatto leadership of Cape Verde origin. In addition, differences of political opinion arose. After Cabral's death, his brother Luiz became president and Aristides Pereira was made the secretary-general of the party.

For a while, a number of rival movements were active, the best-known being the Frente para a Libertação e Independência da Guiné Portuguesa (FLING) based in Senegal. Created in 1963 and led by Benjamin Pinto-Bull, it enjoyed the support of Senegal's regime until 1967. FLING never developed a guerilla army and, as its name indicates, was opposed to the inclusion of the Cape Verde islands in an independent Guinea-Bissau. FLING was revived after the coup in Portugal in 1974, but the new Portuguese regime ignored it as a negotiating partner.

22

The white regimes

In addition to the white regimes of South Africa and Rhodesia, the opponents of the liberation movements include—as potential parties to the conflict—certain groupings among the white populations of Angola and Mozambique. A further category of potential participants in the conflict would be those foreign powers whose financial interests in the region lead them to support one or the other. These countries will be discussed in the context of the polarization process. (See page 40.)

In the *Republic of South Africa,* the government has been led since 1948 by the Afrikaner-supported National Party. The present Prime Minister is J. B. Vorster, who succeeded H. F. Verwoerd (assassinated in 1966).

The head of the Republic is the State President N. J. Diederichs. Legislative power is vested in a Parliament consisting of the State President, a Senate and a House of Assembly. Members of the Senate and House must be white citizens.

The territory of *Namibia* is represented in the South African House of Assembly by six members elected by registered white voters of the territory, and in the Senate by four white Senators. On 13 October 1966 the security and apartheid laws of South Africa were extended to Namibia, retroactive to 1950.

The non-white populations of South Africa and Namibia do not participate in the parliamentary democratic system briefly outlined above, but are ruled according to a different system. (See page 37.) No black African political parties are represented in the white parliament.

Rhodesia is also ruled as a parliamentary democracy, following the British structure. The ruling party since UDI in 1965 has been the Rhodesian Front, led by Prime Minister Ian Smith. The Parliament has 66 seats, of which the Rhodesian Front won 50 in the general election of 1970. The British government stated in 1970 that Rhodesia's assumption of a republican status was illegal, as was also its 1965 declaration of independence.

In *Mozambique,* even before the change of regime in Portugal, a new "third force" movement was allowed to appear, with discreet Portuguese backing. This was the Grupo Unido de Moçambique (GUMO) led by a former COREMO member, Mrs Joana Simeão. GUMO advocated the establishment of a Portuguese Commonwealth, and its ideas bore, in fact, a close resemblance to those later presented by General Spinola. Its existence may have reflected an attempt by the Caetano regime to find a new and more acceptable negotiating partner than FRELIMO, in the face of the continuing guerilla advances. After April 1974, however, GUMO expelled Mrs Simeão, who was accused of being a DGS informer under the Caetano regime.[12]

[12] DGS (Direção Geral de Segurança); formerly the PIDE (Polícia Internacional e Defesa do Estado)=the secret police. "International" in this case means that these special police also operated in the Portuguese colonies. The DGS was disbanded after the April 1974 coup in Portugal.

References

1. Davidson, B., *The Liberation of Guiné*, (Harmondsworth, UK, Penguin Books, 1969).
   (a) —, Foreword by Amilcar Cabral, p. 11.
2. Yost, C. W., *The Conduct and Misconduct of Foreign Affairs*, (New York, Random House, 1972) p. 133.
3. *White Paper on Defence and Armament Production 1973*, Republic of South Africa, Department of Defence (W.P.E. 1973). Preface by Defence Minister P. W. Botha, p. 1.
4. *Times*, UK, 25 May 1973.
5. *Statesman's Yearbook 1974/75*, (London, Macmillan) p. 1297.
6. *Africa Diary*, New Delhi, No. 2, 8–14 January 1974, quoting speech by the South African Minister of Mines, Dr. P. G. Koornhof, to the Transvaal Chamber of Commerce and Industries.
7. *Dagens Nyheter*, Sweden, 14 July 1974.
8. *Rand Daily Mail*, South Africa, 30 November 1973.
9. *African Development*, UK, May 1974.
10. *Portugal: An Informative Review*, Portugal, December 1973.
11. *Daily News*, Tanzania, 4 May 1974.
12. *Nelson Mandela Speaks*, South African Studies 4. (London, undated, Publicity and Information Bureau ANC South Africa) p. 102.
13. *Rand Daily Mail*, South Africa, 15 February 1975.
14. Mondlane, E., *The Struggle for Mozambique*, (Harmondsworth, UK, Penguin Books, 1969) p. 219.
15. Cabral, A., *Revolution in Guinea* (London, Stage I, 1969).
    Speech at the Tricontinental Conference in Havana, January 1966, pp. 74–75.
16. Myrdal, G., Prologue: "The Beam in Our Eyes", in *Asian Drama*, Vol. 1 (New York, Pantheon, 1968) pp. 31–34.
17. *Regional Arms Control Arrangements for Developing Areas*, (Cambridge, Mass., 1964, Massachusetts Institute of Technology, Center for International Studies, C/64–25).
18. Gibson, R., *African Liberation Movements: Contemporary Struggles Against White Minority Rule*, (London, Oxford University Press, 1972, The Institute of Race Relations).
19. Mlambo, E., *Rhodesia: The Struggle for a Birthright*, (London C. Hurst & Co., 1972).

Part I. Conflict determinants

Square-bracketed references, thus [1], *refer to the list of references on page 67.*

For the following description of situational factors determining the conflict in Southern Africa between the African people and the white regimes, a four-fold categorization has been made. First, a division was made between local and international conflict determinants—that is, between socioeconomic factors at work inside the countries concerned and factors determining outside interests in Southern Africa. These categories were, in turn, subdivided into specific economic and political factors. The final category, called the polarization of forces, should be regarded as appearing after the establishment of the basic structure of local and international conflict determinants.

Chapter 1. Local conflict determinants

I. *The racial dimension*

Inequalities in the distribution of economic, political and social rights prevail in many nations, but the distinctive feature in Southern Africa is the racial dimension: it is, in general, literally possible to *see* who belongs to the privileged class, as the system is based on the separation of the races.[1]

The key to the political system in South Africa is the doctrine of white supremacy known as the *apartheid system*,[2] which is defined as a system of separate development.

Its origins go back to the traditional Boer ideology, based on Calvinism and the white man's mission in Africa. The Nazi race doctrine has also influenced the apartheid ideology of today. The system of separation of the races has been progressively applied in Namibia by the South African government, and a local variation of apartheid is developing in Rhodesia. In the former Portuguese colonies, white supremacy was embedded in the system of colonial power. The Portuguese colonial governments' persistent claim of having welded diverse multiracial elements into a single Portuguese civilization was denounced as a myth during the course of the wars in Portuguese Africa and later by the new government of Portugal.

Thus, despite differences between countries, it is apparent that a common structure of racial discrimination prevails throughout the area. It is also evident, as will be shown, that the similarities in the actual living conditions of the Africans (in the labour system and in the granting or denial of voting rights) are greater between the countries—and are, in any case, of more practical importance—than possible variations in theory.

In the *Republic of South Africa,* the apartheid system separates by law not only the white, Coloured, Indian and Bantu peoples from one another, as will be shown below, but also emphasizes the division of the African Bantu population into different peoples.

---

[1] There are much-publicized anomalies, involving individuals in South Africa who appear to be white but have been declared by court order to be "non-whites" because of mixed racial origin generations back. Also the Japanese in practice enjoy a special status of "honorary whites". This is because of Japan's growing commercial importance and the necessity of allowing Japanese businessmen to operate in white areas and establish normal relations with their white South African partners. This praxis may at first glance appear absurd, but it may contain graver implications if a parallel is drawn with Nazi Germany, when the Japanese enjoyed the status of "honorary Aryans".

[2] "Apartheid" is an Afrikaans word meaning *separation.*

The Native Land Act, 1913 reserves certain areas for the black population.

The Industrial Conciliation Act, 1924 excludes black African workers from its definition of "employee".

The Land Resettlement Act, 1936 fixes the quota of land to be allocated to the black population at 13.7 per cent of the total area.

The Suppression of Communism Act, 1950 outlaws the South African Communist Party and any other organization that furthers the aims of communism.

The Bantu Authorities Act, 1951 provides a system of Bantu tribal, regional and territorial authorities within the Bantustans.

The Promotion of Bantu Self-Government Act, 1959 provides the legal framework for the development of the Bantustans into self-governing units and simultaneously abolishes the representation of black Africans by whites in the Parliament.

The Unlawful Organisations Act, 1960 outlaws the ANC of South Africa and the PAC.

The General Law Amendment Act, 1962 makes sabotage a capital crime and calls on the accused to prove his innocence.

The Terrorism Act, 1967 provides for indefinite detention of suspects in solitary confinement, without access to a lawyer.

The General Law Amendment Act, 1969 establishes the Bureau for State Security (BSS).

The Affected Organisations Act, 1974 empowers the Minister of Justice to restrict the activities of any organization engaged in politics.

The concept of establishing "native reserves" long predates the rise to power of the National Party in 1948. As early as 1838, when the Boer Republic was established in Natal, legislation was enacted denying Bantus and Coloureds the right to be in settled areas of the Republic except as servants of the whites. The different African peoples are expected to develop their own nations in the so-called Bantustans, established in 1913 under the Native Land Act. The Land Resettlement Act of 1936 fixed the quota of land to be set aside for the blacks at 13.7 per cent of the total area. This act, which provides the framework of the Bantustan scheme, is also a cornerstone of the apartheid system and resulted—paradoxically—from international pressure on South Africa, via the League of Nations, to improve conditions for the African population in the country. According to the act, nine separate Bantustans or homelands for the African peoples were to be created and ruled by African chiefs and African parliaments. In 1951, the Bantu Authorities Act was passed, providing a system of Bantu tribal, regional and territorial authorities. These were given limited administrative, executive and judicial functions and restricted legislative powers. The limitations to black self-government are evident in the Transkei which is the

27

most advanced Bantustan: external affairs, defence, internal security, postal services, immigration, currency, banking, customs and excise, information and the Transkei constitution itself are controlled by the South African government. In 1959 the main ethnic groups received legal recognition when the Promotion of Bantu Self-Government Act was passed. It provided for the development of the Bantustans into self-governing national units, each with a white commissioner-general who would represent the government of the Republic of South Africa. Because the act envisages eventual political autonomy for the Bantustans, and because white representation of the Bantustan population in the white governing bodies was adjudged a retarding factor in this development, the representation of the Bantu by whites in Parliament was abolished as of 30 June 1960.

The African opposition holds that the Bantustan development scheme never was a serious plan, but the South African regime insists on its feasibility. The official view, which has been stated, for example, by the Minister of Information, Connie P. Mulder, is that the white population in South Africa is not a minority, but a *majority,* since the four million whites outnumber each tribe. Further, it is claimed that the creation of independent Bantustans will provide equal opportunities for all the peoples in South Africa, but within their separate territories.[3] According to Mulder,

The basic . . . objectives of our policy include self-determination for the various nations in South Africa, protection of the identity of all ethnic groups and the elimination of domination of one people over others. This is a totally different picture from the one accepted by so many United Nations commentators [1].

Divergent opinions about the apartheid system exist among the whites in South Africa, however, and these will be described when the economic factors involved are examined.

The creation of Bantustans—alternatively known as homelands, or reserves—involves the removal of Africans from the white area where, officially, they have the status of temporary sojourners. Africans in the white area have no political or economic rights, except the right to work. If their families live in the white area they are expelled to a Bantustan. In 1968, it was estimated that 38 per cent of all the blacks lived in reserves. In 1970 this figure had risen to 47 per cent. By 1974, more than 1 600 000 Africans had been moved from the white area into Bantustans, but the

---

[3] The names of the nine Bantustans in existence by 1974 and their respective ethnic groups were:
Bophuthatswana – the Tswana tribe
KwaZulu – Zulu
Basotho Qwa Qwa – South Sotho
Lebowa – North Sotho
Vendaland – Venda
Gazankulu – Shangaan/tsonga
Transkei – Xhosa
Ciskei – Xhosa
Swazi – Swazi

proportion of blacks in the reserves had declined to 40 per cent of the total. When the scheme is completed, over two million will have been resettled, in what amounts to the largest transfer of people undertaken by a government in peacetime. The overall design is to separate the four main racial groups—white, Coloured, Indian and Bantu—into separate jurisdictional compartments.

No land is set aside for the Coloured and Indian communities; instead, they are allocated limited residential areas in the urban centres. Prior to 1959, Coloureds had their own (white) representatives in Parliament, but even this right was abolished, simultaneously with the withdrawal of the Bantu's right of representation by whites. The Indian National Council and the Coloured Representation Council, which govern these two groups, have no voice in Parliament.

The legislation implementing the apartheid system is highly complex and detailed and covers literally all aspects of life for the non-white population. The pass laws provide for complete control over the movements of Africans: the latest report of the South African Commissioner of Police shows an average of 1 690 prosecutions *every day* for pass offences [2]. Major legislation includes the Suppression of Communism Act, 1950 and the Terrorism Act, 1967.

The apartheid system was legally extended to *Namibia* upon the recommendation of the South African Odendaal Commission, which worked out the plans between 1962 and 1964. In Namibia, 11 homelands, covering 39.6 per cent of the total area, will be created for the African peoples. The whites would receive 44.1 per cent of Namibian land. The remainder, including the rich diamond areas, would remain under direct South African control.

In *Rhodesia,* the major legislative measures to protect the *status quo* have been the Unlawful Organizations Act, 1959, the Emergency Powers Act and the Law and Order (Maintenance) Act, 1960. New pass laws for Africans were introduced in November 1973. Since that time, pressure to segregate university education has increased.

Under the Land Tenure Act, which dates from 1969, the African population will be resettled and separate white and African areas created. This act is denounced by the African opposition as an attempt on the part of the regime to construct a Rhodesian variation of the apartheid system, the difference being that the African areas in Rhodesia are not planned to become autonomous units.

Thus, the existing systems in South Africa, Namibia and Rhodesia are not merely defending the *status quo;* they are also working progressively towards a complete physical separation of whites from Africans.

The practical result of this general policy has been the *de jure* and *de facto* creation of two social classes inside each nation: one rich and highly privileged, composed of whites and another that is poor and oppressed, composed of Africans. The apartheid system aims at perpetuating the reservoir of labour for the white economy, and it must be assessed not theoretically but by the reality of the resultant misery endured by the black population.

Until its fall in 1974, the Portuguese regime claimed that the "multiracial" policy in its colonies differed entirely from apartheid in South Africa. As one example of its liberal policies it cited the Africanization of the Portuguese colonial army. Demographic factors alone may well have demanded an Africanization policy at that time, however, because of the growing shortage of manpower that arose as a consequence of emigration from Portugal. Approximately 1.2 million Portuguese had emigrated to the EEC countries since 1961, and it was difficult for Portugal to supply the 200 000 men required by the armed forces unless Africans were enlisted.

Some writers do acknowledge that there has been a certain basis for Portugal's claim of a multiracial policy, at least during one period in history, but most maintain that very little of this more liberal policy survived the imposition of military rule in Portugal in 1926.[4] No physical separation of the races was enforced by law in Portuguese Africa however.

Some specific factors relevant to the Portuguese political system will be further examined below. It is sufficient here to say that the idea *per se* of creating a Portuguese culture in Africa carried with it the notion that this culture was superior to that which the Africans possessed. The Portuguese "civilization mission" permeated the ideology of the Salazar and Caetano regimes. The establishment of the colonies was regarded as a major accomplishment without which a mere disorganized, primitive country would have existed. Marcelo Caetano emphasized this idea in a radio speech to the nation. "Portugal", he said, "*made* Angola. Portugal *created* Mozambique" [3].

II. *Economic factors*

Income distribution

Despite the white regimes' oft-repeated claim that they are conducting a policy in the best interests of all the people living in the area, all investigations—including those made by bodies representing these regimes—show that the Africans still form the poorest strata in these societies.[5]

Specific information on the differential between black and white wages in *South Africa* is hard to provide, because there are no general wage or distribution statistics covering the entire African population in South Africa

[4] See, for example, Basil Davidson, *The Liberation of Guiné,* [13a].
[5] See, for example, the annual surveys, published by the South African Institute of Race Relations in Johannesburg, called *A Survey of Race Relations in South Africa.* A substantial amount of information has also been published by various United Nations bodies.

and Namibia; nor have any general statistical surveys been conducted in the Bantustans. The statistics that exist apply to particular economic fields—for example, the mining industry, on which most data have been collected; or to one particular area, for example, the Transkei Bantustan, or they cover the situation in a specific foreign company active in South Africa. General statements about income distribution in the entire Republic of South Africa are thus statistical inferences, based on particular investigations. Speculation has arisen about the reasons for this absence of statistical data in a modern country. *The Statesman's Year-Book 1974/75* had this to say:

The registration of Bantu essential data was introduced on a compulsory basis many years ago. However, despite serious efforts on the part of the registering authorities, *the Bantu are still largely reluctant to have their essential data registered.* Consequently no complete vital statistics are available for this population group [4]. (*SIPRI italics.*)

In 1972, a leading South African economist, Dr Francis Wilson, published an extensive study of the gold mining industry and disclosed that African wages in the industry in 1969 were no higher in real terms than in 1911, although white wages had risen 70 per cent during the same period [5]. Other investigations support this general information: the white-black wage ratio was 11.7: 1 in 1911 and 20.1: 1 in 1969.[6] A general estimate of income distribution in 1969, issued by a South African source, said that Africans, who make up 68 per cent of the population, received only 18.8 per cent of all income, whereas the whites, who compose 19.2 per cent of the population, received 74.0 per cent of all income [6]. The average monthly *per capita* income in 1969 for whites was $133.00 as compared with $9.80 for Africans. According to another general estimate in 1974, approximately 70 per cent of the total African population is living below the Poverty Datum Line (PDL) [7].[7]

In *Rhodesia,* the white-black wage ratio by 1974 was nearly 11: 1, according to Finance Minister Wrathall [8]. Wage information does not, however, include the rural African population living on subsistence farming. The income of this group is substantially below the average: in 1965, the annual *per capita* income for African workers was reported to be $359, but the *per capita* annual income for Africans living in rural areas was only $28 [9 a].

A survey conducted by the University of Rhodesia's social studies faculty in 1974 showed that in terms of detailed Poverty Datum Line studies, the African workers were generally underpaid. Average wages ranged from $83 a month for workers in the manufacturing industry to $118 for schoolteachers. The PDL in Salisbury in January 1974 ranged from $61

[6] See, for example, *Consolidated Gold Fields Limited: Anti-Report CIS,* [70] and *Sechaba* [71].
[7] The PDL is the calculated level of wages that a family in South Africa needs in order to survive. The PDL measure was established by survey groups at South African universities and is used also in Rhodesia.

for a family of two to $162 for a family of eight, according to the survey [10].

In the former Portuguese colonies, where the majority of the African people still reside in rural areas, statistical information on income distribution was even more fragmentary than in South Africa and Rhodesia. In 1960, minimum wages were established by law and varied in 1965 between $34 and $204 per month for semi-skilled and skilled workers. The monthly rural wage paid for unskilled labour in Angola averaged $7.50 in cash and $11.60 in allowances. In Mozambique, rural salaries varied from $8.80 to $17.20 per month [11].

Social services

The distribution of opportunities and services closely follows the structure of income distribution and stands in inverse proportion to the need. For example, in *Namibia* in 1967, where the ratio of whites to non-whites was 1:7, there were 27 hospitals and six health centres for whites, and 39 hospitals and 38 health centres for seven times as many non-whites. There was not a single African doctor in the entire country. Only two out of 10 African children attended school, usually a missionary rather than state-supported school, and few were able to continue studying for more than two years [12]. In *South Africa* in 1972, there were 11 universities for whites, three for Bantus and one each for Indians and Coloureds. There are two educational systems: for white children schooling is free and compulsory; for non-white children, not even the primary schools are free, and books and other necessary materials have to be paid for, making it impossible for many parents to afford even a minimum of education for their children.

The situation in *Portuguese Africa* reflected that of metropolitan Portugal itself, which lags far behind Western Europe in education and health services: in 1960 only 11 Africans from Portuguese Guinea had acquired graduate status at universities and high schools in Portugal [13 b].

Labour legislation

The Africans in *South Africa* are prohibited from forming registered trade unions or negotiating wages or other working conditions.

There are two important white trade-union organizations in South Africa: the Confederation of Labour, which is decidedly pro-apartheid, and the Trade Union Council of South Africa (TUCSA), which is more multiracial in the sense that, although the executive leadership is white, Coloureds and Indians may hold membership. When TUCSA was formed in 1954, its decision to exclude African unions gave rise to a controversy that has continued over the years. Between 1962 and 1967 non-registered African unions were permitted to affiliate, but these were once again excluded in

1967 and still again in 1969, mainly because a number of white trade unions resigned in protest against the admission of Africans. In 1973, TUCSA's Executive Committee declared that it did not intend to challenge the provision of the South African Industrial Conciliation Act which excludes Africans from membership in registered trade unions. In 1974, conditions changed once again, as will be described in Part IV.

Non-registered African trade unions have been in existence since the beginning of the century. In 1954 they combined to form the non-racial South African Congress of Trade Unions (SACTU), but until 1973 all strikes by African workers were illegal. Conditional and limited strike-rights for certain categories were proposed by the government in the summer of 1973. Detailed information about the strength of the African trade unions that participated in the first mass strikes in 1973 is classified. Union membership is low. There are 22 black trade unions with 40 000 members [14]. Similar conditions prevail in *Namibia*.

In *Rhodesia,* organized African labour has not developed any significant strength. In Portuguese Africa, as in metropolitan Portugal, trade unions, strikes and demonstrations were illegal until April 1974.

The migratory labour system and forced labour

The migratory labour system, sometimes called the contract labour system, or—in Portuguese Africa—the forced labour system, prevails throughout the area.

In *South Africa,* each African officially belongs to a Bantustan and is classified as a migratory worker when working in a white area. Usually he is employed on a one-year contract. Those Africans who are actually recruited from a Bantustan are not allowed to bring their families into the white area. African workers have no right to choose jobs: they are simply recruited through the employers' central agencies that are in complete control of African labour outside the Bantustans and can send workers wherever they are needed. In the Bantustans there is very little industry or arable land, and unemployment is high.

Despite the fact that South Africa has its own African labour reserve, its mining industry must still import foreign migratory workers. Under an intergovernmental agreement, Portuguese Mozambique supplied 100 000 workers per year to the South African mines. South Africa paid a recruitment fee of $6.00 per African worker to the colonial government. Their wages were paid to the government of Mozambique, which deducted taxes and paid the recruits upon their return. Forty to 50 per cent of the wages of these so-called "labour units" were paid in gold, at fixed prices, to the government in Portugal, which could then sell the gold at market prices for a considerable profit.

Over 40 per cent of *Lesotho*'s male population, 25 per cent of *Malawi*'s,

20 per cent of *Botswana*'s, and 8 per cent of *Swaziland*'s, worked in South Africa by early 1974.

Since the German colonial period, the administrative area reserved for the whites in Namibia has been known as the Police Zone. Africans are not allowed to move from one place to another or to change employment without permission within the zone, nor are they allowed to leave their homelands unless they have a labour contract. Prior to the outbreak of the SWAPO-organized mass strikes in 1971, a contract labour system controlled the recruitment of Africans from the homelands into the zone.

When slavery was formally abolished in *Portuguese Africa* in 1878 a system of forced or contract labour took its place. The large, European-owned plantations and industries contracted Africans through central agencies. All *indigenas* had to work six months per year for the state, a company or an individual. The forced labour system was officially terminated in 1961, but Africans continued to be employed under contracts whenever the authorities deemed this to be in the "national interest", especially in Angola. The contract labour system was never very widespread in Portuguese Guinea.

In *Rhodesia,* forced labour for Africans aged 12–60 was introduced in February 1974.

Job reservations

In *South Africa* and *Namibia,* a variety of job reservation measures restrict the opportunities for non-whites to become skilled workers. The government controls the job reservation system and can grant temporary exemptions wherever there is a shortage of white labour. The preservation of this system is one of the main demands of some white trade unions.

In *Rhodesia* and *Portuguese Africa* no formal rules prevent Africans from doing qualified work, but the social conditions of the average African serve as a natural barrier to advancement.

Land ownership

Outside the Bantustans in *South Africa* and *Namibia,* land ownership by Africans is prohibited by law. Inside the Bantustans, blacks are prohibited from owning land individually. A few African farms which came into existence in the Transvaal under the more liberal legislation before 1948 are known as "black spots", and the intention is to remove them because they are in the white area. In South Africa, the Bantustans cover approximately 14 per cent of the total area but contain no mineral wealth, no highly fertile agricultural districts and no major cities. Only the Transkei, set up in 1963, consists of an unbroken geographical area and has a coastline. Altogether by 1973 the nine Bantustans contained 260 scattered parcels of land. The

Kwazulu Bantustan, for example, consists of 29 separate pieces. In 1955, a South African government commission calculated that the Bantustans would be able to support 2.3 million people [15]. By 1974 they had a population of seven million.

No black Africans in Namibia may own property in the Police Zone, where the only fertile land is located. White-owned farms cover 47.3 per cent of the country. The Africans are also prohibited by law from selling agricultural or other products to other Bantustans [9b].

In *Rhodesia,* under the Land Apportionment Act as amended in 1941, 38 per cent of the total area, including the most cultivable land, has been allocated for the white community. Under the Land Tenure Act of 1969, specific African areas are being organized: the first two Rhodesian "Bantustans" were established in November 1973.

Prior to April 1974, Portuguese civil law generally prohibited individual African ownership of land in rural areas. Furthermore, African farmers were not allowed to hold more than a few hectares of land anywhere, although Europeans could obtain concessions of up to 50 000 hectares and foreign companies still more. In *Angola,* for example, the average European coffee farmer owning 100 hectares could have an annual income of $28 000, but an African farmer was restricted to only one or two hectares, and consequently earned only around 2 per cent of that amount. By 1971, 60 per cent of the cultivable land in Angola consisted of large farms, belonging almost exclusively to Europeans [16].

The economic strategy of the white regimes

The white regimes have usually responded to demands for improvement of African economic conditions by pointing to such on-going reform pro-grammes as the various Bantu development schemes in South Africa and Namibia and the reforms in education and health services which were initiated in the Portuguese colonies after 1961. But the ruling National Party in South Africa has been quite outspoken in opposing any fundamental changes in the economic conditions of the African population. Prime Minis-ter Vorster has said, for example, that he fears "elements who are propagating communism in a disguised form. They are advocating a reallo-cation of assets, which would amount to a form of Socialism and *would mean the end of South Africa*" [17]. (*SIPRI italics.*)

This assumption, that a redistribution of income and social opportunities would, in fact, bring about a fundamental change in the present structure in South Africa, actually seems to be in agreement with the view held by a wide range of critics of the apartheid system, ranging from the leftists to the liberals. Their view is that South Africa's economic prosperity is in fact based on the constant supply of cheap black labour and is therefore de-pendent on the continuity of the apartheid system. Cheap labour and low

35

social costs are the sole reasons for South Africa's attractiveness to foreign investors.

But divergent opinions have also emanated from the South African political establishment—chiefly from members of the Progressive Party but also from liberal economists in South Africa and elsewhere. These critics of the apartheid system hold that economic considerations alone call for the development of a multiracial society based on more equable economic conditions. They consider the Bantustan scheme to be economically unrealistic and demand its abolition. South Africa is beginning to suffer from a shortage both of skilled and unskilled labour, and this despite the recruitment of African workers from other countries. The proportion of the labour force in the manufacturing industry, in particular, continues to decline [18]. Skilled African workers will be needed, these critics say, to sustain the economy. They regard the separate development plan for the Bantustans as a waste of potential labour. Thus, for economic reasons, the liberalization of the apartheid system is being advocated. The extent to which a liberalization of political conditions is being considered will be discussed below.

South Africa's present economic strategy is to create a "co-prosperity sphere" in Southern Africa, ideally taking the form of a federation of Botswana, Lesotho, Swaziland, Malawi, Rhodesia and Malagasy—with South Africa as the dominant power in this economically integrated bloc. Portuguese Africa was included in this strategy prior to the 1974 coup. Despite Zambia's clear opposition to apartheid, the extensive economic relations between the two countries have caused the South African government to consider this country as a potential ally. In 1968, Prime Minister Vorster expressed his conviction that the time will come when Zambia and South Africa "will understand each other not only because of good relationships, but because of the need for Southern Africa to be kept free of Communist infiltration . . . We will be obliged to close our ranks—and here I include Zambia" [19].

The Caetano regime in Portugal had pursued a parallel line, which ideally would have resulted in the creation of a "Lusitanian Commonwealth" involving Brazil and the African colonies, with Portugal as the leading power. The Portuguese dream of establishing such an intercontinental commonwealth was based on concepts that were not only anachronistic but contrary to the South African design for the area. Any real understanding and cooperation between Portugal and South Africa was probably impossible for historical reasons; theoretically, if such cooperation had existed, it could have provided the colonial governments in Portuguese Africa with the traditional and legal basis for demanding military protection from South Africa after the 1974 coup in Portugal.

South Africa's politico-economic plan for a co-prosperity sphere was expressed in the so-called "dialogue policy". The aim of this policy was, obviously, to establish South Africa as an accepted partner on the African continent and neutralize black African opposition to its internal apartheid system. The prospect of substantial economic gains was held out to those black African states that would be willing to normalize their political relations with South Africa. The dialogue policy was most energetically promoted between 1968 and 1971 and temporarily evoked a certain amount of response from some of the Organization of African Unity (OAU) member states, such as Malawi and the Ivory Coast.

III. *Political factors*

Opportunities for the non-white population to participate in political life are non-existent or minimal in all the countries concerned. But the Portuguese colonial system allowed for more African representation after 1961 than did the apartheid system of South Africa. A certain difference in development also exists between Rhodesia and South Africa: in Rhodesia there is no question of excluding Africans from parliamentary representation, while in South Africa and Namibia there is no question of allowing African representation.

The franchise

Africans in *South Africa* and *Namibia* cannot vote or hold office except in the Bantustans. The Parliament of the Republic of South Africa is elected by whites. Previous legislation that permitted a small number of blacks to have indirect representation has been rescinded. In 1969 the few Coloureds in the Cape who were allowed to vote were removed from the common electoral rolls. They now vote on separate rolls which deprives them of any direct representation in the government of the country. All whites above the age of 18 have the right to vote, however, and to be elected to the governing bodies in the Republic. At present, the House of Assembly consists of 166 members, 160 of whom are elected by white voters in the Republic and six by white voters in Namibia.

No white party has yet endorsed the idea of "one-man one-vote". The United Party stands firmly for white leadership in South Africa. Its reformist aim is restricted to the creation of a federal political system in which power and responsibility would be divided more fairly between the white community and the Bantustans.

The liberal Progressive Party describes itself as a modern and enlightened force in South Africa. It primarily represents financial interests. Harry Oppenheimer, chairman of the Anglo-American Corporation of South Africa, was one of its first prominent members. Its sole member of Parliament up to 1974 was Mrs Helen Suzman. The Progressive Party favours extending a qualified franchise to non-whites, based either on education or income.

According to Mrs Suzman, such a scheme, when coupled with the introduction of compulsory and free education for the blacks, would eventually lead to one-man one-vote, but only after a period of 10 or more years.

After the 1970 elections, in which the ruling National Party still enjoyed a firm majority, it was predicted that the most serious future challenge to the present regime would come from the extreme right-wing Herstigte Nasionale Party,[8] rather than from the more liberal opposition parties.

In *Rhodesia* the new republican constitution of 1970 did not change the previous situation: 50 of the 66 seats remained reserved for whites. The ruling Rhodesian Front still held all 50 seats in the 1974 elections. The African franchise is qualified: in 1974 only 10 000 could vote. The Coloureds have the same voting rights as the whites. Within white politics, the two more liberal opposition parties—the Centre Party and the Rhodesian Party—have minimal support, while the strength of the rightist opposition Rhodesia National Party is growing.

There is no black parliamentary party. The sole representation of Africans in Parliament has been by independent black or white liberal candidates.

In the *Portuguese colonies,* any African could in theory acquire the same political status as a Portuguese, under what was known as the *assimilado* system. After absorbing what was officially deemed to be an adequate amount of Portuguese civilization and passing a literacy examination in the Portuguese language, an African could become an *assimilado* and theoretically acquire all of the privileges of Portuguese citizenship, including the right to vote. The vast majority of Africans, who never achieved this status, remained classified as *indigenas* and were still denied the franchise, and qualified Africans never grew large enough in number to influence the structure of the colonial regimes.

Obviously, no democratic system could be developed in the African colonies by a metropolitan power itself lacking democratic practices. No opposition candidates or opposition parties were allowed before the 1974 coup either in Portugal itself or in its overseas territories.

Non-white representation in South Africa and Namibia

In the native reserves in *South Africa* and *Namibia* black legislative assemblies are replacing the earlier territorial authorities and are being vested with certain extended legislative and administrative powers. Executive power rests with a council, usually consisting of six members of a department. White officials will serve the Bantustan governments until trained Bantu citizens are able to take over. However, these African parliaments and governments do not, and will not, have any power over foreign or economic policy, the judiciary or defence matters.

[8] "Herstigte" is Afrikaans for *re-established.*

The Coloured People's Representative Council consists of 40 elected and 20 appointed members. The Council's Executive has legislative powers and is responsible for the management of finance, education, community welfare, pensions and local government in the rural areas and settlements to which the Coloureds are restricted. The South Africa Indian Council is a statutory body consisting of 30 representatives of the Indian communities. It *advises* the South African government on the economic, social and political interests of the Indian population.

Coloureds and Indians are allowed to form political parties. The opposition Labour Party and the Natal Coloured Teachers' Association are influential among the Coloured communities. They object to the classification of "Coloured" people as a separate population group and demand citizenship rights equal to those of whites. Under the Prohibition of Political Interference Act, the various non-white political parties representing the different races are specifically prohibited from cooperating with one another.

In the political field, South Africa is willing to cooperate with any African government, but only on South Africa's own terms and without interference in its internal policy towards its African population. When justifying the apartheid policy as a *political* ideology, the ruling party becomes evasive, calling attention to the threat of Communism rather than to concrete political conditions within the Republic. Prime Minister Vorster said in 1973, for example, at the celebration in Cape Town of the 25th anniversary of National Party rule, that the country's enemies *"do not so much desire the franchise for all its peoples, as possession of the country itself for its strategic position"* [20]. (*SIPRI italics.*) The anti-Communist or anti-Socialist component in the apartheid ideology, possibly its only clearly distinguishable and definable component, is closely related to the important question of foreign political interests in the area, which will be discussed below. Another type of argument indicates that the whites fear that any sharing of power will automatically eliminate their privileges. In a statement to Parliament in 1968, Prime Minister Vorster illustrated this when he said:

It is true that there are blacks working for us. They will continue to work for us for generations, in spite of the ideal we have to separate them completely. Surely we all know that? . . . The fact of the matter is this: We need them, because they work for us . . . but the fact that they work for us can never—if one accepts this as one's own criterion one will be signing one's own death sentence now—entitle them to claim political rights. Not now, nor in the future. It makes no difference whether they are here with any degree of permanency or not . . . *Under no circumstances can we grant them those political rights in our territory, neither now nor ever.* [21]. (*SIPRI italics.*)

Chapter 2. International conflict determinants

Several factors explain world interest in Southern Africa. Large investments of foreign capital have been and are being made, and in view of future
energy crises the huge reserves of vital and strategic minerals in the area will
become even more valuable. There are also important foreign political and
geostrategic considerations, such as NATO's interest in the sea route round
the Cape of Good Hope and the issue of the militarization of the Indian
Ocean.

I. *Foreign economic interests*

Structure

When considering the Southern African conflict in its global perspective,
foreign economic interests stand out as the major factor favouring the
maintenance of the *status quo* in South Africa, Namibia and Angola, and to
a lesser degree in Rhodesia.

Being a modern, highly developed country in the Western sense, South
Africa's economy is closely linked in all fields to that of the major Western
industrial nations, mainly through the activities of large multinational concerns. These concerns mostly represent British and US capital. South Africa
is regarded as one of the safest countries in the world for foreign investments and, according to a survey published in 1974, is one of the few where
the investment climate is improving.[9] This was not always the case. Following the Sharpeville massacre in 1960, there was general fear of a massive
civil insurrection. The result was the withdrawal of foreign capital until it
became clear that the repressive measures taken by the government had
succeeded in pacifying the black population. South Africa, in its turn, is one
of the major investors in neighbouring countries. South African capital, in
conjunction with foreign investment, has been placed in Namibia, Angola,
Mozambique and Rhodesia, although, for obvious reasons, Portuguese capital played a more important role in the economy of Portuguese Africa. The
economy of colonial Portugal was to a large extent foreign-controlled; here,
too, British and US capital played a vital role. Although Portugal was a

---

[9] This is the opinion of a pioneer in risk-evaluation systems, Professor F. T. Haner of the
University of Delaware's Department of Business Administration. In his latest Business
Environment Risk Index for 1973, South Africa rates "very high" on most of his scales which
measure the degree of safety of foreign investments. One of the basic criteria used is "political
stability".

relatively underdeveloped European country, it was attractive to foreign investment for much the same reasons that South Africa still is—namely, the cheap labour supply and generous taxation rules. Portugal was in the paradoxical situation of being at one and the same time the last empire in the world of the classical type and also a colony depending on the investments of more modern economic empires for its survival.

Generally speaking, the same multinational Western financial interests are present throughout the area, indeed throughout the continent. The scale of foreign investments and banking as well as the activities of various companies in Southern Africa have been documented in several studies.[10]

The structure of foreign capital in Southern Africa follows the usual pattern: companies are set up as wholly- or partly-owned subsidiaries of a parent company, an arrangement which offers them the opportunity to circumvent, for example, an arms embargo (see Part III). In general, indirect investment has been declining in favour of direct investment in subsidiaries. This is especially evident in the development of British interests in South Africa. US investment only began on a large scale after 1945 and took the form of direct investment in US subsidiaries. Unlike the British subsidiaries, the US branch companies in South Africa are wholly owned by their parent US corporations.

Around the mid-1960s, the manufacturing sector in South Africa overtook mining as the main recipient of foreign capital, indicating that South Africa had achieved an industrial economy and was no longer a mere supplier of raw materials to the industrialized world.

The operations and interests of Western companies in Southern Africa are protected by normal business discretion and are not automatically made public in their home countries, not even to their governments. But occasionally their activities are brought out into the open. In 1970, a campaign was launched in the United States to force US firms either to disengage completely from South Africa or to adopt industrial policies in line with US practices. Only Polaroid made concrete improvements in their workers' labour conditions, but some companies within the motor and oil industries promised substantial reforms. Again, in 1973, a report published in the UK by the *Guardian* caused considerable official embarrassment when it revealed that a substantial number of British companies in South Africa were paying below-subsistence wages. The result of public and parliamentary pressure was a noticeable improvement in the employment conditions of some black workers in British-owned industries. Similarly in autumn 1974, the Swedish government was reported to be greatly surprised when it was revealed that some 18 Swedish companies, acting through one of Sweden's largest private banks, were operating in South Africa.

[10] See, for example, *The South African Connection: Western Investment in Apartheid* [22] and *U.S. Business Involvement in Southern Africa* [72]. There are also several UN publications on the subject.

Traditionally, the whole area has been dominated by British financial interests, but during the last decade several other foreign countries—representing US, West German, Swiss, Japanese, French and other capital—have moved in. South Africa's main trading partners are at present the UK, followed by the EEC countries, Japan and the USA, in descending order. Of the EEC countries, FR Germany was the largest partner; France's share remained relatively small despite South Africa's arms imports from this country.

Natural resources

Foreign capital is traditionally invested in mining and other industries, which together produce almost all the exports from this area. The examples below illustrate the magnitude of foreign financial interests. In South Africa, gold is still the major export item, followed by diamonds and coal. Rich reserves of diamonds have also been found in Namibia, but the major export item there is uranium. In Angola, oil has become the major export item.

Gold and diamonds

The largest single employer of labour in South African mines, apart from the government itself, is the Anglo-American Corporation of South Africa, whose chairman is Harry Oppenheimer. This company controls 40 per cent of the gold production. South African state holdings, especially in gold mining, continue to rise, but 42 per cent of the shares in Anglo-American were still held in Britain and other European countries in 1970 [22 a]. One of Anglo-American's subsidiaries, De Beers Consolidated Mines of South Africa, controls in turn the largest and most profitable enterprise in Namibia, the Consolidated Diamond Mines of South West Africa. De Beers has a near monopoly on the world trade in diamonds, controlling some 80 per cent. The real ownership of De Beers was estimated in 1969, by the company itself, to be spread as follows: South Africa, 44 per cent; continental Europe, 25 per cent; the United Kingdom, 25 per cent, and others, 4 per cent [9c]. In Namibia, the second largest diamond producer is the Marine Diamond Corporation, which is closely associated with Anglo-American and mainly owned by South Africa, the UK and the USA. In Angola, De Beers, in association with Portuguese capital, controls the Angola Diamond Company, Diamang, which is the country's largest private employer.

Uranium

The huge, international British-run Rio Tinto Zinc Corporation (RTZ) controls, among other things, uranium production in Namibia at the Rossing site near Swakopmund. In 1970, 43 per cent of the Corporation's profits came from its South African subsidiary, Palabora Mining [22 b]. In 1968, the consortium, Rossing Uranium Ltd., was formed in association with RTZ and South African and French capital, specifically to exploit the estimated 100 000 tons of low-grade uranium at Rossing. Subsequently, the Urangesellschaft of FR Germany also invested in the project. In 1969, agreements for the sale and supply of uranium were concluded with FR Germany, Switzerland and Japan. South Africa is now the largest supplier of uranium to Japan. Under an agreement reached in 1970, Rossing will supply 7 500 tons of processed uranium to Britain beginning in 1976.

In 1970, the Urangesellschaft signed a contract with the Portuguese Commission for Nuclear Energy for the mining of natural uranium in Angola and Mozambique in a concession area totalling 6 300 km².

Other strategic minerals

Multinational companies are also involved in the extraction of other strategic minerals in the area.

The London-based Lonrho Ltd. operates in Rhodesia, Mozambique and South Africa where its activities include platinum mining. US capital controls the Tsumeb Corporation in Namibia, the main producer of copper, zinc and lead. In Rhodesia, three local companies owned by the Union Carbide Corporation of the United States control most of the large chromium deposits. Union Carbide is also engaged in vanadium mining in South Africa. Krupp of FR Germany financed the huge Cassinga iron mining project in Angola.

Oil

Oil prospecting and exploitation in Southern Africa are conducted almost exclusively by large multinational oil companies. The largest of these in Angola is the Gulf Oil Corporation of the United States. Through its wholly-owned subsidiary, Cabinda Gulf Oil, it has acquired concessions that run until the year 2010. The Angolan oil, which contains a high percentage of wax, is refined in Trinidad and then exported to the USA, Canada and Japan. In exchange, under the Gulf agreement, the USA supplies Portugal with oil of a more suitable quality than the Angolan product.

In 1974 the Portuguese-Belgian company Petrangol-Angol entered into association with three US companies to intensify the oil prospecting that is under way on the continental shelf of Angola's Cuanza basin. The Portuguese government has the right to acquire the equivalent of 37.5 per cent of all oil found in Angola, and 100 per cent of it in case of war or an energy crisis [23]. A Belgian-Portuguese company applied in early 1974 for permission to build a refinery with an annual capacity of 10 million tons in São Vincente on the Cape Verde islands. In Mozambique, nine applications for oil prospecting rights were received after July 1973 from Norwegian, South African, Swedish and US companies [24]. No oil has been found in Namibia and reports of an oil find in South Africa have not been confirmed.

Agriculture

In the past, foreign companies have to a very large extent controlled the commercial cultivation and export of such income-producing crops as coffee, sugar, cashew nuts, cotton and rice in Portuguese Guinea and Mozambique. Even today, they retain this position of power in Angola and Rhodesia. In Rhodesia, for example, Lonrho Ltd. alone owns almost one million acres of land. The production of tobacco in Rhodesia, which accounts for a large part of the country's export earnings, is British-controlled. In Angola and Mozambique sugar production is a foreign monopoly. The largest sugar company in Mozambique is the British-owned Sena Sugar Estates. Cashew nut production there is mainly controlled by the Anglo-American Corporation. South African capital is also heavily involved in agricultural production in these countries, marking one of the differences between industrial and less developed economies.

Transport and communication

Another difference between South Africa's economic status and that of the less developed countries of the area is its control and ownership of transport and communication, which are state-owned in South Africa. In the underdeveloped nations foreign firms predominate in this sector as well as in agriculture and industry. The oil pipeline connection across Mozambique, that links Rhodesia with the port of Beira, is owned by Lonrho Ltd. of London. The Benguela railway in Angola, running from Zaire through Zambia to the port of Lobito, is owned by the British Railway Company which, in turn, is 90 per cent owned by Tanganyika Concessions, a British mining and investment group. The entire communications network in Angola is controlled by International Telephone and Telegraph of the USA (ITT). The ITT is also active in South Africa.

Port and harbour installations also involve foreign financial interests. The Portuguese LISNAVE shipyard, which is jointly owned by a Portuguese-Dutch-Swedish consortium, set out in 1973 to build a major modern military harbour in the port of Nacala in Mozambique. The project collapsed when the Swedish government influenced the two Swedish shipyards holding 24.5 per cent of the shares to request withdrawal of LISNAVE from the Nacala project in order to avoid political embarrassment. It has not been possible to find out exactly how this governmental intervention was implemented, but LISNAVE did withdraw from the project on the recommendation of the Swedish shareholders. Instead, a US-French-

44

Japanese consortium declared its interest in investing $45 million over a five-year period for the modernization of 26 ports in Mozambique, presumably including the military port of Nacala.

Special projects

Huge development projects have been undertaken by South Africa and Portugal with foreign financial backing.

Construction of the Cabora Bassa dam, a vast hydroelectric project in the Tete district of Mozambique, was initiated in 1969 by South African and West European consortiums. The waters of the Zambezi river are being dammed up in order to supply electric power to South Africa and to permit extensive farming in Tete. The first stage will be completed in 1975, with the formation of a lake 220 km long. The installation of high-tension power transmission lines to South Africa has already been completed, ahead of schedule. The ZAMCO consortium in charge of the project is based in Lisbon and is composed of West German, French, Italian, Portuguese, South African and Swiss companies. ASEA of Sweden withdrew from the consortium at the request of the Swedish government.

The Cabora Bassa project illustrates several aspects of foreign economic interests—for example, the close collaboration between colonial Portuguese and South African capital, working together with Western financial and industrial trusts. Specifically, it demonstrates South Africa's economic expansion to the north. Before 1974, the Cabora Bassa project was often described in terms of its strategic significance to white Africa: the great lake would form a natural barrier to prevent the FRELIMO guerilla armies from advancing south of the Zambezi river in Mozambique. White immigrants would populate the irrigated Tete area and also form a human barrier to the north.

The Cunene Dam project, on the border between Angola and Namibia, has received comparatively less publicity than Cabora Bassa, but it illustrates the same aspects, and again, especially South Africa's economic expansion. South Africa is the principal financer of the Cunene Dam. Non-African investments have come mainly from FR Germany and Portugal. A campaign initiated by the World Council of Churches discouraged British companies from joining.[11]

In Portuguese Africa, foreign companies concluded special security agreements with the Portuguese to preserve law and order, including the use of their own police and security forces to protect their property in Angola and Mozambique. Special funds were allocated for the support of the Portuguese armed forces.

[11] See, for example, *The Cunene Dam Scheme and the Struggle for the Liberation of Southern Africa* [73].

II. *Foreign political interests*

The political dimension of foreign economic interests in Southern Africa takes the form of anti-Communism in theory, and support for and actual cooperation with the white regimes in practice. Also present are geostrategic considerations of the need to protect the Cape Route and the need to counter a perceived Communist threat in the Indian Ocean. This foreign political interest is closely intertwined with that of the white regimes in the region.

Anti-Communism

During the cold war in the 1950s, outright statements about "African inferiority" and "white superiority" were replaced by another theme. Anti-Communism became the popular justification for retaining the *status quo* in Portuguese Africa, Rhodesia and South Africa. In official statements, if not in practical policies, the anti-Communist theme faded in the West after 1960. In Southern Africa, however, it has consistently been reinforced. The liberation movements there are called "Communist agents", and, as was exemplified earlier, demands by the African opposition for equal political rights and redistribution of income are denounced as proof of foreign "Communist penetration" of African organizations. Replying to these charges, Amilcar Cabral stated that "the people are not fighting for ideas, for things in anyone's head. They are fighting to win material benefits, to live better and in peace, to see their lives go forward, to guarantee the future of their children" [25].

The anti-Communist theme has possibly been used primarily in the hope of convincing the West that the white regimes in Southern Africa are the representatives of democracy in the area. The arguments and statements of those regimes have often been repeated by supporters outside Africa. The chief basis for the opinion that all African opposition groups, and especially the liberation movements, are Communist agents is the fact that the Socialist bloc provides most of the military aid to these movements. FRELIMO was, for example, hardly ever mentioned by the Caetano regime without the epithet "Chinese-led Communist". The following description by a supporter of the Ian Smith regime in Rhodesia is typical: "With the tentacles of Communist-backed terrorism thrusting deeper into Southern Africa, the defence policies of the white-ruled states have been brought, inevitably, to the verge of total cooperation" [26]. The assumption that a direct, causal relationship exists between the supply of arms and political influence on the part of supplier ᴼver recipient was repudiated by the President of FRELIMO, Samora Machel, who said:

FRELIMO's orientation and personality is Mozambique. I know people suggest we are communists because most of our aid comes from Moscow and Peking. But they

46

are the only people who will really help us. Both Russia and China have fought armed struggles and whatever comes from their struggles and is relevant to Mozambique, we use [27].

The anti-Communist theme has at least two functions: one is to create support for the white regimes among their own African and white populations and among the liberal African states; another is to ensure support from the major Western powers. If a qualitative analysis were made of all relevant public statements, especially those by spokesmen of the South African government, the result would probably show that the anti-Communist theme is adapted in diverse ways to serve these two purposes. Inside Africa, the Communist threat is frequently described as a *Chinese* threat, and the most commonly cited illustration is China's relationship with Tanzania, as exemplified in the construction of the Tanzam railway.[12] This railway, linking landlocked Zambia with Tanzania, was built by some 15 000 Chinese army engineers, whose mere presence in the area is regarded with apprehension. Their number is consistently and incorrectly cited in South Africa as 200 000. South African Defence Minister Botha warned his fellow citizens: "We must not forget the Tanzam railway. China has built it mainly for strategic, not economic reasons. *Will China be tempted one day to dump its surplus population in Africa?*" [28]. *(SIPRI italics.)*

In order to win support from abroad, especially from NATO and the United States, a variation of the anti-Communist theme is used. In this context the Communist threat takes the form of a *Soviet* naval presence in the Indian Ocean. Soviet relations with both Atlantic and Indian Ocean coastal states are said to be creating a presumed sphere of influence stretching from Cuba, across Africa, to Bangladesh. It is claimed that the target of Soviet military designs in Southern Africa is the supply route of oil and other strategic materials to the West around the Cape of Good Hope. The *NATO Review* has described this threat:

The South Atlantic vacuum is increasingly tempting for the Soviets. The role of Cuba must be added to the development of Conakry as a naval base. Thanks to its geostrategic key position, South Africa occupies an extremely important blocking position for the Soviet Navy's offensive plans, and it would be in the well-understood defence interests of Western Europe and the USA to take account of this fact [29].

No theoretical combination of a Chinese and Soviet threat in the area has been elaborated in detail, but it could be inferred that two alternative conclusions are possible if this line of thought is carried through: either the conception of a Communist threat leads to a classical theory of conspiracy, even presuming the existence of a Sino-Soviet master plan for the conquest

[12] Also known as the Great Uhuru Railway or the TAZARA. (Uhuru=freedom, in Swahili.) The Tanzam Railway project is the largest development aid project ever undertaken by China in a foreign country. The agreement to build it was concluded in 1968, after the West had rejected the project as uneconomical.

of Southern Africa, or the ultimate aims of China and the Soviet Union in the area are seen as separate—China aims at the conquest of territory in Africa and the Soviet Union aims at control over the oil supplies and the Cape Route.

Geostrategy

As with foreign economic interests in Southern Africa, the foreign strategic interests described below are Western interests. This is so for two major reasons. First, the continent of Africa was by tradition a Western sphere of interest. Relations between the newly independent African states and the Socialist bloc have been viewed as pointing to a "foreign influence" in Africa, ever since Egypt in 1955 entered into major economic relations with the Soviet Union. This line of thought, adhered to by those Western powers that have major economic and strategic interests in Africa—but not necessarily shared by other Western powers—obviously does not recognize the policy of nonalignment adhered to by many new African states. Second, the Western strategic interest in Southern Africa is shown by the widely publicized debate about the need to protect the southern hemisphere, the oil supplies along the Cape Route and military control of the Indian Ocean.

No corresponding material has appeared about a Soviet or Chinese strategic interest in the area. The claim that such an interest exists is based on inferences, drawn from Soviet and Chinese relations with some African and Indian Ocean littoral states, and from the presence of Soviet naval units in the area.

The Cape Route

The need to protect the Cape Route is often singled out as the main Western geostrategic interest in Southern Africa. For many years South Africa's main foreign policy objective has been to achieve the position of a highly important strategic ally of the West and thereby to acquire the support of the major Western powers, either within a formal alliance or on a bilateral basis. Similarly, the Caetano regime in Portugal emphasized the usefulness to NATO of the Portuguese possessions in Africa. Military planners in the West and several of the NATO commands have frequently expressed their approval of extending NATO's sphere of interest south of the Tropic of Cancer, thereby echoing or parallelling the argumentation of the white minority regimes in Southern Africa. The Nixon administration that came into office in the United States in 1969 and the Conservative government that took office in Britain in 1970 both showed greater interest than their predecessors in Southern Africa from the point of view of protecting Western security. Sir Alec Douglas-Home, the British Conservative government's Secretary of Foreign Affairs, stated the need for an alliance with South Africa, in particular, but also with Portugal in Africa:

With the closing of the Suez Canal and the permanent routing of the oil of the Persian Gulf around the shores of Africa and the simultaneous appearance of a Soviet submarine fleet which is oceanic in range, South Africa's geographical position assumes new strategic significance. The policing of the South Atlantic and the West of the Indian Ocean becomes important both to Britain and to Western Europe. *These areas in effect* (although they may not formally be made so) *are an extension of NATO's responsibility* for the security of Europe [30]. (*SIPRI Italics.*)

The length of the Cape Route varies somewhat with the context of the discussion. When the US Department of Defense describes the Cape Route it may actually stretch from the Philippines to North America. In NATO debates it usually extends from the Persian Gulf, round the Cape of Good Hope, via the Cape Verde islands to the Tropic of Cancer, where the NATO Iberian Atlantic Area Command (IBERLANT) takes over responsibility. The IBERLANT thus covers much of North Africa; its duties include ensuring that Western Europe is continuously supplied with the goods necessary for its existence.

NATO member countries provided the persistent military support which enabled Portugal to wage a war in Africa until 1974. As an organization, NATO never applied any pressure on Portugal to leave Africa. On the contrary, its interest in Portuguese Africa as an ally has been expressed on several occasions, for example in this extract from its Parliamentary Report of autumn 1972: "Portugal as a member of NATO should be in a position to make available its facilities on the Azores, the Cape Verde Islands, Madeira and São Tomé, and to contribute on the African continent to the protection of the Cape Route, if NATO should request it" [31].

The Portuguese themselves had little strategic use for the Cape Verde islands. The United States, on the other hand, uses the Cape Verde base facilities for its submarines on duty in the Atlantic Ocean and for the important communications station that it maintains on the island of Sal. The communications centre also comprises a relay station for the main submarine cable linking Portugal with South Africa. In addition, Sal has an airport with a 300-metre runway, which is the only place where South African Airways planes flying between Europe and Southern Africa are permitted to land. Another airport, on the island of Praia, is being improved to receive long-distance jets. There are smaller airports on the islands of São Vincente, São Nicolau and Fogo. On São Vincente, the Porto Grande harbour with 915 metres of wharves ranks third after Lisbon and Lourenço Marques in tonnage handled within Portuguese territory. There are port installations on several of the other islands as well.

The possibilities for controlling Atlantic traffic from Guinea-Bissau and Angola, as well as the strategic importance of Angola's Atlantic coastline and Mozambique's Indian Ocean coastline, have often been stressed. In early 1974, when it became evident that the Portuguese armed forces were in no position to counter the PAIGC's army in Guinea-Bissau, an unusually large number of reports appeared claiming that PAIGC control over the country would mean, in effect, that the Soviet Union would acquire access to both the naval base in Bissau and to Cape Verde. In August 1974, shortly before Guinea-Bissau became independent, a leading PAIGC military commander declared, however, that the PAIGC would never allow any foreign military base to exist on Cape Verde [32]. Much concern was also expressed about Soviet relations with Guinea-Bissau's immediate neighbour to the south, the Republic of Guinea. The British press, in particular, repeatedly pointed out that the civilian airport in Conakry in Guinea had been transformed into a fully operational base for the Soviet "Badger" and "Bear" long-range aircraft. It was said that British warships could therefore no longer operate in the South Atlantic without Soviet approval and that the strategic importance of Simonstown had increased considerably [33]. All such reports have been denied by the Guinean government.

In the main, the West has followed two approaches in its strategy for protecting the Cape Route. Both are closely related to South African strategy. One idea was to establish a special South Atlantic Treaty Organization (SATO) and the other was to extend NATO's responsibility into the southern hemisphere. The possibility of creating SATO, with South Africa, Argentina, Brazil and Australia as leading partners, seemed quite feasible at the end of the 1960s. South Africa's Foreign Minister Muller paid repeated visits to Brazil and Argentina and conceded that his talks with the foreign ministers of these countries centred around "the communist penetration of the South Atlantic" [34]. But SATO's prospects soon vanished, for reasons quite beyond the control of South Africa or its major supporters. In 1972 a Labour government came into power in Australia, and in 1973 Juan Perón returned to Argentina. Foreign policy in those two countries was no longer favourable to a military alliance with South Africa.

Already in 1970, the former Deputy Chief of Staff of the Netherlands stated in Durban, South Africa, that NATO was considering the idea of supporting South Africa in the defence of the Cape Route, and even of associating South Africa with NATO. A chain of military bases was then envisaged, stretching from the Cape Verde islands to Iran. Portugal's contribution to this chain was to consist of the ports of Moçâmedes, Lobito and Luanda in Angola, and, most importantly, the high-capacity ports of Nacala, Beira and Lourenço Marques in Mozambique. It was also reported that the Caetano regime had offered the United States the use of the port of Nacala, which is large enough to accommodate the entire US seventh fleet. The State Department's response was "less than enthusiastic", however, for reasons to be described below [35].

In Guinea-Bissau, the naval base at Bissau was of some military significance, and in Angola the Portuguese Navy was based at Santo Antonio do Zaire, on the south bank of the Congo river. Even a small naval force in control of this latter base is sufficient to seal off all Congo river traffic.

The centre of the envisaged chain of bases to protect the Cape Route remains the South African naval base at Simonstown, which was a British naval base since 1895. In 1955 it was handed over to the South African government under the Simonstown Agreement. Under the agreement, however, the British continued to use the base and were responsible for the supply of naval weapons and equipment to ensure the defence of the Cape Route. In 1972, South Africa's first submarine base, Drommedaris, which was constructed by a Danish shipyard, opened at Simonstown.

Access to and use of Simonstown is a focal issue in the West's discussion of the protection of the Cape Route and the security of the southern hemisphere. South Africa has repeatedly offered the use of Simonstown to NATO and the United States. But no major Western power has yet found it politically feasible to enter into an open military agreement with South Africa. Such military cooperation as exists remains indirect. It is known that military intelligence, for example, has been exchanged for many years. The United States maintains a guided missile tracking station and a NASA space tracking station in South Africa.

The high-capacity communications station at Silvermine, built in the southern Cape Peninsula ostensibly as a British commitment under the Simonstown Agreement, is capable of tracking Indian Ocean and Atlantic shipping along the entire Cape Route. The station provides NATO and the United States—via Cape Verde—with information about the movements of Soviet naval units in the area.

NATO interest in the Cape Route remained confined to a relatively small group of countries within the organization until 1972, when a report, drafted by a subcommittee of the Military Committee of the North Atlantic Assembly and entitled "The Soviet Maritime Threat", was presented to the Assembly in Bonn. This report, which was based on the theory that a serious threat to the security of Europe was developing in the southern hemisphere, was accepted by the Assembly, which recommended that the North Atlantic Council give SACLANT, the Supreme Allied Commander Atlantic, a plan for the protection of vital shipping lanes in the Indian Ocean and the South Atlantic, including surveillance and communications.[13] The Assembly also recommended that the North Atlantic Council complete a detailed survey of the present oil requirements of North America and the NATO member states in Europe and draw up a 10-year forecast.

The SACLANT contingency plan was first revealed in a United Nations report which was circulated to parliamentary circles in the Hague in May 1974. It was subsequently confirmed by the NATO Press Service, which stated that the authorization for the study was given to SACLANT as early as October 1972 [36].[14]

---

[13] The Supreme Commander Atlantic is at present US Admiral Ralph Cousins. SACLANT's headquarters are in Norfolk, Virginia.
[14] This contingency planning subsequently received much publicity, mostly in the context of

The NATO Assembly is only an advisory body, however, and the contingency planning by SACLANT does not yet mean that NATO, as an organization, has actually taken on the responsibility of protecting the Cape Route. Nonetheless, it does illustrate a growing concern, already expressed before the energy crisis of 1973, about guaranteeing the supply of strategic raw materials to the West.

Before the 1973 war in the Middle East and the ensuing Arab oil boycott against Western Europe, the United States, South Africa and Portugal, the monthly volume of oil shipped round the Cape from the Persian Gulf amounted to some 20 million tons, about 90 per cent of which was destined for European ports [37]. Most of Europe's oil comes from the Persian Gulf states.

The large supertankers carrying up to 350 000 dead weight tons (dwt) now, and more in the future, will have to continue to use the Cape Route, even after the Suez Canal is reopened; because the Canal is limited to ships in the 60 000-dwt class at most.

The oil boycott in late 1973 suddenly highlighted the strategic importance of the Cape Route to the West. It also underlined the importance of oil, not only to military planners but to the general public in the industrialized world. It became obvious that these societies were much dependent on this single source of energy, and that a sudden reduction of oil supplies could bring about severe economic disruption.[15]

Vital commodities other than oil also follow the Cape Route. About 20 000 ships call at the Cape each year and another 14 000 pass without calling [38]. According to a survey commissioned by the US Navy, the United States imports 100 strategic minerals, 16 of them in amounts exceeding 100 000 tons annually. Forty of these minerals are required for normal peacetime use in US industry. About 50 per cent are shipped along the Cape Route [39].

The assured supply by sea of oil and other essential minerals in the event of a global conflict is a primary problem for the strategic planners of NATO and the United States. In this context, the Cape Route has become the most important naval area in the world.

The Indian Ocean

From the foregoing description of foreign strategic interests in the Cape Route, it is evident that the issue of protecting this route is linked closely to that of safeguarding the Indian Ocean. In terms of its strategic importance to the West, the Indian Ocean issue is argued on the same basis as is the Cape

revealing the existence of a change in the United States' policy towards Southern Africa—the "Tar Baby" option. (See page 66.) The United Nations report was prepared by Sean Gervasi and commissioned for the UN General Assembly's Decolonization Committee. The report has not yet been adopted and is not, therefore, an official document.
[15] For a discussion of the importance of oil, see *Oil and Security* [74].

Route. Emphasis is placed on the need to use South Africa as a military partner against a Communist threat in the Indian Ocean

The protection of the Cape Route is primarily a NATO strategic interest, whereas the military significance of control of the Indian Ocean is more specifically a US interest, in terms of the US global power rivalry with the Soviet Union.

The United States, of course, remains the major force within NATO, but the presentation of the development of a NATO interest in the Cape Route is of importance in this study insofar as it provides material for considering the possibility of direct NATO involvement in Southern Africa. Similarly, the focus here is not on US policy vis-à-vis the Soviet Union. Rather, the reason for including a more detailed presentation of the Indian Ocean issue is to examine whether the US military interest in the Indian Ocean is such that it may ultimately guarantee the existence of the present regime in South Africa.

The militarization of the Indian Ocean has become a highly controversial issue in the West.[16] The following presentation of the Indian Ocean issue concentrates on three aspects, the Western and Eastern military interest and naval deployments in the Indian Ocean, and the official policy of the majority of the Indian Ocean littoral states as formulated in the proposal to neutralize the Indian Ocean and to declare it a "nuclear-free zone of peace".

Western presence in the Indian Ocean

The mere fact that much of the oil and other strategic raw materials needed in Europe and the United States are shipped from the Far East or from the Persian Gulf round the Cape of Good Hope is, in itself, not enough to create a strategic problem, unless a plausible military threat to this supply route exists. The British decision to withdraw its military forces from "east of Suez" by 1971 prompted Western strategists to seek ways to fill the "vacuum" in Southern Africa and in other areas east of Suez. The appearance of Soviet naval units in the Indian Ocean on a permanent basis in 1968 provided what was considered to be the factual evidence of a threat.

The South African regime has consistently warned that when the British withdrew from the Indian Ocean, the Soviet Union would move in. In the words of Admiral H. H. Bierman, the Commander-in-Chief of South Africa's defence forces:

Communist penetration into the Southern Hemisphere, and the threats that this portends, have caused the Southern Hemisphere, and particularly the Indian Ocean to emerge dramatically from a position of relative obscurity and to assume a con-

---

[16] For a thorough presentation of this issue, see *World Armaments and Disarmament, SIPRI Yearbook 1975* [42 a].

spicuous position in the East-West power struggle. The focal point in this changed perspective is occupied by Southern Africa—and the Republic of South Africa [40].

But the United States and Britain signed an agreement on the development of a naval base on the British-controlled island of Diego Garcia in the Chagos archipelago in the Indian Ocean well before the British withdrawal from the area. In 1967, US naval strategists were developing a southern hemisphere plan aimed at securing supplies of raw materials from the ex-colonial Third World areas, in particular from the Far East and Africa.

A 1970 School of Naval Warfare research team, including five naval officers and one US Air Force colonel, concluded that cooperation with South Africa on naval defence matters would be necessary in the future, despite the existing differences of political opinion between this country and the United States. According to Admiral Elmo Zumwalt, the US Chief of Naval Operations, this strategy included the development of a US naval presence in the Indian Ocean, and also an extensive communications build-up for the "worldwide command and control network for naval operations supporting national requirements" [41].

The military reconnaissance network established between the United States and South Africa extends over Iran to Indonesia. In this context, the potential role of Iran cannot be overestimated. Iran has become the leading military power in the Persian Gulf, having embarked very early on a military policy of its own when the British left the Gulf. The Shah of Iran allowed the United States to set up an important reconnaissance centre on the island of Abu Musa in the Persian Gulf. The construction of the $600-million naval-air complex at Chah Bahar, close to Iran's border with Pakistan, is already under way. This will become the largest military base in the Indian Ocean. As Iran develops a role in the Indian Ocean, it may also establish closer links with South Africa. A first step in this direction may have been taken in 1974, when Iran announced that it would supply oil to South Africa despite the Arab boycott. An informal axis, consisting of the USA, South Africa and Iran, for the military surveillance of the Indian Ocean seems to be in the making.

Since the Indo-Pakistani War in 1971, the US Navy has maintained several task forces in the Indian Ocean. In spring 1974, the carrier "Kitty Hawk", with a 90-aircraft complement, spent two months in the Indian Ocean. In all, US deployment in March 1974 amounted to six destroyers and destroyer escorts, one nuclear attack submarine, one amphibious assault ship, one oiler and several naval patrol aircraft. This deployment includes the US Middle East Task Force, consisting of one amphibious ship and three destroyers based at Bahrein. The "Kitty Hawk" and several of its escorting destroyers temporarily left the Indian Ocean again in April 1974 and returned to the Pacific. According to US Secretary of Defense Schlesinger, the United States plans for such a force to visit the Indian Ocean regularly. During November 1974, a new US naval task force headed by the aircraft carrier "Constellation" entered the Indian Ocean through the Malacca Straits. It was accompanied by three destroyers and a support ship and came to participate in the largest naval exercise ever held in the Indian Ocean. The participants were the USA, Iran, Pakistan, Turkey and the UK [42 a].

In March 1973, the US communications centre at Diego Garcia opened, and the following January a plan was announced for the construction of a $20-million air and naval base support facility there. The Diego Garcia harbour was planned to accommodate aircraft carriers and Polaris submarines. However, the Diego Garcia plan was temporarily halted by the British Labour government.

The US announcement of its intentions to develop Diego Garcia brought international attention to the possibility of a naval arms race ensuing in the Indian Ocean between the United States and the Soviet Union. In South Africa, where this development was closely followed, it set off a series of semiofficial visits to the USA. In January 1974, South Africa's Minister of Information, Connie P. Mulder, called on Admiral Ray Peet at the Pentagon's International Security Affairs Office, which is responsible for planning US strategy in the Indian Ocean. Soon afterwards, in April 1974, the South African Commander-in-Chief, H. H. Biermann, visited the USA (on a tourist visa) and was received by Vice-President Gerald Ford, Senator H. Byrd, Governor Ronald Reagan of California and other high defence officials and politicians. The unconfirmed purpose of his trip was said to be to discuss the effects of the coup in Portugal on security in the Indian Ocean. Reportedly, the Pentagon and some US governing circles feared that the Soviet Union might acquire shore bases in independent Angola, Guinea-Bissau and Mozambique [43].

In his first news conference after accepting the Presidency, Ford announced that he favoured a limited expansion of the Diego Garcia base, where some 275 Americans were then serving at the communications station. President Ford said that he did not "view this as any challenge to the Soviet Union which is already operating three major naval bases in the Indian Ocean" [44].

Other Western powers are occasionally present in the Indian Ocean. The United Kingdom retained one guided missile destroyer, five destroyer escorts, and six support ships in the area until 1975. These are now to be withdrawn. In September 1973, France created a new naval command extending from Djibouti in French Somalia to the Kerguelen islands in the southern Indian Ocean and from the West African coast to Malaysia.

In October 1974, a new French naval task force, code-named "Saphir", appeared in the Indian Ocean to relieve the previous one. The new force was composed of the aircraft carrier "Clemenceau", one frigate, one destroyer and two tankers. The "Clemenceau" carries the Crusader all-weather interceptor aircraft, the Etendard attack and reconnaissance plane, the Breguet-Alizé antisubmarine warfare (ASW) plane and Super Frelon helicopters. The French government is opposed to either US or Soviet domination of the Indian Ocean [45].

Eastern presence in the Indian Ocean

THE USSR

No official statements have been made by Soviet statesmen, the Soviet press or other media to the effect that the Soviet Union has any strategic interests in the Indian Ocean. On the contrary, such official statements as have been made deny that the Soviet Union has any military interests in this area.[17] General S. Kozolov, political observer of the Novosti Press Agency, has declared that the Soviet Union has only *maritime* interests in the Indian Ocean. The Suez Canal is one such maritime interest. Its reopening would provide the Soviet Union with a cheaper communication route between its own European and Asian ports than land transport affords. The USSR would also gain cheaper access to friendly nations, such as North Viet-Nam. According to General Kozolov no rivalry exists between the Soviet Union and the United States in the Indian Ocean, despite the negative US response to previous Soviet proposals for some kind of understanding regarding military deployment in the area. Furthermore, he pointed out that, strategically, US deployment in the Indian Ocean would be irrelevant in a global conflict, as the USSR long ago acquired a retaliatory capability for such a conflict.

General Kozolov also charged that the real objective of establishing and maintaining US naval bases in the Indian Ocean might well be the domination of the Indian Ocean nations [46]. At a press conference in Port Louis, Mauritius, on 16 October 1974, the commander of a visiting Soviet naval squadron said that the Soviet naval presence in the Indian Ocean was based on geographical factors alone: the Soviet Navy, he said, has to travel through the Indian Ocean when moving between the eastern and western ports of the Soviet Union. He declared further that the Soviet Union was ready to treat the Indian Ocean as a zone of peace and would maintain no base there [47].

But some circles in the West and in China insist that the Soviet Union does indeed have a strategic interest in the Indian Ocean. As proof they cite the fact that the Soviet Union has access to several naval bases in the area and has kept a substantial naval deployment there, totalling 30 ships in 1974. According to the US Chief of Naval Operations, "Soviet tentacles are going out like an octopus into the Indian Ocean" [48].

The Chinese view most often concentrates on accusing the Soviet Union of military expansion in the Indian Ocean. Two illustrations are commonly

[17] See, for example, references [75–76].

offered: that the Soviet Union has acquired anchoring, bunkering and repairing facilities for its ships at the Indian ports of Vishakhapatnam and Port Blair, and that Soviet vessels have been assisting Bangladesh in clearing the Chittagong harbour [49].

The series of naval courtesy visits to Indian Ocean ports in 1968 marked the beginning of a continuous Soviet presence in the area, with a peak strength of some 30 ships.

According to Australian Defence Minister Barnard, in a written reply to Parliament, the following number of Soviet vessels had visited the Indian Ocean between August 1973 and November 1974; four cruisers, eight destroyers, four diesel-powered submarines, four minesweepers, two landing ships, 29 auxiliaries and 20 miscellaneous vessels employed in minesweeping operations in Bangladesh and the Red Sea [42 b]. Since 1971 all of the minesweepers and most of the support ships have been engaged in clearing the Chittagong harbour in Bangladesh. At one time the Soviet salvage fleet at Chittagong totalled 24 ships [50]. In August 1974, the helicopter-carrier "Leningrad" arrived via the Cape Route in the Indian Ocean from its usual attachment to the Soviet Mediterranean squadron. It was accompanied by one tanker, one supply ship and one cruiser, and carried 18 Mi-8 minesweeping helicopters on board. Reports that the "Leningrad" would serve as the command ship for two nuclear submarines and other vessels have not been confirmed [51]. The "Leningrad" was supposed to participate in the clearing of the Suez Canal.

The Soviet naval bases, which are alleged to be located in Berbera in Somalia, on the South Yemeni island of Socotra, in Umm Qasr in Iraq, in the Indian port of Vishakhapatnam, and at Chittagong in Bangladesh, are cited only slightly less frequently as proof of Soviet strategic interests in the area.

It is known that the Soviet Union has placed mooring buoys off the Seychelles islands, Malagasy and Mauritius. Soviet ships also have access to port facilities in Aden, Hodeida, Mogadishu and Berbera, as well as to Iraqi and Indian ports. In South Yemen some 500 Soviet military technicians are expanding the Aden harbour. All information about naval bases is denied by the Soviet Union itself and also by the Indian Ocean states concerned.

In Somalia, the Soviet Union has access to a repair centre at the port of Berbera. In addition, it has been engaged in expanding the harbour facilities in Ceila and Misimaio. By 1974 the Soviet Union had also become the major arms supplier to Somalia, to which it delivered over a number of years MiG-15, MiG-17 and MiG-19 aircraft, plus 250 tanks and 300 armoured cars. Some 600 Soviet military advisers and instructors were stationed in Somalia. Reports published by the *New York Times,* that the Soviet Union had built a large, long-range communications centre in Berbera to direct its warships in the Indian Ocean and that over 2 500 Soviet military technicians were stationed in Somalia, were denied by the Somali government on 17 May 1973 [52].

Iraq had received a total of 350 combat aircraft and over 1 000 tanks from the Soviet Union by 1974, but according to the Iraqi government no Soviet naval base rights had been granted. Those Soviet warships that occasionally visit Umm Qasr do so on a permission-only basis.

Reports that India had given base facilities to the Soviet Indian Ocean fleet were denied by Indian Foreign Minister Swaran Singh in 1973. "These reports are totally unfounded", he said. "The Soviet Union has never asked for, nor been given, any base facilities. There is no military contract in our friendship treaty" [53].

CHINA

It was widely reported during and after 1970 that China was erecting a missile-tracking station on the island of Zanzibar, Tanzania, and that the Indian Ocean would become a new Sino-Soviet rivalry area. China was said to be planning to test-fire its first ICBM over the Indian Ocean. These reports originated from Indian parliamentary sources. It has also been claimed that China's naval construction programme is aiming at establishing a future significant naval presence in the Indian Ocean [54]. However, according to the United Nations' special report on the militarization of the Indian Ocean, of July 1974, China has no naval bases or naval deployment in the area [55]. No reports confirming the existence of a missile-tracking station on Zanzibar appeared, and Tanzania denied before the UN in 1974 that any such project existed. The only fact that can be substantiated regarding Chinese interests in the area is that China enjoys friendly relations with Tanzania, where it is responsible for the build-up of the air force, as well as with Pakistan and Ceylon.

The Indian Ocean Peace Zone

In 1971, Sri Lanka proposed in a letter to the UN Secretary-General that the Indian Ocean should be developed into a "zone of peace". Support for this proposal has since come from Australia, Bangladesh, China, India, Indonesia, Iraq, New Zealand, North Viet-Nam, Pakistan, South Yemen and Thailand, although the position of Australia and China is somewhat ambiguous. Australia supports on the one hand the South East Asian nations in their campaign for a zone of peace; on the other hand, it provides the USA with communications facilities on the North West Cape and the Cocos islands.

Although China has supported the Sri Lanka proposal since 1971, the Soviet Union alleged in 1974 that China in fact supports a US naval presence in the Indian Ocean. Official Chinese statements in 1974 continued to condemn the "two super-powers' naval race in the Indian Ocean" [56].

Chinese criticism of the Soviet naval deployment in the Indian Ocean seemed, however, to be more closely related to China's opposition to the Soviet plan for an Asian collective security alliance than to any support of the United States.

Finally, two proposals for safeguarding the Indian Ocean against an arms race between the two dominant powers may merit attention, as both would in one way or another affect South Africa as a military power in the area.

1. In September 1972, India's former Navy Chief, Admiral A. K. Chatterji, writing in an anthology on *India and the World*, suggested the establishment of an international Indian Ocean naval force, to be composed of units from the littoral Indian Ocean states. Its purpose would be to prevent great-power rivalry in the Indian Ocean.

2. The second proposal, advanced by the Shah of Iran during a visit to Australia in 1974, proposed a collective security arrangement among the Indian Ocean littoral states. He made clear that the purpose of this arrangement would be to reduce the US and Soviet presence in the Indian Ocean, replacing their naval presence with that of such nations as Iran and Australia [57]. Although South Africa was not mentioned, it can be assumed, considering the developing trade axis between this country and Iran, that South Africa would play an important role in a local Indian Ocean naval force.

Chapter 3. The polarization of forces

The expression "the polarization of forces", as the concept is usually applied in social science, means roughly that the parties to a given conflict are consolidated into two opposing sides. All of the local and international conflict determinants singled out thus far for investigation may be present in a nation or region without giving rise to open conflict, *if* the opposing parties are splintered into many interest groups—that is, if there is no polarization of forces. On the other hand, before the outbreak of every international or civil war fought to date, two clearly discernible sides, each regarding the other as the enemy, have always developed. The fact that there are always groups within a given population or among nations who abstain from taking sides does not matter in this context, if only the two discernible hostile parties are large enough to influence effectively the escalation of the conflict. The following description of the process of polarization, made in 1944 by a social scientist, adequately defines the concept:

Whether the process of change involves the resolution of cross-pressures, the influence of opinion leaders or external events, or mutual interactions, the result of change is increased consistency, both within groups and within individuals. As these processes mold and modify opinions, the group members find themselves in closer agreement with each other; there is thus the simultaneous movement toward increased homogeneity within groups and increased polarization between groups [58].

The notion that a polarization of forces is developing in Southern Africa is widespread and has been expressed on several occasions, for example, by the Somali Ambassador to the UN, Mr Farah, who warned a UN committee in 1972 that in Southern Africa "the sides have begun to line up for . . . racial war" [59].

The extent to which the polarization process has developed in Southern Africa will now be investigated at three levels—internally, regionally and internationally.

I. *The liberation movements*

Consolidation

Polarization has proceeded quite differently in different countries. The stage of creating a guerilla army is regarded here as the last phase in a sequence of events which begins with the organization of non-violent opposition to the prevailing political system and which takes the form of strikes, demonstrations and similar measures. In 1974, armed uprising was developing rapidly in Namibia and was in the making in Rhodesia, but it had not appeared in the Republic of South Africa.

However, the mere existence of guerilla forces within a given territory does not necessarily reflect a polarization of forces among the African opposition. In *Guinea-Bissau* and in *Mozambique* the consolidation of the disparate African opposition groups into one liberation movement, the PAIGC and FRELIMO, respectively, took place quite early. In *Namibia,* SWAPO is developing from a tribal organization into a nationwide liberation movement. But in *Angola* the unity of three liberation movements, the MPLA, the FNLA and UNITA, after a long history of intermovement rivalry as well as intramovement struggles, remains unstable.

In *Rhodesia,* the merger of the ANC with ZAPU and ZANU may create a black united front against the whites—provided that the ANC does not break up again.

In *South Africa,* however, the ANC and the PAC remain separate. The outbreak of well-organized strikes, large demonstrations and other forms of protest from 1973 illustrates instead an earlier stage of consolidation within the African population.

At the regional and international levels, the African liberation movements tend to present a united front against the white regimes. Particularly close relations have been maintained for historical and ideological reasons between the Socialist-oriented PAIGC, MPLA and FRELIMO. SWAPO in Namibia is supported by UNITA and the MPLA, who are active in the south of Angola, and FRELIMO has actively aided ZANU by allowing transit through Tete in Mozambique. In 1967 a formal military alliance was announced between ZAPU and the ANC of South Africa. This was later parallelled by an alliance between ZANU and the PAC. The status of these two formal alliances was uncertain, however, at the end of 1974.

Regional support for the liberation movements

From the time of the Angolan uprising in 1961, it became obvious to the newly formed African liberation movements that they could not expect assistance from the Western powers. The OAU became, from the time of its establishment in 1963, the major instrument for channelling material and military aid to the liberation movements. It also became their spokesman to the world outside Africa.

The purpose of the OAU was and remains the liberation of the entire African continent from white rule, but its strategy has varied. Contrary to what is sometimes alleged, the Lusaka Manifesto did not contain an unconditional acceptance of South Africa's offer of political and economic cooperation. But it *did* contain the declaration that if South Africa should respond positively to demands for the abolition of apartheid, Black Africa would favour peaceful negotiations rather than armed warfare.

But already by 1971, a reversal to a more militant position was apparent. The idea of a dialogue between the white-ruled countries and independent Africa failed to yield any practical results. That year, a certain restructuring of the OAU's military aid policy took place. The immediate aim was declared to be the liberation of at least one Portuguese colony by September 1974. Military aid should be channelled first of all to those liberation movements which had been able to establish and consolidate themselves within a contested territory and which had achieved significant military advances. These movements were the PAIGC in Guinea-Bissau and FRELIMO in Mozambique. At the OAU summit meeting in Rabat in June 1972, a token declaration of war on the white South was issued, and subsequent official declarations have been increasingly militant in tone. At the opening session of the Liberation Committee of the OAU in 1974, President Sekou Touré of the Republic of Guinea called on all African states to enter into open warfare against Portugal, Rhodesia and South Africa. President Idi Amin of Uganda outlined a plan for each of the 42 member states of the OAU to organize two battalions each, under a special African High Command, for the coming liberation war. According to this plan, Uganda would place seven regiments at the disposal of such an all-African army [60].

This development within the OAU represents a polarization of the independent African nations, in that a number of traditionally pro-Western countries departed from the ideas of a peaceful settlement of the Southern African conflict and decided in favour of a definite commitment to the liberation movements. These countries include Ethiopia, Nigeria, Senegal and Zaire. It should be pointed out that the OAU never was a monolithic bloc, being composed of member states with differing political systems. Its early militant position was supported by a few member states that represented early Pan-Africanism, such as Ghana under Nkrumah, and Guinea and Tanzania. From the outset the two most radically nationalistic states in Africa—Algeria and Egypt—firmly supported revolutionary war against the white regimes. In this context it may be relevant to point out that there is no Communist regime among the OAU members, and indeed that very few Communist parties exist in Africa. The trend in political developments in independent Africa has been for one-party states to evolve. Single-party states have often been misinterpreted by Western liberals as being identical with Communist one-party states. The term "radical" in the African context refers rather to the degree to which the newly independent states have broken away from their colonial past. The foreign policy advocated by the OAU member states is that of nonalignment.

Complementary to this political development are the efforts by Africans to achieve a form of regional economic cooperation, separate from both the

62

existing Western cooperation structure and the South African co-prosperity scheme. Several countries have taken measures aimed at establishing more control over their economies. Complete or partial nationalization has been carried out in Algeria, Guinea and Somalia. In Uganda, the government has taken over more than 500 British companies. Nigeria and Zambia have adopted measures to increase state participation in the economy. This is not the general trend, however, looking at the region as a whole.

In 1961, Amilcar Cabral warned at the third All-African Peoples Conference in Cairo, that "the practice of African solidarity reveals some hesitation and improvisation which our enemies have been able to exploit in their favour" [61]. The OAU's military aid policy during the 1960s did arouse some criticism; there were charges of malpractices, especially concerning the criteria for recognition of representative liberation movements. But the structure of the OAU makes practical difficulties inevitable. Despite these, the OAU has developed into a significant political force in Africa.

The financial and military contributions of the OAU member states to the Liberation Committee have varied considerably. Algeria, Egypt, Tanzania and Zambia have been the most regular and reliable contributors.

The fact that independent African states have allowed alien liberation movements to operate from their territories has been vital to the continued existence of these movements. The PAIGC was based for many years in the Republic of Guinea, and since 1968, also in Senegal; the MPLA, SWAPO ZANU and ZAPU all initiated their operations in Zambia, where the South African ANC and PAC are also based; FRELIMO had its headquarters in Tanzania, and the FNLA has been stationed in and supported by Zaire. The MPLA has also gained access to the Congo Republic.

International support for the liberation movements

At the international level since early 1961, the entire Socialist bloc has come out in support of the liberation movements. None of the OAU member states are arms producers, and virtually all of the arms and other military equipment delivered to the liberation movements are of Soviet, East European, Cuban or Chinese origin. These supplies have been delivered either second-hand from such countries as Algeria and Egypt, or through the OAU Liberation Committee. However, the bulk of the equipment has been supplied to certain movements on a bilateral basis. The most sophisticated equipment has come from the Soviet Union. But China, DR Germany, Yugoslavia, Bulgaria and Romania have often been referred to by the liberation movements as important donors of military aid, and not surprisingly, in view of the general African foreign policy of nonalignment.

However internationally, what seemed to be a clear example of polarization, with the Socialist states aiding the liberation movements against the

63

white regimes and the West, has in effect developed away from that situation. In 1964 the Scandinavian countries began extending humanitarian aid to some liberation movements, and the sums allocated have been increased each year. Denmark, Norway and Sweden started by giving educational and humanitarian aid to FRELIMO, the PAIGC and the MPLA. Canada and Finland joined this group in 1974. The British Labour Party had committed itself to supporting the liberation movements and had set up a fund for this purpose even before the Labour government came into power in 1974. All aid from Western powers has been strictly non-military.

At the non-governmental level in the West, protest organizations have developed into opinion-making factors, especially in Britain, the Netherlands and the USA. The work of the Angola Committee in Amsterdam and the Anti-Apartheid Movement in London may serve as examples.

II. *The white regimes*

Consolidation

The complete disintegration of the Portuguese regime in Africa became evident in April 1974 when it was clear that there was no support left in Portugal for the Caetano regime.

No such disintegration within the white power establishments has manifested itself in Rhodesia and South Africa, however. In these countries the position of the ruling Rhodesian Front and National Party remained unchanged.

At the regional level, a certain informal military cooperation existed between South Africa, Rhodesia and colonial Portugal, especially in the field of military intelligence. Before 1974 there seemed to be a drive under way towards a formal military alliance. As early as 1967, South Africa established a formal military presence in Rhodesia, to counter the ANC guerilla units fighting with the Rhodesian ZAPU. According to a South African official, Mr Gerdener, who was then the administrator of the Natal province, the Rhodesian and Portuguese territories had at that time become South Africa's first line of defence [62]. Rhodesia served as a buffer zone, separating South Africa from unfriendly African states. In 1973, Prime Minister Vorster still justified the presence in Rhodesia of South African paramilitary police units, equipped with helicopters, on the grounds that South African terrorists—meaning the ANC of South Africa—were operating together with the Rhodesian terrorists, and said that he "would rather meet them on the Zambezi than on the Limpopo" [63].[18] Despite this common security interest, no formal military alliance has been established

[18] The Limpopo river runs along the border between South Africa and Rhodesia. The Zambezi runs along Rhodesia's border with Zambia. Thus, this statement indicates why South Africa felt responsible for the defence of Rhodesia.

between Rhodesia and South Africa and there have rather been cases of friction between the respective governments, beginning with Ian Smith's UDI declaration in 1965. The action of the Smith government in closing its border with Zambia in 1973 without consulting South Africa was considered to be an unwise panic measure; moreover, it damaged South African trade with Zambia. South Africa extended military aid over the years to the Portuguese in Angola and Mozambique and repeatedly offered to enter into some kind of formal military cooperation agreement with Portugal. But the consolidation of the white regimes did not develop sufficiently to override the fundamental differences between colonial Portugal and South Africa. Spokesmen of the Portuguese colonial regime stated on many occasions that no military agreement would be made with South Africa because Portugal did not care to enter into "unnecessary alliances" [64]. As the guerilla armies advanced in Mozambique, increasingly sharp criticism of Portugal's capacity to handle the insurgency was heard in Rhodesia and South Africa.

As for independent Africa, not one African state can really be regarded as an ally of Rhodesia or South Africa. The South African regime considers Botswana, Lesotho, Swaziland and Malawi to be neutral in the Southern African conflict, mainly because Malawi stood out as the state most receptive to the dialogue policy, and the BLS-countries (Botswana, Lesotho and Swaziland) were in no position to adopt any militant policy against South Africa. However, the governments of these countries—all of which depend entirely on South Africa for their economic survival—have declared their opposition to apartheid. At the OAU Liberation Committee meeting in Dar es Salaam in 1972, Malawi voted for the proposal that free transit for men and material to the battle zones should be allowed by countries adjacent to contested territories in Southern Africa.

International support

It is hardly surprising that those Western powers with the highest economic interests at stake in Southern Africa are also the ones that, in fact, have guaranteed the survival of the white regimes by, first of all, helping to build up their armed forces. These countries are Britain, France, the United States, Italy and FR Germany. NATO member states provided over the years virtually all of the armaments needed by the Portuguese armed forces in Africa, including much equipment specifically designed and equipped for use there. But such support as there is, is unofficial and was undertaken in defiance of the arms embargoes adhered to by the same powers that supply the military equipment. Furthermore, this policy is by no means uncontested within the Western states concerned. It became more apparent in 1974 that a difference of opinion existed within the ruling circles in the United States, and this has received much publicity.

US policy towards Southern Africa has changed with each different administration. The Kennedy administration emphasized the US tradition of anticolonialism and stressed the need to support an anti-apartheid policy. The Nixon administration relaxed this policy considerably in practice, by allowing dual-purpose equipment to be sold to Portugal and South Africa—for example, aircraft that can have a dual civilian and military role—and by lifting the ban on the import of chrome from Rhodesia. These practices were revealed in 1973 during the congressional hearings before the Subcommittee on Africa, on the implementation of the US embargo against Portugal, Rhodesia and South Africa. In 1974, two US columnists, Jack Anderson and Tad Szulc, revealed the existence of a classified survey undertaken in 1969 to present various options for the United States in Southern Africa. According to these reports, the Nixon administration decided on the option later known as "Tar Baby", which called for a relaxation of attitude against the white regimes. It was based on the assumption that the African opposition was not to play any decisive role in Southern Africa [65–66].

Further, in the course of the debate in the United States over the build-up of the Diego Garcia base and the militarization of the Indian Ocean, a sharp cleavage became apparent between the CIA and the State Department on one side, and the Department of Defense—specifically the Navy Command—and Presidents Nixon and Ford on the other. In August 1974, the CIA Director, William Colby, testified before the Armed Services Subcommittee on Military Construction that without a substantial US military build-up in the Indian Ocean there would be no Soviet build-up, and that the Soviet Union would, in fact, prefer an agreement limiting naval deployment in the area [67]. The CIA Director described the Soviet access to the ports of Berbera, Umm Qasr and Aden, which the Department of Defense and President Ford claimed were Soviet naval bases, as insignificant.

The State Department's official view was said to be that it was still premature in 1974 to assume that the future independent governments of Angola and Mozambique would actually turn out to be pro-Soviet [68]. Furthermore, the State Department's reply to South Africa's earlier attempts to secure support for the colonial regimes in Portuguese Africa was decidedly negative and was accompanied by a declaration that the United States would not become involved in any war in Africa and would continue its arms embargo against South Africa [69].

In the United Kingdom, Labour governments have declared themselves in favour of arms embargoes and Conservative governments have reversed this policy. But the Labour governments have not been able to exert any fundamental influence on South Africa. This became especially evident during the Rhodesian crisis of 1965, when the African call for British military intervention against the Smith rebellion proved entirely unrealistic.

Finally, while the NATO headquarters and some NATO members have shown interest in the Portuguese territories in Africa and in extending

NATO's area of responsibility to the Cape Route, this interest has aroused the strong opposition of several member countries, notably Canada, Denmark, the Netherlands and Norway.

It has often been stated, in answer to those who favour a Western military build-up in the area, that the Cape Route is too vast to be policed—the area between the Cape and the ice line to the south is too large to be covered by anything like the present Soviet naval forces in the Indian Ocean. The Soviet Navy does not possess sufficient logistical or other support there to enable it to threaten the east-west traffic round the Cape of Good Hope. Alternatively, if there is a realistic prospect of increasing Soviet political influence in Southern Africa, there is no logical reason to assume that Western insistence on a militarization of the area will adversely affect such an influence. Thus, it would be an oversimplification to conclude that the polarization of forces in Southern Africa has led to a situation in which the entire Western world supports the white regimes. It is rather certain groups in the West that provide such support, despite the existence of opposition within the respective countries.

References

1. *New York Times,* USA, 14 May 1974.
2. *Financial Mail,* South Africa, 26 July 1974.
3. *International Herald Tribune,* USA, 30 March 1974, quoting radio speech by Marcelo Caetano, 28 March 1974.
4. *Statesman's Yearbook 1974/75* (London, Macmillan) p. 1290.
5. Wilson, F., *Labour in the South African Gold Mines 1911–1969* (London, Cambridge University Press, 1972).
6. *Financial Mail,* South Africa, 18 April 1969, quoting research report by Market Research African, South Africa.
7. *Apartheid and the British Worker,* 2nd edition, updated to May 1974 (London, The Anti-Apartheid Movement).
8. *Africa Diary,* India, 5–11 February 1974, p. 6833.
9. *Foreign Economic Interests and Decolonization* (New York, United Nations Office of Public Information, 1969).
    (a)—, p. 20.
    (b)—, p. 19.
    (c)—, p. 10.
10. *X-Ray,* UK, Vol. 5, No. 1, December 1974.
11. Abshire, D. M. and Samuels, M. A., eds, *Portuguese Africa. A Handbook* (London and New York, 1969) p. 170–71.
12. de Sousa Ferreira, E., *Portuguese Colonialism from South Africa to Europe: Economic and Political Studies on the Portuguese Colonies, South Africa and Namibia* (Freiburg, Aktion Dritte Welt, 1973) p. 105.
13. Davidson, B., *The Liberation of Guiné* (Harmondsworth, UK, Penguin Books, 1969).
    (a)—, pp. 23–29.
    (b)—, p. 28.
14. *Rand Daily Mail,* South Africa, 15 February 1975.
15. *New York Times,* USA, 4 February 1974.

16. *Financial Times*, UK, 19 July 1971.
17. *Africa Diary*, India, 9–15 July 1973, p. 6544, quoting speech by Prime Minister Vorster on 24 April 1973.
18. *A Survey of Race Relations in South Africa 1973* (Johannesburg, January 1974, South African Institute of Race Relations) p. 244.
19. *Star*, South Africa, 28 September 1968.
20. *Africa Diary*, India, 28 May–3 June 1973, p. 6488.
21. *House of Assembly Debates* (Hansard) 24 April 1968.
22. First, R., *et al.*, *The South African Connection: Western Investment in Apartheid* (London, Temple Smith, 1972).
    (a)—, p. 85.
    (b)—, p. 11.
23. *Marchés Tropicaux*, France, 8 February 1974.
24. *Facts and Reports*, Netherlands, No. 5, 2 March 1972, quoting a radio report in Portuguese from Lourenço Marques, 22 January 1974.
25. *Africa*, UK, No. 38, October 1974, p. 11.
26. Christopher Munnion reporting from Salisbury, *Daily Telegraph*, UK, 7 June 1974.
27. *Guardian*, UK, 2 February 1970, quoting Samora Machel.
28. *NATO's 15 Nations*, Belgium, April/May 1972. Interview with Defence Minister P. W. Botha.
29. *NATO Review*, Belgium, June 1974.
30. *Daily Mail*, UK, 3 July 1969.
31. *Agenor*, Belgium, February 1973, quoting NATO Parliamentary Report, Autumn 1972.
32. *Daily News*, Tanzania, 15 August 1974.
33. *Daily Telegraph*, UK, 25 March 1974.
34. *Star*, South Africa, 12 April 1969.
35. *Washington Star News*, USA, 26 January 1974.
36. *Observer*, UK, 19 May 1974; *Washington Post*, USA, 2 May 1974.
37. *Armies & Weapons*, Italy, June 1973.
38. Martin, L., *Arms and Strategy: The World Power Structure Today* (London, McKay, 1973) p. 229.
39. *International Herald Tribune*, USA, 25 July 1974.
40. *Armies & Weapons*, Italy, June 1973.
41. *Petroleum Press Service*, London, November 1970, p. 438.
42. *World Armaments and Disarmament, SIPRI Yearbook 1975* (Stockholm, Almqvist and Wiksell, 1975, Stockholm International Peace Research Institute).
    (a)—, p. 124.
    (b)—, p. 126.
43. *Christian Science Monitor*, USA, 10 May 1974.
44. *Far Eastern Economic Review*, Hong Kong, 13 September 1974.
45. *Le Monde*, France, 15 October 1974.
46. Quoted in *Times of India*, India, 20 February 1974.
47. *Times*, UK, 17 October 1974.
48. *Far Eastern Economic Review*, Hong Kong, 27 May 1974.
49. *Hsinhua News Agency*, newsletter, Stockholm, 22 November 1973, Item No. 112135.
50. *International Herald Tribune*, USA, 3 August 1974.
51. *Flight International*, 8 August 1974.
52. *International Defence Studies and Analyses, South Asia*, India, May 1973, quoting Reuter dispatch.
53. *International Herald Tribune*, USA, 7 December 1973.

54. *Times of India,* India, 24 August 1970.
55. UN General Assembly document A/AC. 159/1/Rev., 11 July 1974.
56. *Hindustan Times,* India, 22 September 1972.
57. *New York Times,* USA, 29 September 1974.
58. Lazarsfeld, P., *et al., The People's Choice* (New York, Columbia University Press, 1944, preface to 2nd edition) p. xxxvii.
59. *Standard,* Tanzania, 2 October 1972.
60. *Times,* UK, 2 April 1974.
61. *Africa,* UK, No. 38, October 1974, p. 18.
62. *Africa Diary,* India, 14–20 January 1968.
63. *Times,* UK, 17 August 1973.
64. *Financial Times,* UK, 7 March 1973.
65. Szulc, T., "Why Are We in Johannesburg?", *Esquire,* USA, September 1974.
66. Anderson, J., "Kissinger's Tilt", *New York Post,* 11 October 1974.
67. *International Herald Tribune,* USA, 3 August 1974.
68. *Daily Telegraph,* UK, 2 May 1974.
69. *Christian Science Monitor,* USA, 12 May 1974.
70. *Consolidated Gold Field Limited: Anti-Report CIS* (London, Counter Information Service, undated).
71. *Sechaba,* Vol. 8, No. 6, June 1974, p. 9. Based on the Government Mining Engineers' *Annual Reports* (1911–1961), South Africa, and the Department of Mines' *Mining Statistics* (1966–1969), South Africa.
72. *U.S. Business Involvement in Southern Africa,* Hearings before the Subcommittee on Africa of the Committee on Foreign Affairs, US House of Representatives, May, June, July 1971, Parts 1 and 2 (Washington, US Government Printing Office, 1972).
73. *The Cunene Dam Scheme and the Struggle for the Liberation of Southern Africa,* OIKUMENE, World Council of Churches Programme to Combat Racism, December 1971.
74. *Oil and Security,* SIPRI monograph (Stockholm, Almqvist & Wiksell, 1974, Stockholm International Peace Research Institute).
75. Melkov, G., "Sources of Tension", *Krasnaya Zvezda,* 9 June 1974.
76. *Pravda,* 27 August 1974, 5 September 1974.

Part II. A general pattern of conflict escalation

Square-bracketed references, thus [1], *refer to the list of references on page 111.*

In Southern Africa a general pattern of conflict escalation, from reformism to revolution, has been developing over the past 20 years.

African resistance to white rule began when the first European colonizers arrived on the continent. It then took the form of local wars against the intruders. The significance of those past wars in Africa is evidenced by the fact that such European colonizers as, for example, Cecil Rhodes and the German Count Caprivi, were celebrated as first-ranking military heroes in their home countries. But when opposition again developed among the African population after World War II it did not take the form of armed resistance but used instead the methods of reformism. Where reformism failed, the conflict escalated into armed revolt. Reformism prevailed throughout the area until the end of the 1950s, but beginning in 1960 the prospect of armed revolution became a reality in Southern Africa.

The stage of conflict escalation differs from one country to the other, but events in one country also influence developments in the whole area. Thus, military and political events in Portuguese Africa are of relevance to what happens, and what will happen, in Rhodesia, South Africa and Namibia. The development from reformism to revolution is not "inevitable" or pre-determined in any objective sense, however, but under given conditions armed revolution is the logical consequence of the failure of reformism. With substantial changes of those conditions the alternatives to revolution are multiplied.

The following section describes this escalation from reformism to revolution as it proceeded in Portuguese Africa and the degree to which it has developed in Rhodesia, South Africa and Namibia. The concept of reformism is also applicable to measures taken by the white regimes in response to the demands by the African populations.

Chapter 4. Reformism

I. *Portuguese Africa*

In the late 1940s various cultural organizations were created in Lisbon among the African students from the Portuguese colonies. Their initial aim was to revive the ancient African culture. "Towards the 1950s", Mario de Andrade recalls, "the little community of students and intellectuals who were then in Portugal became sharply aware of the need to act against the Lusitanian image of the black man and to trace out a path to national self-assertion" [1].

A Centre for African Studies was set up in Lisbon. Among its members were several men who were later to become leaders of liberation movements in Africa: Amilcar Cabral, Agostinho Neto and Mario de Andrade. The sector of the African population providing this embryonic leadership for the future nationalist organizations consisted exclusively of *assimilados* and was very small indeed. In 1950 in Guinea-Bissau, less than 2 per cent of the total population was classified as "civilized"—that is, assimilated. In Mozambique there were only 4 555 *assimilados* among six million Africans. In Angola in 1958, only 135 355 persons out of a population of 4.5 million were registered as "civilized"; of these, only 56 000 were African or other non-white *assimilados*. Forty-seven of these had achieved entry to the universities of Portugal [2].

Along with the concept of nationalism, the African intellectuals absorbed the ideas of majority rule, anti-colonialism and Socialism. When transferred onto the African scene, these ideas resulted in the growth of political organizations in the colonies.

In *Angola,* several cultural organizations had appeared before World War II. One early example was the Liga Angolana, a predominantly mulatto organization founded in 1913. After 1945, some of these cultural groups were transformed into political parties. The Angolan Communist Party was founded in 1955 by Mario de Andrade and Viriato da Cruz, among others. This party merged with a number of radical groups in 1956 to form a united nationalist front, which, in turn, merged with still more groups later the same year to become the MPLA. The real strength of the MPLA was among the urban population, and its members, in the main, were mulatto intellectuals, a few *assimilados* and some European liberals. Among the founders of the MPLA were Agostinho Neto, its future president, and the Guinean statesman Amilcar Cabral. The MPLA's initial strategy was to create a clandestine urban organization, and it confined its activities to Luanda and other urban centres. Its orientation was highly intellectual. The MPLA's first secretary-general was Viriato da Cruz, who had been the editor of the *Mensagem* review, the rallying point for African nationalism until it was banned by the Portuguese Governor-General. The MPLA had not yet become a mass organization when the Portuguese secret police, the PIDE, began making mass arrests in 1959 of all suspected subversive elements in Angola. These detentions severely decimated the MPLA activists during the crucial period when the Portuguese military command was bringing in army reinforcements to forestall a nationalist uprising.

Such an uprising was anticipated, not only from the clandestine MPLA city organizations, but from another kind of nationalist movement—Bakongo nationalism—developing in the rural areas in northern Angola and aimed initially at reviving the ancient kingdom of the Congo. In 1957, however, the Bakongo nationalist movement was transformed into an all-Angolan movement, the União das Populações de Angola, later to become the FNLA, led by Holden Roberto.

In the rural south of Angola, this movement also managed to recruit successfully among the Ovimbundu and Cuanhama peoples. The latter is a subgroup of the Ovambo living in Namibia. (This tribal connection provided the basis for the later cooperation between SWAPO of Namibia, the UPA, and its breakaway movement, UNITA, in the south of Angola.) Thus, there was no initial basis for any contact and collaboration between the MPLA cadres and the UPA representatives.

When Angola's neighbour to the north, the Belgian Congo, achieved independence in June 1960, events in Angola were profoundly influenced. The various nationalists' demands for independence were stimulated and the Portuguese determination to extinguish any nationalist organization within Angola was strengthened.

On 22 January 1961, a Portuguese opposition leader and former colonial official in Angola, Henrique Galvão hijacked the liner "Santa Maria" in an attempt to bring world attention to the nature of Portuguese rule in Africa. Many Angolan nationalists, including the MPLA leaders assumed that Galvão would join their cause and on 4 February several hundred MPLA militants attacked a police station and a prison in Luanda to free the political prisoners in anticipation of a major revolt. This attempt ended in a full-scale massacre of Africans and mulattos by the police and armed Portuguese civilians. The MPLA was forced into exile.

The UPA movement, working independently of the MPLA, had managed by this time to secure support from Algeria and to set up headquarters in independent Congo. The Portuguese government's refusal to negotiate decolonization caused the UPA to abandon the policy of non-violence that it had professed until 1961, and in March of that year a vast UPA-led uprising spread throughout northern Angola.

The Portuguese reaction was massive. Large numbers of reinforcements were rushed in from Lisbon, including the first air force units ever to be stationed in Africa. Before 1959, Portugal had only 2000 troops in Angola plus 6000 local police. By the end of 1961, 50000 troops had been brought in. Several months of large-scale massacres followed. The UPA forces attacked not only the Portuguese armed forces but also white settlers, mulattos and Africans belonging to other tribes, and the Portuguese struck out indiscriminately against all Africans in the area. Eventually, the rebellion was crushed. But the UPA, which emerged as the leading Angolan nationalist movement, was as equally opposed to the Portuguese as to the MPLA. The outright hostilities between these two nationalist movements began at that time and are still continuing.

Thus, the events in Angola in 1961 marked the transition from reformism to revolution. No further opportunity remained for the nationalist movements to conduct political work inside Angola. From their separate headquarters both the UPA and the MPLA concentrated on preparations for a future war of liberation. The Angolan insurrection also marked the beginning of Portugal's colonial wars in Africa that were to continue until 1974, and shattered the Portuguese image of racial harmony in its African colonies.

In *Guinea-Bissau* the majority of the *assimilados* were mulattos of Cape Verdean origin, who were traditionally active as administrators and enjoyed a certain upper-class status in the colony. This fact compounded the initial difficulties of the emerging African nationalists, because it made it necessary for them first to weld a bond of confidence between the mulattos and mainland-born Africans, and then between the nationalists—many of whom were intellectuals—and the rural population. When the PAIGC was founded in Guinea-Bissau in 1956, its first undertaking was to create an urban underground organization. There was no classic urban-industrial proletariat in existence at that time. The 25000–30000 African city wage-earners were mostly former peasants, employed as artisans or semiskilled workers.[1] Successful recruiting to the PAIGC was effected only among the dock and transport workers, where it led to the formation of a clandestine African trade union. This phase of early PAIGC activity included a wave of strikes, beginning in 1958, which culminated in the massacre at Pidgiguiti in Bissau on 3 August 1959. The striking dock workers there were attacked by Portuguese officers and civilians who opened fire—after the African troops in Portuguese service had refused to do so—and killed 50 strikers. The Pidgiguiti massacre marked the end of the PAIGC's reformist period and the beginning of armed resistance. A new PAIGC strategy was formulated in September 1959, which concentrated on the mobilization of the peasant population for armed warfare, and the PAIGC headquarters were moved to

[1] See also Gérard Challiand, "*Lutte Armée en Afrique*" [87] and Richard Gibson, *African Liberation Movements* [88].

74

the neighbouring Republic of Guinea, which had become independent of France in 1958.

In 1960, the PAIGC appealed to the Portuguese to open negotiations for the establishment of a parliamentary system of self-rule—with full African representation—in Guinea-Bissau. On 13 October 1961, Amilcar Cabral urged the Salazar regime to follow the decolonization example of other colonial powers in Africa. The Portuguese response was to bring in the secret police, the PIDE, along with military reinforcements. Mass arrests were made of suspected PAIGC members, among them Rafael Barbosa, the chairman of the organization's central committee. In late 1961, the Portuguese armed forces in Guinea-Bissau already numbered 5 000. The Angolan uprising in 1961 caused the Portuguese military command to reinforce troop strength in the other colonies.

The mobilization of the peasants proved to be a highly difficult task. According to Amilcar Cabral, the rural population was not by tradition the revolutionary class in Guinea-Bissau:

The conditions in China were very different: the peasantry had a history of revolt, but this was not the case in Guiné, and so it was not possible for our party militants and propaganda workers to find the same kind of welcome among the peasantry in Guiné for the idea of national liberation as the idea found in China. All the same, in certain parts of the country and among certain groups we found a very warm welcome, even right at the start. In other groups and in other areas all this had to be won [3].

The PAIGC's initial campaign succeeded among the Balante people, but the Fula chiefs remained loyal to Portugal and asked for and obtained arms to create an African anti-guerilla militia. Two years of planning, propaganda and mobilization in the countryside, coupled with a sabotage campaign in the towns, preceded the first PAIGC military attacks against the Portuguese at the end of 1962. In January 1963, the PAIGC headquarters in Conakry issued a formal declaration of war against Portugal.

In *Mozambique,* resistance to colonial rule took a somewhat different course from that in Guinea-Bissau and Angola. Much as in the other colonies, intellectuals (such as the poet Marcelinho dos Santos) prevailed among the leadership. But in Mozambique the most vigorous protests came from African workers and peasants. Already in the 1930s several strikes by the dock workers in Lourenço Marques had taken place. In 1947, strikes by dockers and plantation workers were followed by an abortive uprising which resulted in mass arrests and deportations of Africans to the island of São Tomé. In 1956, 49 dock workers were shot by Portuguese troops during another strike in Lourenço Marques.

In the Cabo Delgado province, in the north, a special form of resistance was developing at about the same time. In the 1950s, peasants organized their own cooperatives in an attempt to rationalize the production and sale of agricultural products. Profits were to be reinvested in the cooperatives. The Portuguese authorities imposed financial levies on these associations and kept all peasant meetings under police surveillance. This led to the politization of the peasant cooperative movement. Agitation spread among the Cabo Delgado peasants and when, in April 1960, members of the Makonde people tried to form an association, a large demonstration took place in the district town of Mueda. More than 500 Africans were shot by Portuguese troops, and the peasant leaders were arrested and deported. Dr Eduardo Mondlane, who became the first president of FRELIMO, said that this massacre at Mueda, which passed virtually unnoticed in the outside world, caused FRELIMO to decide at the time of its formation in 1962 to resort to armed warfare:

By 1961 two conclusions were obvious. First, Portugal would not admit the principle of self-determination and independence, or allow for any extension of democracy under her own rule ... Secondly, moderate political action such as strikes, demonstrations and petitions, would result only in the destruction of those who took part in them. We were, therefore, left with these alternatives: to continue indefinitely living under a repressive imperial rule, or to find a means of using force against Portugal which would be effective enough to hurt Portugal without resulting in our own ruin [4].

When the three Mozambican nationalist movements in exile in Tanzania merged to form FRELIMO in June 1962, the leaders were already convinced that armed struggle was the sole method by which independence from Portugal could be achieved. Recruits were sent to the United Arab Republic and Algeria for military training. Within Mozambique, conditions already existed which enabled FRELIMO cadres to recruit and mobilize for the coming war. Most of the leaders who organized FRELIMO were members of underground forces inside Mozambique. A secondary school, the Mozambique Institute, was established in 1963 in Dar es Salaam, Tanzania, to provide education for the numerous Mozambican refugees living there, and many of the first FRELIMO soldiers came from among these exiles.

The Portuguese increased their armed forces in Mozambique from 16 000 in 1961 to 35 000 in 1964. Opposing them was FRELIMO's initial army of 250 men.

In September 1964, the FRELIMO headquarters in Dar es Salaam declared war on Portugal and the first guerilla troops began moving from Tanzania across the Ruvuma river into the Cabo Delgado province in Mozambique.

The Portuguese reforms

The Salazar regime in Portugal, which was in power from 1932 until 1968, embarked upon a reform programme of sorts in Africa in 1961, partly in response to international pressure and partly to forestall the already apparent development towards militant African opposition in the colonies. On 6 September 1961, as the situation in Angola was slowly being brought under control, all Africans were given full Portuguese citizenship. The status of *indigenas* and *assimilados* was formally abolished, and the colonial governments began to expand health services and educational opportunities for the Africans, who had been severely neglected until then. At the same time, Dr Antonio Salazar vowed that he would fight to the death for the survival of the Portuguese presence in Africa. When Marcelo Caetano succeeded Salazar in 1968, he promised greater autonomy and administrative reforms for the colonies. This trend towards a certain liberalization was firmly supported, in particular by the military commander in Guinea-Bissau at that time, General Antonio de Spinola. Throughout his period of service in the colony, Spinola emphasized the necessity of conquering the "hearts and minds" of the Africans.

Relatively great efforts, compared to those in the past, were made to set up schools and health centres in the rural areas. Africanization of the army in Africa was accelerated in all three colonies. The *aldeamentos* scheme, conceived by the military commander in Mozambique between 1968 and 1973, General Kaulza de Arriaga, was presented as part of an overall development policy favourable to the Africans, that would provide them with better housing, education and health services. *Aldeamentos* were the Portuguese equivalent of the fortified villages used successfully by the British in Malaya in the early 1950s and the strategic hamlets later set up by the United States in Viet-Nam.

In 1972, greater autonomy was granted to Angola and Mozambique. Their status was changed from "overseas territories" to "autonomous states", but they still remained within the Portuguese nation-state. The new legislative assemblies set up in these two colonies in May 1973 provided a measure of self-government unknown before and increased African representation somewhat. But these reforms proved insufficient to stem the militant opposition that had arisen against Portuguese rule in Africa. The franchise was based on literacy, and only about 1 per cent of the Africans were literate. No opposition candidates were allowed. A large number of the assembly members were not elected at all but appointed, according to the corporate principles of the Portuguese state system [5a]. The governor-general was still selected by the Portuguese, and the new legislative assemblies had jurisdiction only over internal affairs, not over external or defence matters.

Thus, in Portuguese Africa, reformist methods had already been abandoned by the African nationalists by the beginning of the 1960s, and the Portuguese reform programmes which were started in 1961 provided too little and came too late to influence the course of events.

II. *Rhodesia*

The course of armed resistance to the Portuguese in Angola and Mozambique served as a model for the Rhodesian liberation movements, ZANU and ZAPU. But the Rhodesian situation is still in an intermediate phase between reformism and revolution, and it is too early to judge whether or not the possibilities for the success of reformism have diminished to the same degree as they did in Portuguese Africa. In Rhodesia, African political opposition within the country and guerilla warfare waged from outside have developed simultaneously.

After the UDI declaration in 1965, the British government held repeated negotiations with the Smith government on the principles for granting independence to Rhodesia. But the so-called Settlement Proposals were not agreed upon until the Conservative government came into office in 1971. The 1971 proposals did offer African majority rule, but at a date generally considered distant—possibly around the year 2055—since they outlined a very gradual extension of the franchise to the Africans. Both the OAU and the UN General Assembly rejected these proposals, stating that the basis for a settlement between Britain and Rhodesia should be one-man one-vote, applied to the entire Rhodesian population. The British government appointed a special commission headed by Lord Pearce to investigate African opinion in Rhodesia on the Settlement Proposals issue, because of its insistence from 1965 onwards that any proposal for independence should be acceptable to the people of Rhodesia as a whole.

The African National Council (ANC) was set up in 1971 to convince the Pearce Commission that the Settlement Proposals were unacceptable to the Africans. It succeeded, and the proposals were temporarily shelved. Subsequently, in 1973, the Smith government conducted talks with the ANC, but these came to a halt in May 1974 when the ANC rejected the new proposals which would have given 22 seats, or one-third of those in Parliament, to the Africans. Bishop Muzorewa declared that the ANC would accept nothing less than majority rule and, moreover, would take no further initiatives to negotiate with the Smith government.

This rejection was interpreted as evidence of a new militancy and determination on the part of the ANC, following the coup in Portugal and the prospect of Angola and Mozambique achieving independence. Up to this time, relations between the ANC and the two exile liberation movements, ZANU and ZAPU, had been relatively hostile since the liberation movements had all along demanded majority rule and at times suspected that the ANC might accept less than that. ANC policy after May 1974 was to boycott all measures proposed by the Smith government—such as the proposal for a round table conference of Africans and whites to reach a constitutional solution, but from which ZANU and ZAPU representatives would be excluded.

While the ANC stands out as the most prominent African political group, two new movements representing other viewpoints were created in mid-1974. One was the African Progressive Party and the other was the National Settlement Forum, both favouring the Smith regime's proposal for a round table conference from which representatives of the liberation movements would be barred.

Sir Alec Douglas-Home, the British Foreign Secretary at that time, warned that unless a settlement was reached between the Smith government in Rhodesia and Britain, the mounting tension in Rhodesia was likely to result in a civil war and emphasized that Britain would stay out of such a war [6]. But Ian Smith persisted in trying to organize the conference, despite its rejection by the ANC, explaining that after 10 years of international isolation he was prepared "to ride it out for another ten" [7].

The African political opposition to the Smith regime, represented mainly by the ANC, has been complemented by the increasing consolidation of African labour in Rhodesia. For example, in October 1974, 5 000 African workers at Wankie Colliery, Rhodesia's main coal producer, went on strike over wage demands, bringing production to a standstill.

The Smith government has not embarked on any programme since 1965 that could be called reformist, not even in the sense that the Portuguese colonial regime did. So, with the possible exception of the offers of a very long-term progressive extension of the franchise to Africans, legislation in Rhodesia since 1965 has been retrogressive, worsening the living conditions of the Africans, as has been described in Part I.

III. *Namibia*

In Namibia the evolution of the African opposition is similar to that of Rhodesia: there was an increasingly consolidated political opposition at work inside the country, complemented by an advancing guerilla movement operating in northern Namibia and the Caprivi Strip.

The origins of SWAPO date back to 1957 when the Ovambo Peoples Congress was formed, initially to represent Ovambo opposition to the contract labour system. In April 1959 this organization was transformed into the Ovamboland Peoples Organization, which later in the same year became the nationwide movement SWAPO. SWAPO demanded the termination of the UN mandate for South African rule of Namibia. In 1963, SWAPO began sending recruits abroad for military training.

A second movement came into being in May 1959, when the South West African National Union (SWANU) was established to represent the Herero people. At one point SWAPO and SWANU came close to creating a joint movement, but tribal loyalties prevailed. Later, when the SWANU leadership split away from the tribalist Herero Council of Chiefs, the latter created a new organization for their people in 1964, the National Unity Democratic Organization or NUDO. The Rehoboth Volksparty and the Volkstem represent other African peoples who have a long tradition of opposition to white rule in Namibia.

Throughout the 1960s, an intermovement rivalry prevailed between SWAPO and SWANU over which of the two could rightfully claim to represent the Namibian people. In 1963, SWANU refused to organize the military units recommended by the newly created OAU, which meant that it was deprived of future OAU support. A leadership crisis in 1969 further weakened SWANU, while SWAPO became increasingly influential, both politically and militarily. In December 1971, SWAPO organized the first mass strikes against the contract labour system and won a partial victory for the Africans. By 1972, SWAPO was estimated to have 150 000 members among the Ovambos [8]. That same year the various political movements in Namibia set up a joint National Convention, with SWAPO as the dominating force.

The policy of the African opposition is to convince the United Nations and world opinion that the African people wish to be represented as Namibians and that they reject the South African ideology of separate development for the different tribes in Namibia.

During 1972 and 1973, political confrontation was escalating in Namibia. The South African government's elections in the Bantustans were widely boycotted, especially in Ovamboland. Severe rioting took place in March 1973, involving some 5 000 African workers in the Katatura township outside Windhoek—the scene of the strikes in 1971 and 1972—in protest against the convening of a multiracial advisory council set up by the South African government.

By the end of 1973, the talks between the UN Council for Namibia and the South African government on the subject of Namibia's future independence were broken off by the Council, which had come to regard its task as hopeless. South Africa had in the meantime regained tight control over migrant labour and a period of mass arrests of SWAPO leaders and members began. Public floggings of Africans accused of terrorism were widely reported, even in the South African press [9]. A special law—the Development of Self-Government for Native Nations of South West Africa Amendment Act of 1973—made the South African police responsible for maintaining internal security in the territory. At the beginning of 1974, another new South African law made it illegal to publish information about police actions against the radical SWAPO Youth League. Thus, the situation of the African nationalists in Namibia was rapidly deteriorating just before the coup in Portugal. Sean McBride, the first UN Commissioner for Namibia, took office in 1974 and stated in Lusaka on 21 February that:

One feature of the present worsening of the situation in Namibia which is worrying is the failure of the press and media in many parts of the world to inform public opinion adequately of the repression which is taking place and of the attempts that have been made to suppress SWAPO . . . The international press must not allow the South African authorities to cajole it into what amounts to a conspiracy of silence [10].

IV. *The Republic of South Africa*

For almost half a century, from its creation in 1913 until 1960, the ANC of South Africa adhered to a policy of non-violence. The movement was originally influenced by the ideology of Mahatma Gandhi, who lived in South Africa from 1893 until 1914. Defiance campaigns, protest meetings, demonstrations and petitions were the methods used to fight the apartheid system. In 1952, a defiance campaign involving 8 500 ANC members was conducted during which the Africans used white buses, white park benches and other facilities reserved for whites in the same way as black Americans were to protest in the United States 10 years later. Some 500 ANC leaders were arrested, African students were expelled from the universities, and new legislation was passed prohibiting African strikes and demonstrations.

Despite these counteractions, African political efforts continued, reaching a height in 1960 when the newly-created PAC added its activities to those of the African opposition in the country. That year, a nationwide disobedience strike took place, including mass meetings where passports were burnt. On 21 March, a PAC-organized demonstration against the pass laws was staged in Sharpeville, near Johannesburg. The South African police was called in and opened fire on the crowd, killing 69 Africans and wounding some 200 more. The Sharpeville massacre filled the same function for the ANC and the PAC that the incidents in Portuguese Africa had for the liberation movements there: both organizations adopted a strategy of armed revolution and established military wings. In 1961, after a state of civil emergency was declared by the South African government—during which time more than 20 000 Africans were arrested—both the ANC and the PAC became exile organizations.

The mass arrests, the increasingly repressive legislation and the implementation of the Bantustan scheme severely decimated the African opposition movements and restricted their activities for more than a decade. The South African government may have managed during this time to convince both the outside world and itself that the only threat to apartheid rule came from the guerilla movements in exile. But in the early 1970s, African resistance within the Republic of South Africa began to re-emerge and manifest itself in three main ways: in the form of African trade-union protest actions, in the form of student protests, and in the form of pressure applied to the white government by some of the African Bantustan chiefs to make it fulfil in practice the letter of the Bantustan legislation that foresees the creation of independent African nations within South Africa.

The consolidation of African labour that has taken place is reflected by a sharp increase in the use of the strike weapon. In 1971, only 25 strikes by Africans were recorded, involving 2 620 workers. In 1972, there were 22 strikes involving 3 756 workers [11]. But in January 1973, a strike in Durban, involving over 60 000 Africans, signalled the beginning of an unprecedented wave of work stoppages that spread to Witwatersrand, Port Elizabeth and East London. The most militant sector was made up of textile industry workers.

As a result of the 1973 labour problems, the government and the employers' associations called for a review of the African wage system. A revision brought a number of wage increases and a new Bantu Labour Regulation Act which, for the first time in the history of South Africa, granted some categories of African workers the right to strike under certain specified conditions. However, these rights are severely limited, and the African trade unions still have no power to influence the wages of Africans. In January 1971, another extensive textile workers' strike broke out in Durban, resulting in the temporary arrests of more than 10 000 Africans. The Trade Union Council of South Africa (TUCSA) organized a special fund to pay their fines. The strike also won the official support of the Zululand Bantustan authorities. Further large-scale strikes continued throughout 1974 and led in most cases to wage increases.

During 1973, strikes and demonstrations among the foreign African workers in the mining industry developed into serious confrontations, in which more than 60 Africans were killed.

Since 1971, five organizations have been founded to promote trade unionism among the African workers. The first was the Johannesburg-based Urban Training Project, founded in 1971. In 1973 over 700 African industrial workers attended courses run by its African and white trade-union teachers.

Durban's Institute for Industrial Education which functions as a training centre also came into existence after the mass strikes in 1973. In the same year, the Central Administration Services were set up in Natal by some of the registered trade unions to be responsible for the task of organizing trade-union activity among Africans. Also in 1973 the Western Province Workers' Advice Bureau was created to organize African workers by the establishment of workers' committees. In 1974, Johannesburg's Industrial Aid Society was founded.

These embryo labour organizations are able to operate legally because the revised Bantu Labour Relations Regulation of 1973 provides for the creation of African workers' and liaison committees in factories. This legislation was passed in an attempt to forestall worse labour market disturbances than those which occurred in 1973.

In May 1972, large-scale African student protest demonstrations took place, led by the non-white South African Students Organization (SASO). For the first time white students, mainly from the English-speaking community, joined in and began to demand free and non-discriminatory education. Large numbers of students were arrested. SASO also played an important role in forming in July 1972 the Black Peoples Convention, the first African political party to arise since 1960.

The mainly white, English-speaking student organization, the National Union of South African Students (NUSAS) has also engaged in anti-apartheid activities. In 1973, as a result of its actions, eight of its leaders were banned for five years.

White students from the Afrikaans-speaking community are represented by the Afrikaanse Studentebond (ASB). It usually supports the government's policy.

The Bantustan chiefs have made increasing use of their positions to demand that the South African government implement the Bantustan scheme. Two leaders in particular, Chief Gatsha Buthelezi of the KwaZulu and Chief Kaiser Matanzima of the Transkei, have pursued a policy of active pressure for more land, greater political powers and for the establishment of local African defence forces inside the African reserves. This policy has been denounced by the other African opposition groups who regard these demands as supporting the government's policy of separate development.

The activities of the Bantustan chiefs have considerably embarrassed the South African government. On 8 November 1972, a summit meeting of homeland leaders took place in Umtata, and agreement was reached in principle to demand complete African administrative control within each homeland. A decision was also made to work against racial discrimination in all its forms, and in particular against the pass laws and the migratory labour system. Chief Buthulezi reportedly said that "none of the architects of separate development could ever have dreamed that their policy would be used as a platform on which to build black solidarity" [12a].

After this meeting, six Bantustan chiefs participated in a conference on federalism, convened in East London during November 1973 by the editor of the *Daily Dispatch* and attended by representatives of white opinion, including members of the Progressive Party and Verligte Aktion. Chief Buthelezi outlined the idea of a "federal union of Autonomous States of Southern Africa", to be composed of the homelands, Botswana, Lesotho, Swaziland and, in addition, the Republic of South Africa. The conference issued a declaration of consensus which stated that a federal solution guaranteeing equal rights for all individuals in the separate states would be the best way to deal with South African problems [12b].

Both the Indian and the Coloured populations have become increasingly unified among themselves. In 1974, the militantly anti-apartheid Coloured Labour Party obtained a majority in the Coloured Representative Council, after which the Council demanded restoration of coloured representation in the South African Parliament, a right which was abolished in the 1950s.

Governmental reforms

The government of South Africa has shown very little response to African demands and has taken few reformist initiatives of its own, unless the Bantustan development scheme is so regarded. The Bantustan plan would increase investment in these reserves by means of concessions and assistance with capital costs and the disbursements involved in moving to the homelands. At present, these expenses are paid by the Africans themselves. Technical and developmental aid is also planned. Despite the promotion of the so-called development scheme, all investigations conducted by the South African authorities themselves show that conditions are worsening in the homelands. Acute poverty, malnutrition and high infant mortality prevail in all the areas. This situation is progressively aggravated by the forcible removal of old, ill and incapacitated persons from the white areas.

The government's response, such as it is, has mainly concerned the manifestations of so-called "petty apartheid". The gradual abolition of petty apartheid in the urban centres is partly a response to pressure for reform which has come from such sectors of the white community as are represented by, for example, the Progressive Party. In the April 1974 elections, the Progressive Party, which until then had occupied only one seat in Parliament, surprisingly won another six at the expense of the more moderate United Party and received 6 per cent of the votes. The right extremist Herstigte Nasionale Party took only one of the 84 seats. This could be described as opposition by modern capitalism to what is condemned as an anachronistic form of apartheid that is detrimental to economic development. This type of opposition to the present rule in South Africa, which has its counterpart in foreign countries, is manifested in the tactics of "peaceful pressure" adopted since 1973 by a number of companies operating in South Africa. The Polaroid Corporation of the United States, and the British-controlled Barclays Bank, the largest bank in South Africa, can be cited as examples. Wage increases and more skilled jobs for Africans have been approved by these concerns, whose declared aim is to effect a change in the apartheid structure by means of gradual reforms. The adherents of this "bridge-building" strategy, for example Harry Oppenheimer and the British Rio Tinto Zinc Company, argue that it will build a link between the Africans and the liberal enterprises and cause the apartheid system to wither away by creating an African middle class that will in the future become a potential governing elite.

Against this policy of peaceful pressure for change, the African nationalists hold that such reformist measures as there are, do not in any way challenge the apartheid system but, on the contrary, strengthen it:

Once recognizing the tight connection between foreign capital and the regime, the pressure for peaceful change that the companies claim is their policy, can be seen in truth for what it is—an attempt to whitewash the regime, to confuse the world by giving some minor, and effectively irrelevant concessions, while at the same time maintaining their profitability. In one sense, and in one sense alone, the western companies involved in South Africa and Namibia have built bridges. They have built them between their own governments in the west and the regime in Pretoria, between the economies of Britain, France, West Germany, Japan, the United States and so on, and the apartheid economy. The traffic across the bridges has not been subverting the apartheid regime from inside, as proponents of this theory claim, but has been in the other direction. It has, in fact, enabled apartheid to grow stronger, by trying to defuse, confuse and destroy the actual pressure for change that comes from elements within the African and Asian world, and some of the metropolitan countries [13].

The influence of the coup in Portugal on the South African system response will be described in Part IV.

Chapter 5. Revolution

I. *Portuguese Africa*

By the time of the coup in Portugal and after more than a decade of war the military situation in the Portuguese colonies had reached a point where neither side seemed likely to win a military victory within a reasonable time. In Guinea-Bissau, the PAIGC controlled most of the rural areas, whereas the Portuguese held the capital and other urban centres as well as a number of fortified posts throughout the territory. Each attempt by either side to improve its military position brought heavy losses. In Mozambique, the guerilla armies of FRELIMO had advanced south of the Zambezi river, once declared by General Kaulza de Arriaga to be the ultimate limit where the guerillas would have to stop. FRELIMO revealed that its official aim was to reach the Save river south of Beira during 1974. In Angola a certain degree of pacification—made possible by the controversies between the MPLA, the FNLA and UNITA—had been achieved. The Portuguese were therefore able to divert troops from Angola to Guinea-Bissau and to Mozambique.

In August 1973, General Spinola left his post as military Commander-in-Chief in Guinea-Bissau before the completion of his period of service and returned to Lisbon. In his controversial book, *Portugal and the Future*, which was published in February 1974, he drew the conclusion, which eventually turned out to reflect the general point of view held by the Portuguese armed forces, that an exclusive military victory was no longer possible in Portuguese Africa. Even if Portugal had unlimited resources, he declared, the wars would merely be prolonged: "We must smash the myth that we are defending the West and Western civilization" [5b].

The course of events that eventually led to a complete reversal of the optimism voiced by the General when he took up office in Guinea-Bissau in 1967, is summarized below. Further comparison can then be made with the conditions for armed revolution in Rhodesia, Namibia and the Republic of South Africa.

Portugal's military strength

A superficial comparison of the balance of military strength between Portugal and the liberation movements would seem to point to an overwhelming superiority on the Portuguese side in numbers of troops, in quantity and quality of military equipment and in financial resources.

The cost of the wars in Africa

Despite the fact that Portugal was one of the least developed and poorest nations in Europe, the fall of the Caetano regime in 1974 was not preceded by a state of economic chaos and bankruptcy.

Until 1961, Portugal persisted with an isolated nationalist economy typical of the 1930s, which corresponded to the outdated theories of Dr Salazar, former professor of political economy at the University of Coimbra. But from the time of the Angolan uprising in 1961, public expenditure on defence had to be increased each year. It was estimated that since 1962 the Extraordinary Overseas Forces absorbed an average of two-thirds of the total defence budget. To this must be added related expenditures for arms procurement, support and maintenance, investment in arms-related industries, training and the like. The exact yearly cost of the wars in Africa and accurate figures showing the total annual military expenditures are difficult to obtain. Budgetary allocations for the Extraordinary Overseas Forces, reported in the official *Diário do Governo,* Lisbon, include only what are considered to be "extraordinary" defence expenditures. Other allocations for military purposes appear elsewhere. Further, expenditure estimates are usually considerably lower than those actually allocated, and the real situation is not known until two years after the allocation date, when the accounts have been approved. Nevertheless, the figures provided by the *Diário do Governo* do illustrate the rising cost of the wars in Africa [14]. (See table 5.1.) With the above reservations, it has been estimated that military expenditure in Portugal rose from $261 million in 1961 to $450 million in 1972 [15].

In 1974, defence allocations amounted to over 40 per cent of the $1.3 billion national budget. A final indication of the cost to Portugal of its African wars is to be seen in the fact that the military budget of 1975 was reduced by about $210 million—40 per cent of the total military budget [16].

Without funds from abroad, the financial situation might long ago have become untenable. But in 1965 the colonies in Africa were opened to foreign investment, which was needed in order to cover the unproductive public expenditure on defence, and this policy brought certain successful results. Cabinda Gulf paid Portugal an average of $50 million per year, or almost 75 per cent of the official military expenditure of Angola [17]. Other contributions came via the colonial governments' clearing payments in gold from South Africa for the African migratory "labour units" employed in the mines.

Other sources of financial aid played a part in supporting the Portuguese economy. Between 1946 and 1972, the United States provided $571.8 million in aid to Portugal. Of this, $334 million was military aid [18a]. This help increased in direct proportion to the war effort in Africa. The Kennedy administration was more critical, but nevertheless paid for the lease of the Azores base. When Caetano renewed the Azores treaty in 1971, he received

Table 5.1. The rise in Portuguese military expenditure, 1960–74

Escudos mn, at current prices

1960	1961	1962	1963	1964	1965	1966	1967	1968	1969	1970	1971	1972	1973	1974
3023	4922	5744	5724	6451	6680	7393	9575	10692	10779	12538	14699	16046	16736	20910

Source: See reference [87].

$400 million from the Export-Import Bank and an additional $36 million from the US government.

The entire economy of Portugal, in fact, became geared to financing the war effort in Africa. Despite this heavy drain of resources which could otherwise have been used for development, and despite the fact that Portugal's African policy made it unacceptable as a partner in the EEC, the Caetano regime believed that Portugal could afford to carry on the wars in Africa for another 30 years if necessary.[2] In early 1973, Dr Rui Patricio, who was then Defence Minister of Portugal, stated at a press conference in Cape Town that "Portugal has the financial resources to wage anti-terrorist wars in Africa indefinitely" [19].

Arms procurement

Portugal is not a major arms-producing nation. Until 1974 its own armaments industry was confined to small arms and ships. All other equipment had to be imported. Foreign arms deliveries proved crucial for sustaining the Portuguese empire in Africa. From the register of arms supplies to Portugal, 1950–1974, given on pp. 212–15, it can be seen that NATO and the USA supplied virtually all armaments during this period, and in many cases they were shipped directly to Africa. This was consistently denied until April 1974 by the Western powers, who persisted, against all evidence, in declaring that no arms suitable for deployment in Africa were being supplied to Portugal.[3]

In early 1974, the Portuguese Air Force consisted of some 800 aircraft including 150 combat planes, all supplied by NATO countries. The navy included four submarines, eight frigates, six corvettes and some 130 other surface ships. The army was equipped with US tanks, French and British armoured cars and US howitzers. The United States, Britain, France and FR Germany accounted for the major share of Portugal's arms imports.

[2] See, for example, Neil Bruce, "Portugal's African Wars" [54], and "*Southern Africa in Perspective*" [89].
[3] The term "NATO arms", widely used in press reports and studies describing the appearance of these weapons in Africa, means two things: either weapons produced according to NATO specifications and used as standard weapons by the NATO member states, or merely arms supplied to Portugal by a NATO country. In both cases, the military transfers have been made as bilateral agreements. NATO has no central body for arms distribution.

In addition to those US weapons listed in the register on page 212, it was revealed during the House Hearings before the Subcommittee on Africa in 1973 that the United States had exported herbicides with a combined civilian-military use to Portugal and sent crop-spraying planes directly to Angola and Mozambique. Napalm and phosphorus bombs of US origin were also used in Africa. The US Department of Defense argued that the military assistance programme to Portugal was justifiable, as it contributed to Portugal's role in the NATO common defence effort and promoted US interests since "it helps us to maintain some influence with the Portuguese military, an important political force in the country" [18b].

After 1961, it became increasingly difficult for Portugal to acquire major arms from Britain, however, and a request for a large number of Strikemaster armed jet trainers was refused in 1973.

The arms deliveries took place despite the fact that several NATO countries, including the United States, decided to insert a clause into their arms transaction agreements, after the Angolan uprising in 1961, prohibiting the use of NATO arms outside of the NATO area. However, there was no requirement that the Portuguese government inform NATO of its assignments either of troops or weapons to Africa.

By 1969, France had become a major arms supplier, gradually taking over the role of the UK and the USA for certain categories of arms. Portugal was the third largest importer of French military equipment. Frigates and submarines especially equipped for tropical waters were ordered from France in 1973. In January 1974, it was reported that France had agreed to sell a new batch of Alouette and Puma helicopters and Panhard armoured cars, destined for use in Angola. Military sales agreements were also concluded with Spain and Brazil. In early 1974 the Portuguese Air Force concluded an agreement for the purchase of 28 Casa C-212 light transport planes from Spain. Japan and Belgium were also becoming important suppliers: between 1971 and 1972, Belgium delivered military equipment worth more than eight million Belgian francs to Portugal [20].

Domestic arms production

The Portuguese arms industry has played an important role in equipping the armed forces with light weapons and munitions. At the time of the coup, work was under way to expand domestic production capacity, using know-how and technology largely provided by the same NATO countries that supplied the armaments.

The *light weapons industry* was established with US aid under the Marshall Plan. Beginning in 1961, this industry was expanded and modernized. Material and monetary aid came from FR Germany, which financed the establishment of two ammunition factories in Portugal, the Fábrica de Material de Guerra de Braço de Prata, and the Fundação de

Oeiras. FR Germany sold the licence-production rights for the NATO standard G-3 gun, produced since 1961 at the Braço de Prata factory. It also financed the Beja air base, which was used by the West Herman Air Force until 1973. Furthermore, when Portugal failed in 1961 to obtain a production licence for the Israeli-designed Uzi submachine-gun, also a NATO standard weapon, FR Germany resold 10 000 Uzis to Portugal, which explains the subsequent appearance of this weapon in Portuguese Africa [21].

The *shipbuilding industry* is advanced in Portugal. In 1961, the LISNAVE shipyard was set up, under the ownership of two Swedish, two Dutch and two Portuguese shipyards, with 51 per cent of the shares being held by the Portuguese.

A company which has grown up alongside LISNAVE is the Electricidade Naval e Industrial SARC (ENI). It specializes in the design and supply of a wide range of marine electrical equipment, automation systems, radio communications and navigational aids. There are two major shipyards other than LISNAVE: the Viana do Castelo, and SETENAVE. The former only builds ships under 5 000 dwt. With two British companies involved, work started in December 1962 on the SETENAVE shipbuilding and repair yard to be completed in early 1975. This new yard is 65 per cent owned by CUF, a major Portuguese company, and LISNAVE.

In all, around 80 small patrol boats and landing craft have been built in Portugal since 1964. All of these have been used in Africa. In late 1973 a new 300-ton patrol boat, the "Save", was launched at the Alfeite shipyard in Lisbon.

Plans to expand the *aircraft industry* were well under way by 1973. The Oficinas Gerais de Material Aeronáutico at Alverca, established with financial and material aid from FR Germany, had designed a twin turboprop light transport aircraft, the ADAC, which used French engines. In the same year, it was announced that FR Germany had decided to cancel its agreement for the use of the air base at Beja. The contract was to have run until 1981.

As a *quid pro quo* for cancelling this contract, FR Germany agreed to finance the construction of a $10-million aircraft factory at Beja, through Messerschmitt–Bölkow–Blohm GmbH [22]. The annual planned production capacity was 48 planes. At the beginning of 1973 a subsidiary of the US Cessna Aircraft Corporation set up an aircraft repair facility in Portugal.

In early 1974 it was announced that Brazil had sold the production licence for its T-23 Uirapuru military trainer to Empresa Iberica de Material Aeronáutico. The transaction covered 100 aircraft, of which 50 were to be operated in Angola and 30 in Mozambique. At the same time, the French company Crouzet SA (Valence) opened a subsidiary in Portugal for the assembly of machine tools and equipment for the aerospace industry.

Military vehicles were not produced in Portugal until 1973. Then it was announced that an armoured car, known as "Chaimite", was being built with unspecified foreign assistance and was in use in Angola [23]. This could well be a licensed version of the French Panhard armoured car.

Manpower

While outside financial and material aid may have offset the otherwise unbearable costs of the wars in Africa, another factor remained which constituted a major problem for colonial Portugal. This was manpower. The emigration of labourers, that had begun in the 1950s for economic reasons, was followed by another wave of emigration of young men due for military service in Africa. By 1974, some 100 000 deserters were living in France, Belgium and Sweden [24]. It is estimated that since 1961, a total of 1.6 million Portuguese—out of a population of 8.8 million—have left the country [25].

In mid-1967 the maximum conscription term for all three services was increased to four years. The normal term of service in Africa for soldiers was two years. By 1974, over 160 000 Portuguese soldiers were stationed overseas.

Since 1961, Portugal's contribution to NATO in Europe has been negligible in comparison with the size of its armed forces in Africa. When it joined NATO in 1949, Portugal had six army divisions, all stationed in Portugal. In wartime, two divisions would be under NATO's SACLANT command. In 1961, the number of Portuguese army divisions to be placed at NATO's disposal was officially reduced to one, and the same applied to its contribution to the Spanish–Portuguese Iberian Defence Treaty. The actual strength was far less: in 1961, the NATO division's strength was reduced to 50 per cent and the Iberian's to 30 per cent [26]. By 1962, out of an overall army strength of 150 000 men, only 10 000 soldiers remained in Portugal: the rest were in Africa with what must be regarded as full NATO knowledge, if not open support. It was disclosed, for example, during the 1973 Hearings before the Subcommittee on Africa in the US House of Representatives that a total of 474 Portuguese officers and men were trained in the United States between 1968 and 1973 [18c].

The deployment of Portuguese troops in Africa had by 1974 reached a total of over 160 000 troops and had shown a continuous annual rate of increase since 1961. However, because metropolitan Portugal itself suffered from an increasing shortage of manpower during and after 1961, in particular manpower of draft age, it could not possibly have filled the needs for more troops in Africa from its own population beyond a certain limit which had probably been reached already by 1965. Portugal and its colonies were officially one unitary state on matters of defence until April 1974, and thus, locally enlisted African colonial troops are included in this figure. The Africanization of the armies in Guinea-Bissau, Angola and Mozambique, presented as proof of the multiracial policy of colonial Portugal, was in fact simply a solution of the manpower problem.

The numbers of metropolitan troops in Africa and of African troops serving with the Portuguese have been much disputed by the parties to the conflict. The liberation movements and their supporters have tended to present inflated figures of the size of the Portuguese metropolitan armed forces, and the Portuguese have tended to inflate the number of African troops loyal to them. Apart from prestige reasons, a further cause of uncertainty about the actual numbers of African troops became clear during the first negotiations between the PAIGC and the new Portuguese military junta in London in May 1974—namely, the lack of any reliable statistical information on Africans enrolled in the Portuguese Army. Further confusion arose because there were actually three categories of African troops: conscripts, volunteers in special commando units, and militia troops.

The colonial Portuguese Army was a conscript army. Military service was compulsory for the white colonial population and initially for those Africans classified as "civilized". Conscription was later extended to all male Africans, after they had acquired the status of Portuguese citizens. There were several reports, however, of forced recruitment of Africans. For example:

Many Africans try to avoid military service by escaping to the slums in the cities. There the police make raids at regular intervals, and those whose papers are not in order are sent to military service. And they get 18 months extra service on top of the usual three years. "Nearly 80 per cent of all Africans I have trained, have had this long service", said a lieutenant [27].

Most Africans who volunteered for military service with the Portuguese belonged to one of two categories: either to a tribe traditionally hostile to the people dominating the liberation movements, such as the Macua in Mozambique and the Fula and Mandinka in Guinea-Bissau, or to those detribalized Africans living in the urban centres, for whom military service would provide a chance to escape unemployment and secure a livelihood.

The defence of the three colonies was paid for according to a common arrangement whereby the air forces and navies were entirely financed from the Portuguese military budget, whereas the local governments covered part of the army allocations out of their budgets.

The use of weapons in Africa also followed an arrangement common to the three colonies: aircraft could be moved between the territories, so that different types appeared from time to time. Further, the civilian airlines were under an obligation to assist the air force with planes for troop transportation whenever requested. As to the navy, the large warships in service in Africa, like frigates and corvettes, remained under the central command of the Portuguese Navy rather than under the local military command and were also moved between the territories.

Guinea-Bissau

In Guinea-Bissau military spending rose considerably during the last years of the war, from $6.3 million in 1972 to 8.6 million in 1973. Nearly all of this increase was allocated to the navy [14]. Official Portuguese figures up to 1968 mention a deployment of 20 000 metropolitan troops plus 6 250 African recruits [28]. General Bettencourt-Rodrigues, Spinola's successor as Commander-in-Chief, speeded up the organization of an African militia. In 1973, a Portuguese journal reported that the total number of African troops in Guinea-Bissau had reached 25 000, of which 15 000 were local militia and the remainder regular army troops. Among the regular African army troops were the African Fusiliers, who were deployed as special units in their tribal areas, and the Commando Battalion, a special counterinsurgency unit with African officers [29]. If it is assumed that the 20 000-man metropolitan force was kept more or less constant, the addition of some 7 000 regular African troops plus some 15 000 militia would bring the total up to approximately 40 000, which is the number of Portuguese troops most frequently quoted. In January 1974, 20 000 Angolan troops were scheduled for transfer to Guinea-Bissau, but this plan apparently did not materialize before the coup.

The Portuguese Air Force in Guinea-Bissau, while it was still in unchallenged control of the air in 1972, operated one squadron of 12 Fiat G91 light jet fighter-bombers, one squadron of T-6 armed trainers used for counterinsurgency, 10 Alouette helicopters and a number of Noratlas transport planes [39]. It is not known whether NATO member countries replaced all the aircraft losses from 1973, but by 1974 at least 12 Dornier Do 27 transport planes had been supplied by FR Germany and were reportedly being armed with machine-guns and rockets for anti-guerilla operations [31].

The navy comprised small units of patrol and landing craft as well as river gunboats used along the coast. Army equipment included 155-mm US cannon and 81-mm and 106-mm mortars [32]. Since 1961, napalm bombs and fragmentation and phosphorus bombs were used on rural areas that were under PAIGC control.

The Cape Verde islands

The Cape Verde islands had not been affected by the war at the time of the coup, but the PAIGC had a strong clandestine organization on the islands. Portugal had nonetheless taken strong measures to protect the islands against possible future attack from the mainland or from a local insurrection. Mass arrests were conducted after a minor uprising on the island of Praia in 1962. Defence spending continually rose, increasing from $2 million in fiscal year 1973 to $2.6 million in fiscal year 1974, according to the official *Diário do Governo*.

According to general speculation, in the event of an actual military defeat in Mozambique or in Guinea-Bissau, or both, the colonial regime of Portugal had planned to entrench itself on its island possessions in the Atlantic Ocean.

The cost of the war in Mozambique over the years became an increasingly heavy burden on metropolitan Portugal. According to General de Arriaga, this war alone accounted for 30 per cent of Portugal's defence budget in 1974 [33]. Spending rose from $4.3 million in 1972 to $96.5 million in 1973 [14]. In fiscal year 1974 Portugal allocated $4.7 million for the defence of Mozambique.

Infrastructure development as well as construction work with mixed civilian and military applications would have to be included in an estimate of the real costs of the war. In 1973, 30 airfields and over 150 landing strips were being built all over the country, but the heaviest concentration was in the north. In Cabo Delgado, three new military airfields with a 750-metre runway became operational in March 1973. A highway was being constructed along the Tanzanian border, with a 10-km all-weather airstrip at every tenth kilometre. The Nacala port and other coastal facilities were also to be enlarged, and in 1972 a new naval base became operational at Porto Amelia.

In October 1973 it was reported that a large factory for the assembly of light aircraft was to be built in Mozambique by a Lisbon concern and that it would be partly financed by South Africa and the United States [34]. By early 1974, the plans for this project had reached a fairly advanced stage, with $1 million to be invested during the first phase. The site of the assembly plant was to be Lourenço Marques or Beira, where 40 planes were to be produced each year, starting in mid-1975. The aircraft to be assembled may have been the new indigenous Portuguese design called the ADAC, or a US type, probably a Cessna or a Piper aircraft. The status of this project after the coup is not known.

The Portuguese regular army in Mozambique by 1964 numbered 35 000 troops, very few of whom were Africans. Ten years later, the total number of Portuguese armed forces in the territory was estimated to be 95 000, comprising 65 000 in the army, 3 500 in the navy and 27 000 in the air force [35–36].[4]

Under General Kaulza de Arriaga's command in Mozambique, the Africanization of the army was accelerated, accounting for most of the increase in numbers. About half of the African forces were recruited from peoples living in the southern and central parts of the country who had no tribal affiliations in the war zone in the north. The Macua people, in particular, were regarded for many years as loyal to the Portuguese. As in the other colonies, special African volunteer units were also set up. For example, in 1972, Mozambican financier and businessman Jorge Jardim

[4] The air-force strength of 27 000 is said by Kenneth W. Grundy, in *Guerilla Struggle in Africa* [77], to have come from a Portuguese source, but the figure is not confirmed by other sources. *The Statesman's Year-Book 1974/75*, for example, gives a total strength of only 55 000 army troops in Mozambique, as does *The Military Balance 1974/75*.

backed the organization of an elite corps of 2 000 African parachutists who were used in counterinsurgency operations in the Niassa province.

Of the 65 000 men in the army in 1974, 30 per cent were metropolitan troops, 10 per cent Portuguese Mozambicans and 60 per cent Africans. This means that only 19 500 soldiers were conscripts from metropolitan Portugal itself [37].

In the opinion of one correspondent, reporting on the war in Mozambique in 1973, the strength of the Portuguese Air Force had been consistently overestimated. In reality, he wrote, the air force suffered from constant shortages of manpower and aircraft and lacked an adequate infrastructure [38]. To this must be added the subsequent losses of aircraft in combat, illustrating the development of a guerilla challenge to air control very similar to that which took place in Guinea-Bissau.

By early 1973, the air force consisted of 15 Harvard T-6 and 8 Fiat G91 planes, all used in the counterinsurgency role, five Noratlas and five DC-3 transports, 17 Alouette helicopters and some spotter planes. The fleet of the DETA civilian airline, which according to its contract with the military authorities provided transport charters where necessary, must also be taken into account. In 1972, DETA acquired four turboprop Aero Commanders and three Strike Commanders from the USA. In August 1973, the fourth Boeing 727 was purchased with a $6-million US credit and a Boeing 707 was to be bought, all for troop transports [39–40]. Various ostensibly civilian buyers also purchased aircraft. For example, in 1970, five Bell helicopters were acquired by the Colonial Secretary for Communication, who ordered 12 more in 1973. The purchase was partly financed by an Export-Import Bank loan. Six Rockwell light planes were also bought under the 1973 order, worth $3.3 million [41]. At least 12 Grumman Agcat and 10 Pawnee crop-spraying aircraft were purchased from the United States in 1973–74.

Between 1965 and 1973, the United States sold aircraft ignition systems, electronic measuring and testing equipment, trucks, flight instruments, aircraft spare parts and herbicidal chemicals to Mozambique. All of this equipment was exported from the USA as "non-military" goods [18d].

The local navy in Mozambique operated various river and naval patrol vessels, including two patrol boats armed with 20-mm guns on Lake Malawi. In April 1973, the naval garrison was reinforced by one company of marine soldiers.

Angola

Although the level of military activity in Angola was low compared with Guinea-Bissau and Mozambique, the rising cost of the war could clearly be seen in the budget allocations, which rose from $60 million in 1972 to $81.5 million in 1973 [42].

Related expenditures would have to be included in a calculation of the real cost of the war. For example, in 1973 a $16-million network of airfields was planned [43].

By the end of 1961, the number of Portuguese troops in Angola totalled 50 000. In 1974, army strength was generally quoted at 55 000, of which about 50 per cent was said to be African. After the coup, the actual number of African soldiers was stated to be 17 000. In addition, there were 3 000 men in the air force and 3 600 serving with the navy, all metropolitan Portuguese troops. There was also a 5 000-man police force [44].

By 1974 the Portuguese Air Force in Angola was the largest in the African colonies. It contained more than 100 aircraft, including one squadron of Fiat G91 bombers, units of T-6 armed counterinsurgency (COIN) fighters, Noratlas transports, liaison aircraft and Alouette helicopters. In mid-1971, France supplied the Portuguese Army in Angola with three medium transport helicopters.

In December 1973, the MPLA announced that France had agreed to supply large quantities of arms to Portugal, some of which were directly destined for Angola. These included helicopters, tanks and armoured cars. French sources confirmed the sale of three Alouette and two Puma helicopters to mining companies in Angola [45].

By 1973 the Angolan DTA airlines had bought nine Fokker F.27 Friendship transport planes from the Netherlands. Two Boeing 727s were to be received from the USA in early 1975.

The use of Puma helicopters and army use of M16 rifles in war operations was reported in 1973 for the first time. A factory for explosives and ammunition was to be built with West German participation near Luanda by Explosivas da Trafaria, with a planned annual output of 1 500 tons [45]. West German Parliamentary Secretary of State Gröner, of the Ministry of Economic Affairs, conceded that permission had been granted on 25 March 1972 for Meissner of Cologne to participate in the construction of the Trafaria ammunition plant [47].

The local Portuguese navy in Angola was small, equipped with patrol and coast-guard boats.

The military strength of the liberation movements

Manpower

Numerically, the combined size of the guerilla armies challenging the Portuguese military power was small. The reported strength of the guerilla forces was sometimes inflated when emanating from the liberation movements or from their supporters, at least in Angola. Conversely, such estimates were deflated by Portuguese sources before the coup.[5] The numbers

---

[5] *Remarques Africaines*, Belgium, of 31 January 1975 contained the following information about the current military strength of the three liberation movements: FNLA: 14 000 of which 5 000 in Zaire; MPLA: 5 000 plus 2 000 under the command of Daniel Chipenda; UNITA: 3 000.

given below are estimates that will have to await historical confirmation. In the light of information which became available after negotiations started between the new Portuguese regime and the liberation movements, it became somewhat more possible, however, to establish the relative size of the various armies, as follows: in early 1974, reports from Bissau quoted the PAIGC regular army strength to be 7 000 troops [24]. The regular force was said to include a naval unit and an embryo air force. The militia, which the PAIGC began organizing in 1967, was composed of units of 40 men, and according to the Portuguese authorities in Guinea-Bissau, it numbered only 1 500 by 1974. However, the British writer Basil Davidson estimated its size to be 2 500. The actual number ought to have risen each year, since the militia fulfilled a crucial consolidating function in the areas that were liberated by the PAIGC. Thus, the total size of the armed forces of the PAIGC might well have approached 10 000, which is the most common estimate.

In Mozambique, FRELIMO soldiers numbered about 25 000, including 10 000 regular guerilla troops. This total had also previously been quoted in Portuguese intelligence reports [38]. Women, too, participated in FRELIMO, both as regular soldiers and in the militia.

In Angola, the military status of the three liberation movements—each claiming to be the real representative of the Angolan population and each accusing the other movements alternatively of tribalism, Maoism, of being CIA-financed or of not representing the Angolan people—became somewhat clearer after the coup. The new Portuguese regime announced that it would separately discuss with each movement the problem of how to transfer independence to Angola. It also concluded ceasefire agreements with each of them, which did illustrate, at any rate, that all three were active inside Angola. Actual numbers were still uncertain. The highest estimate ever given of the size of the MPLA's guerilla army, between 50 000–75 000, appeared in *Portuguese Africa: A Handbook,* published in 1969, and was clearly absurd. The official Portuguese estimate was 4 700. After the coup, Portuguese intelligence reported that most of this force was deployed not inside Angola but in the Congo Republic [48].

The official Portuguese estimate of the FNLA's army strength was 6 200. After the coup, the FNLA was reported to have 4 000 troops—only half of whom were armed—deployed in Zaire along the Angolan border, plus a force of almost 2 000 inside Angola [49]. This corroborated reports made in 1973 that General Mobutu, the President of Zaire, was actively aiding Holdeh Roberto, the FNLA leader, to increase the size of the FNLA from 5 000 to 10 000 by recruiting men from among the 800 000 Angolan refugees in Zaire [50].

UNITA was estimated at the time of its foundation in 1967 to number 1 000 men. Later information quoting a guerilla force of 1 000 remained more or less constant until 1974. It has not been possible to corroborate this [51].

Thus, the total number of guerilla troops facing the Portuguese armed forces of over 160 000 men in all three colonies probably did not exceed 40 000–50 000 in 1974. Actual deployment in combat inside the three territories was even smaller. There were, in fact, more Africans serving with the Portuguese than with the guerillas, as the combined size of these African forces would reach a total of some 60 000 men.

Military aid

Compared to the Portuguese, the guerillas were poorly armed and did not possess sophisticated weapons prior to 1973.

US intelligence reports in 1973 predicted that both the Soviet Union and China would increase their arms aid to African liberation movements and that sophisticated weaponry—in particular the Soviet shoulder-launched portable SAM-7 ground-to-air missile—would be supplied. This was later confirmed. During 1974 it became evident in Guinea-Bissau and Mozambique that the guerillas were embarking on a build-up of a conventional military capability. The deployment of SAM-7s can in this respect be said to have been the most significant military development since the beginning of the war.

During the first two years the PAIGC almost exclusively used arms captured from the Portuguese, but after 1964 this movement began to achieve wide recognition as a well-organized and highly disciplined force, both by the OAU member states and other countries, stimulating a continuing increase of military aid from abroad. Thus, in 1964, the first PAIGC units equipped with cannon and automatic anti-aircraft rifles of Soviet and Czech design were formed [52a].

In 1973, the local Portuguese military authorities published a list of weapons found in PAIGC possession during the raids on guerilla bases in Senegalese territory: 122-mm rockets, 60-mm and 80-mm mortars, Kalashnikov automatic rifles and machine-guns [53]. PAIGC troops were also equipped with Chinese recoilless cannon and Cuban bazookas [54]. According to Basil Davidson, in 1973 the PAIGC was about to acquire amphibious tanks and mobile cannon from the Soviet Union [55]. During the same year it received the Soviet SAM-7 ground-to-air missile. Portuguese control of the air was severely challenged for the first time. Reports also appeared in 1973 that 40 PAIGC pilots were being trained in the USSR. In April 1974, the PAIGC took delivery of some MiG-17 fighter aircraft from the Soviet Union. PAIGC pilots reportedly flew the planes from the Soviet Union to bases in Conakry [31].

The immediate support given to the PAIGC by the Sekou Touré regime in the Republic of Guinea was decisive from the beginning of the war. Guinea provided the PAIGC with a guaranteed sanctuary from which its initial operations against the Portuguese could be directed. That this aid contained risks for the Republic of Guinea became evident when the Portuguese bombed several border villages in 1967 and also when they raided Conakry in 1970 and tried to kill both Amilcar Cabral and Sekou Touré. Despite these risks, however, the PAIGC was accepted in 1970 by Leopold Senghor, President of Senegal, who granted it access to Senegalese territory.

Initial military training of the PAIGC soldiers was conducted in the Republic of Guinea, Algeria, Egypt and the USSR. Despite persistent claims by the colonial Portuguese authorities and their supporters that China was aiding the PAIGC, the only detailed information available about Chinese military training activities concerns a group of seven future PAIGC military commanders who spent some months at the Nanking Military Academy during 1961 [52b].

In Mozambique, FRELIMO began receiving OAU aid in 1964 at the start of the war. Eduardo Mondlane listed the USSR, China, Czechoslovakia, Yugoslavia and Bulgaria as FRELIMO's most important sources of supplies.

In 1973, Soviet-supplied 122-mm rockets and heavy mortars were reportedly used in Cabo Delgado for the first time [56].

Tanzania functioned after its independence in 1961 as a sanctuary for refugees from Mozambique and later for FRELIMO, thereby incurring considerable risk. Repeated warnings of preemptive measures were made by the South African regime.

In Angola, the failure to unite the African opposition against Portuguese rule into one dominant movement caused the pattern of military aid and other outside support received by the three Angolan liberation movements to vary. The OAU struggled in vain for many years to determine which movement was the most representative, bound as it was by its policy of recognizing only one dominant liberation movement per territory in white-ruled Africa and of advocating the establishment of a united front. The basic soundness of this policy—considering the OAU goal of liberating the entire African continent from white rule—was borne out by developments in Guinea-Bissau and Mozambique, but such consistency in policy was not evident in Angola. Recognition and military aid were granted periodically to one or another of the competing movements. From the time of the abortive uprising in the north of Angola in 1961, the FNLA—then known as the UPA—received OAU recognition as the sole representative Angolan liberation movement. The OAU denied recognition to the MPLA until 1964, placing its full support behind the FNLA-proclaimed exile government of Angola, GRAE, based in Kinshasa. When the MPLA initiated armed operations in the Cabinda enclave in Angola during 1964, the OAU also extended aid to this movement, but it refused to recognize the third movement, UNITA. UNITA, moreover, was denied recognition from its creation in 1966 until 1974. In 1970, the OAU withdrew its recognition of the GRAE exile government of Holden Roberto. In 1973 it again recognized the FNLA, but this time as a liberation movement on a par with the MPLA, and not as the future government of Angola. Finally, in 1974, UNITA received OAU recognition, but only after the new Portuguese regime had stated that it also regarded this movement as a negotiating partner.

After 1964, the MPLA began receiving Soviet aid, and in 1973 there were confirmed reports that the SAM-7 missile had also been delivered to the MPLA. The colonial Portuguese government in Angola claimed on several occasions that China was providing military equipment to the MPLA, but MPLA sources said that before 1970 their movement had never received Chinese weapons, and after 1970 only via the OAU. The exaggerated size of China's aid was borne out in Portuguese intelligence reports, one of which said that of 483 firearms captured from guerillas in 1970, 326 were of Soviet and eight of Chinese origin.

The FNLA received its military equipment and training first of all from Zaire, formerly Congo-Kinshasa or the Belgian Congo, which has consistently supported this movement, and secondly via the OAU. In the early 1960s, some military aid arrived from Algeria and Tunisia and from private US sources. In addition, according to Holden Roberto, Romania was an important supplier of arms on a bilateral basis. Speaking in Kinshasa in March 1974, on the 13th anniversary of the foundation of the FNLA, Roberto refuted the occasional reports of US support of the FNLA, explaining that such a connection was past history: "In the early days the movement fell within the sphere of influence of the United States, as did the Kinshasa government" [57]. However, he said, conditions had changed, and he now accused the United States of supporting Portugal in Angola and hinted at future reprisals against US companies there.

Regarding Chinese aid, the curious fact emerged that the sole substantial military aid ever provided to an Angolan nationalist movement by the People's Republic was extended not to the MPLA, as had been claimed, but to the FNLA under an agreement reached during the visit of President Mobutu of Zaire to China in 1974. According to the agreement, China was to send 112 military instructors to Zaire to train FNLA guerillas who would form a regular army division of up to 15 000 men. Of these, two-thirds would be equipped with Chinese arms, and the remainder would be fitted out by Zaire. On 2 June 1974, the first group of Chinese military instructors arrived in Kinshasa, followed by a second group in August 1974.

Until UNITA was recognized by the OAU in 1974 it had never received any external military aid, and only some financial aid from Egypt. According to UNITA leader Jonas Savimbi, neither the Soviet Union nor China ever assisted his movement [58].

The social revolution

The aim of the liberation movements in Portuguese Africa was not confined to the retaking of territory. The liberation of territory was rather the precondition for the future social revolution. The war was conducted on a political as well as military level. Propaganda work in the form of political organization and the establishment of education and health centres were considered to be just as essential as military training. A FRELIMO resolution of 1968 says: "Our war is essentially a political war, and its direction is defined by the party. The people's army is part and parcel of the party, and its strategic plans are made by the top leadership of the party [59]."

The balance of strength indicated above between the Portuguese armed forces in Africa and the liberation movements would not suffice to explain the military advances of the liberation movements up to April 1974. Other explanatory factors must obviously be added to that of the significant growth *per se* in the military strength of the guerilla armies. These would include such non-military achievements as the political mobilization and socialization of the population, illustrated by the efforts to organize an embryo future society in the liberated areas of Guinea-Bissau and Mozambique.

The PAIGC and FRELIMO schools, the health centres, the so-called peoples' stores and the administrative village committees offered many Africans living in the isolated and neglected rural areas their first contact with civilization and modern society, determined their loyalty to the liberation movements and resulted in their participation in building a new social and economic structure. This nation-building process became a highly important part of the revolutionary strategy, the aim of which was not merely to liberate the territories from Portuguese rule but also to effect a complete social revolution.

The nation-building efforts of the PAIGC and FRELIMO largely passed unnoticed by the Portuguese colonial authorities and their supporters, and on the rare occasions when their attention was drawn to them, they were ridiculed. According to a government document issued in Dakar, Senegal, by the PAIGC State Commission of Economy and Finance, there were 350 000 people living in the PAIGC-controlled areas by May 1974. This type of information was consistently denied by the Portuguese colonial authorities. General Spinola went so far as to claim that a UN expert group visiting PAIGC areas in 1973 had not been in Guinea-Bissau at all, but in the Republic of Guinea. The social and political dynamics at work in Africa were certainly not understood by the central government in Lisbon which, until the moment of its ousting, persisted in believing that Portuguese civilization could still influence the African populations if only adequate measures were undertaken. These measures included resettlement. By 1973, one million Africans in Mozambique had been moved into 1 000 *aldeamentos,* mostly in the Cabo Delgado and Tete districts, and General Kaulza de Arriaga was confident that when his six-year "development" plan had been completed and all Africans in the country were living in such camps FRELIMO would be crushed [60].

The great emphasis on organizing a new social order and a new society was explained as follows by Dr Eduardo Mondlane:

One of the chief lessons to be drawn from nearly four years of war in Mozambique is that liberation does not consist merely of driving out the Portuguese authority but also of constructing a new country; and that this construction must be undertaken even while the colonial state is in the process of being destroyed. We realized this in principle before we began fighting, but it is only in the development of the struggle that we have learned quite how rapid and comprehensive civil reconstruction must be. There is no question of making a few provisional arrangements and waiting until we control our whole country before deciding how to govern it. We are having now to evolve structures and make decisions which will set the pattern for the future national government. . . . During the two years after the struggle began, the battle to build up services was at least as important as the military one. By 1966 the crisis was past. The worst shortages had been overcome, and embryonic structures had been formed for commerce, administration, health and education. The New Mozambique was beginning to take shape [4c].

In Angola at least one clear distinction could be made between the nationalist movements, despite confusion concerning their military and ideological status: only the MPLA shared the goal of a complete social revolution, manifested in practice in Guinea-Bissau and Mozambique. The principal aim of the other two movements was to achieve national independence without crushing the capitalist economic system.

The military situation by April 1974

Guinea-Bissau

The year 1973 proved to be Portugal's worst in terms of military developments in Guinea-Bissau. The assassination of Amilcar Cabral by Portuguese agents on 30 January 1973[6] resulted in an intensification of the guerilla war, contrary to the expectations of the Portuguese, who had counted on demoralizing the revolutionary forces. In March the PAIGC troops overran the fortified camp of Copa on the eastern front, using light tanks for the first time. In its Operation Amilcar Cabral in May, the PAIGC captured the important Portuguese camp of Guiledje in the south. SAM-7 missiles began being employed in March 1973, and on 28 March 1974 a PAIGC communiqué stated that 40 planes had been shot down during one year. Such high losses were never admitted by the Portuguese authorities, but several other sources stated that about two-thirds of the Portuguese Air Force in Guinea-Bissau had been destroyed before the coup in Portugal [61]. Whatever the actual number, Portugal's air monopoly was finished.

In the liberated Madina do Boé district, the PAIGC National Assembly, which had been elected in 1973, met on 23–24 September that year to

---

[6] President Sekou Touré of Guinea took personal charge of the investigation of Cabral's death and announced in March 1973 the indictment of 50 persons who were called agents of Portugal. During the trials, it appeared that the Portuguese had made use of the latent dissension between mainland Africans and Africans of Cape Verdean origin in the PAIGC rank and file. For more information, see *Africa Contemporary Record* [5f].

approve a constitution and government and declared the independence of the new state of Guinea-Bissau. On 2 November the UN General Assembly voted 93 to 7, with 30 abstentions, to welcome "the recent accession to independence of the people of Guinea-Bissau and the creation of the Guinea-Bissau Republic". The General Assembly also voted to condemn "the illegal occupation of certain parts of the Republic of Guinea-Bissau by Portugal". On 11 November 1973 the new state was admitted into the Food and Agricultural Organization (FAO), but full UN membership was temporarily postponed in the knowledge that the USA and the UK would use their veto power in the Security Council to prevent this.

General Spinola's departure from Guinea-Bissau was interpreted by the PAIGC as a victory. The President of the new state, Luis Cabral, warned during his visit to Senegal one month before the coup in Portugal that "we are capable of taking the war where we wish—even to Portugal if necessary" [62].

Mozambique

In 1961, Dr Eduardo Mondlane was killed in what was then suspected and later confirmed to be a Portuguese intelligence operation.[7] After his death, serious differences of opinion among the FRELIMO leaders came into the open and for a couple of years seemed to threaten the consolidation of this movement.

In 1970, General Kaulza de Arriaga took office in Mozambique and his first task was to launch Operation Gordian Knot, presented as the final solution to the guerilla war in that country. Ten thousand Portuguese troops were used in concentrated attacks on FRELIMO bases in Cabo Delgado. But under the new collective leadership of FRELIMO, with the former military commander Samora Machel as president, the guerillas not only escaped from the Gordian Knot attacks but were able to move south across the Zambezi river and to open a fourth front in the Manica e Sofala province in July 1972, approaching the Salisbury-Beira railway link. In September 1972, FRELIMO troops destroyed 19 aircraft on the ground during an attack on the military camp of Mueda in Cabo Delgado. At the beginning of 1973, General de Arriaga explained the military failures of his armed forces as follows:

We kill 1 300 per year, but this number is made up by local tribesmen being subverted and by continued infiltration from Tanzania. But if the Chinese backers do not escalate the war during the next two years, we shall control terrorism to an acceptable degree [63].

But the guerilla war intensified during 1973. In March, FRELIMO used 122-mm rockets for the first time in an attack on Gago Coutinho near Cabora

---

[7] See, for example, David Martin, "Interpol Solves a Guerilla Whodunit" [90]. Interpol traced the letter-bomb, of Japanese origin, that killed Dr Mondlane, back to Portuguese sources.

Bassa. Four Portuguese aircraft were shot down in Manica e Sofala in August, reflecting the guerilla forces' mastery of more advanced weaponry. The Portuguese reported 14 000 land operations during the first half of 1973, plus 39 000 air strikes and 1 700 naval attacks. Portuguese counterattacks included napalm bombings to clear suspected areas.

More information was available about South African and Rhodesian armed forces activities than about the alleged Chinese aid to FRELIMO: The Rhodesian journalist Peter Niesewand reported in his book *In Camera: Secret Justice in Rhodesia* that Rhodesian troops together with special South African commandos had engaged in counterinsurgency operations in Tete since 1970. By 1973, some 400 light infantry troops were operating in Tete jointly with the Rhodesian Air Force. White phosphorus bombs were dropped on suspected ZANU guerilla bases which FRELIMO reportedly helped to sustain [64–65].

In 1972, it was reported in the British press that South African mercenaries, protected by Portuguese fighter planes, had been spraying FRELIMO-controlled areas with defoliants during a three-month period. FRELIMO'S Vice-President, Marcelinho dos Santos, claimed during his visit to London in June 1973 that South Africa had deployed three battalions around the Cabora Bassa building site. All such reports were firmly denied by the South African authorities.

The war in Mozambique received sudden and extraordinary international attention in mid-1973 when Catholic missionaries told of large-scale massacres of civilians by the Portuguese army and described in particular the massacre of some 400 Africans in the village of Wiriyamo in Tete. After the coup, a UN investigation committee confirmed that massacres had occurred in Wiriyamo, Mucumbura, Inhaminga, Chawola, João and Dak.

On New Year's Eve 1973, FRELIMO derailed a train on the Beira-Salisbury railway and raided isolated farms close to the Rhodesian frontier. After a new attack on Mueda on 20 January 1974, FRELIMO claimed to have destroyed 21 aircraft on the ground: three Fiat G91s, three Dornier transports, seven Alouette helicopters, two Harpoon bombers, and six Harvard bombers [66].

The guerilla attacks on white farmers led to mass demonstrations in Beira by whites who demanded stronger action by the Portuguese armed forces. The district governor there, Colonel Sousa Teles, readily admitted that FRELIMO actually controlled parts of his district and had attacked several *aldeamentos* each night since January 1974 [67]. The Beira-Malawi railway also came under constant attack, mostly near the junction town of Inhaminga.

FRELIMO eventually managed to enter the Mozambique province inhabited by the Moslem Macua people who had initially been hostile to the guerillas. This achievement illustrated the detribalization process that created the real basis for the spread of FRELIMO influence throughout the country. This influence was also at work in the cities of southern Mozambique untouched by the war: as early as 1972, for example, 1 800 alleged FRELIMO sympathizers were arrested in Lourenço Marques [68].

By April 1974, only 10 000 Portuguese troops were still mobile. The rest were tied down in fortified camps in the critical areas of Tete and Cabo Delgado. The air force had been severely decimated, and it seemed that nothing could prevent the guerilla armies from advancing southwards.

In August 1973, General de Arriaga left his post as Commander-in-Chief in Mozambique. But, unlike General Spinola in Guinea-Bissau, he did not conclude that Portugal was unable to win a military victory in Africa, despite the continuous military failures in Mozambique beginning with Operation Gordian Knot. In his book *The Portuguese Answer*, published in 1973, his basic theme was that Portugal would never leave Africa, because Portugal was fighting not only for itself but also to defend the Western world against Communism.

Angola

In 1963, the MPLA had managed to reorganize after its initial heavy losses. It was now established in the Congo Republic and led by Agostinho Neto. A military front was opened in the Cabinda enclave, but the discovery of oil there in 1965 led to the deployment of large numbers of Portuguese troops to protect the foreign companies, and the area was temporarily pacified. Denied access to Zaire, where the FNLA was based, the MPLA units managed to reach the Moxico and Cuando Cubango districts in Angola in May 1966, by using what was called the "Agostinho-Neto trail" from Tanzania across Zambia.[8] The MPLA claimed full control over this area, four times the size of Portugal, and opened new fronts in the Luanda district in 1967 and in the Bié district in 1969. In November 1973, MPLA troops attacked the main Portuguese garrison of Moconje inside Cabinda, 10 miles from the Congo border, after issuing a general warning to the oil companies there. This warning was repeated in 1974 in a communiqué, issued by the MPLA steering committee in Dar es Salaam, and was directed specifically against the following oil companies: Gulf Oil of Cabinda (USA), Texaco (USA), ARGO (USA), Petrofina (Belgium), ANSA (South Africa), CFP (France) and Petrangol (Portugal, Belgium) [70].

The Portuguese-Belgian concern Petrangol-Angol had already declared that it was ready to take over the Angolan oil business from Gulf if this company should give in to either international or guerilla pressure [71]. But during 1973, a serious split within the MPLA leadership divided the guerillas into three groups, two of which challenged the Presidency of Dr Neto and thereby considerably weakened this movement.

According to Portuguese army communiqués, the MPLA was the most

---

[8] See, for example, Basil Davidson, *In the Eye of the Storm* [69].

active guerilla movement in Angola between 1968 and 1970 [72]. A Portuguese intelligence report listed 2 518 military engagements with guerillas that year, 59 per cent of which were ascribed to the MPLA, 37 per cent to the FNLA and 4 per cent to UNITA [73].

The FNLA claimed in 1973 that its military units were fighting on three fronts along the Zaire border and that it controlled an area of 450 km^2 with 900 000 inhabitants in *aldeamentos* [5c]. UNITA had remained entrenched in the Bié district since its foundation in 1966.

After the coup in Portugal in April 1974, it became clear that the liberation movements' claims were inflated but also that the colonial Portuguese regime's claim of pacification had been exaggerated. It was considered unlikely, however, that the liberation movements together controlled more than 20 per cent of the territory.

II. *Rhodesia*

On 12 September 1962 an announcement signed by "The Zimbabwe Liberation Army" appeared in Salisbury, calling for revolution and asking all Africans to join this army within seven days. It has not been established who issued the call; practically all of the leaders of the future guerilla movements, ZAPU and ZANU, had been active in the militant youth uprising of ZAPU in 1962.

When UDI was declared in 1965, the country had been in a more or less constant state of emergency for some years. Between 1963 and 1965 several Africans were arrested upon their return to Rhodesia from military training abroad. It was revealed at a trial on 7 February 1965 of 22 Africans accused of terrorism, that some had received military training in 1964 in Moscow, Nanking and Pyongyang. These first recruits had been unarmed, however, and it was disclosed during subsequent trials that their assignment had been to mobilize the Africans in Rhodesia, in expectation of a UDI declaration by the white rulers. Sabotage tactics and propaganda were the methods used by the African opposition at that time, and their aim was to destroy property rather than wage outright war. These tactics continued to be used for a while after the UDI proclamation, in the hope that the British government would intervene militarily against the white rebel regime.

Both ZANU and ZAPU in 1965 appealed to the OAU for military aid and training assistance, and both were recognized and allowed to set up headquarters in Lusaka, Zambia. They still did not collaborate, however, but worked in parallel.

The military strength of the liberation movements

On 29 April 1966 the ZANU guerilla army launched its first attack across the border from Zambia. Fighting was reported throughout that year at various places, especially on the south bank of the Kariba Dam.

In 1967, the ZAPU guerillas went into action for the first time. Working jointly with the ANC of South Africa, with whom a military alliance had officially been announced, ZAPU sent some 200 troops into the Wankie Game Reserve and fighting continued for several weeks. The exact numbers of ZAPU and ANC guerillas in this force have not been confirmed.

Between 1966 and 1968 neither ZANU nor ZAPU used common hit-and-run guerilla tactics. They chose instead to attack in relatively large groups in a more conventional style, which led to heavy casualties for both movements. The fact that the infiltration from Zambia took place before any preparatory work had been done among the local population in the border areas of Rhodesia also worked to their detriment. By comparison, FRELIMO's strategy was to send their political workers to a new area far in advance of the military units. According to the Portuguese authorities in Mozambique, for example, FRELIMO underground activists had been conducting propaganda work in the Beira district at least two years before the first guerilla units arrived.

No military activity was reported during 1969, as both movements were reappraising their tactics and were under strong pressure from the OAU to unite. In 1971, President Kaunda of Zambia gave the two organizations an ultimatum either to merge or to leave Zambia. FROLIZI was then formed and proclaimed to be a united front, but it was destined in fact to become a third movement. Another abortive military and political alliance between ZANU and ZAPU was announced in December 1972.

At this time, however, a series of more successful ZANU military actions was begun, apparently connected with the FRELIMO advances in Tete in Mozambique. The attacks in December 1972 on Rhodesian farms across the border from Tete were better prepared and conducted, for they were designed to hit at isolated places and thus minimize guerilla losses. The Smith regime had to admit at last that the local population had cooperated with ZANU, and a series of counterinsurgency measures were undertaken. The border closure with Zambia in January 1973 was a direct result of this development, but it failed to stop ZANU infiltration because this time the guerillas did not come directly from Zambia, but via Mozambique. The entire sector between the Salisbury–Lusaka and Salisbury–Tete roads was declared to be an insecure zone and for the first time since 1966 the death penalty was reinstituted for terrorism. Several executions took place during the year, beginning in May 1973.

ZANU units were also active in the Zambezi Valley after December 1972, which led the authorities to resettle forcefully over 8 000 local African inhabitants in strategic hamlets. Among these Africans were some from the northeastern border area with Mozambique, according to the official bulletin of the Ministry of Information in Salisbury [74]. Another measure undertaken by the Smith regime was that of collectively punishing entire African villages in the northeastern war zone in which inhabitants were suspected of

107

aiding the guerillas. This particular policy was questioned by some sectors of the white population. The opposition Rhodesian Party pointed out for example that "reprisal against civilians has been and always will be a major cause of escalation in civil and guerilla warfare" [75].

But harsh methods continued to be used. ZANU sources charged that the Rhodesian troops had begun employing defoliants in order to facilitate their counterinsurgency operations in an area south of the Zambezi Valley [76].

Manpower and armaments

The initial strength of ZANU and ZAPU was hardly more than a few hundred soldiers, and estimates of the size of the Rhodesian guerilla forces in 1974 ranged from 200 to 8 000. Several sources put the joint ZANU and ZAPU force at 200–500 by 1973 [30]. Some, including the South African writer A. J. Venter, say that there was a joint force totalling "several thousands". The fact that estimates ranging up to 8 000 were made illustrates the absence of definite information [77–78].

The preliminary conclusion drawn here, in the absence of any credible numerical confirmation, has to be that the ZANU guerillas must have numbered more than 500, since the military attacks still continued in 1974 and the Rhodesian authorities claimed to have slain 203 guerillas between December 1972 and December 1973 [5d]. But a joint guerilla force of 8 000 deployed in combat would have far outnumbered the Rhodesian regular troops and made a more decisive impact. Furthermore, none of the liberation movements controlled any territory inside Rhodesia. They remained disunited and opposed to each other and also to the African National Council which was negotiating with the Smith regime.

Military aid to ZANU and ZAPU was channelled exclusively through the OAU. Military training took place in Tanzania, Algeria, Egypt, Cuba, the USSR and China. FROLIZI was not reported as being military active at all up to the time of the coup in Portugal. As to the persistent charge that ZANU is "Maoist" in orientation and ZAPU "pro-Soviet", there is practically no evidence of any such ideological affiliation being expressed in the form of military aid, although some of the future ZANU leaders did receive a short period of military education in China.

After 1965, progressively more sophisticated weaponry was brought into Rhodesia, and when the intensive fighting in the Wankie Game Reserve occurred in 1967, the Rhodesian troops captured bazookas, rockets and radio communication equipment from the guerillas. By early 1974, the ZANU troops were equipped with 122-mm rockets, machine-guns and automatic rifles of Soviet origin. In April 1974, ZANU claimed to have shot down three Rhodesian aircraft, including one Canberra bomber [79]. On 8 March 1974, four South African policemen were killed in an attack by ZAPU near the Victoria Falls. This caused the South African authorities to prepare for a change of legislation in order to provide a legal basis for sending South African regular troops abroad. This development, which pointed towards a future deployment of regular soldiers instead of police forces in Rhodesia, was completely reversed, however, by the events in Portugal.

Military aid to the Smith regime

Following the appearance in Rhodesia in 1967 of a guerilla force belonging to the South African ANC, a large contingent of South African paramilitary police troops was deployed in Rhodesia. South Africa became responsible for the security of that sector of the Zambezi frontier which stretches from the Victoria Falls to Lake Kariba. Information varies concerning the exact number of South African police troops in Rhodesia, and it has often been suggested that these were, in fact, regular troops.

In 1973, according to conservative Zambian estimates, there were 2 500 South African paramilitary troops patrolling the Zambezi Valley, and a further 1 000 regular troops were deployed in the interior. ZAPU and ZANU estimates in 1972 gave a total of 8 000 troops [80]. Other sources said that reinforcements of the South African police units along the Zambezi river in December 1972 brought the total to more than 5 000 and by 1973 to 7 000–10 000 [81]. Considering that the Rhodesian regular army numbered only 4 700, the importance of the South African contingents was evident. The South African police units were equipped with Saracen armoured cars, four Alouette helicopters and at least two spotter planes. Their function was similar to that of regular troops.

III. *Namibia and South Africa*

Namibia

In 1967, two years before its formal announcement of the formation of the Peoples' Liberation Army of Namibia, SWAPO carried out armed attacks on the South African forces in the Caprivi Strip. Already in the days of Count Caprivi, the German Chancellor who seized the area for his country in 1890, the Caprivi Strip was described as "a dagger pointing to the heart of Africa". Before the independence of Angola and Mozambique it remained the sole piece of land linking territory under South African control with independent Africa. The South African regime has shown increasing understanding of the strategic advantages offered by military control in Caprivi. Contrary to the provisions of the UN mandate prohibiting South Africa from having regular troops and military installations on Namibian territory, a major air force base was installed at Mpacha and a military base has been constructed at Kamenga in the Caprivi Strip.

When the SWAPO guerilla attacks transformed Caprivi into an insecure zone, the South African authorities ordered the resettlement of some 50 000 civilian Africans from the Strip. In 1974, a plan was revealed to construct an all-weather highway from Grootfontein in Namibia to the major district town of Katima Mulilo in Caprivi in order to limit the effectiveness of SWAPO's ambushes and its mining of the jungle paths. Fighting continued to escalate throughout the year. In January 1973, SWAPO attacked the Kamenga base. In June of the same year, SWAPO claimed to have brought down a helicopter in the west of the Strip, and in November a large guerilla force again attacked the Kamenga base. According to some reports, more than 200 South African soldiers and police were killed in Caprivi during the first half of the year [82].

Guerilla warfare also took place along Namibia's northern border with Angola and on the Kaoko Veld plateau in the northwestern part of the territory, where a SWAPO force had reportedly entrenched itself. This force was said to number 1 500 men in 1970 [77–78] and it seems to have been relatively well equipped and trained. Machine-guns were used in an ambush against an army patrol in Caprivi in April 1973, and land mines were in common use.

South Africa keeps four army companies, totalling around 1 400 men, in the Caprivi Strip and another three in the area around the Cunene Dam building site on the border of Angola [5e].

The exact military status of SWAPO remains disputed. The South African authorities generally deny all information about the military situation in Caprivi emanating from SWAPO or its supporters. The difficulties inherent in reporting from a restricted area are illustrated by this example in point: in mid-1974, international attention was suddenly focussed on the Caprivi Strip when two Swedish free-lance journalists reported on Swedish television about a case which seemed to be similar to the Wiriyamu massacre in Mozambique. The journalists had entered Caprivi with SWAPO units, they said, and had been informed that a massacre of over 100 civilian Africans had taken place on 19 September 1973. South African authorities denied this story and invited a group of Western journalists to inspect the area. This group concluded that the Swedish journalists had not been in Caprivi, and added that they themselves did not "find evidence of the reported massacre" [83].

The point remains that no foreign journalist who visits an area such as Caprivi is likely to be able to produce evidence supporting or repudiating any such opinion. The following description of the war zone by a South African source amply illustrates the difficulties that the Swedish journalists, the 15 foreign reporters, and indeed any outsider must face in determining his exact position in the Strip:

The front line in East Caprivi runs along the Zambezi River from Kazungula in the north west corner of Rhodesia, west of the Victoria Falls, to Katima Mulilo, chief town of the region ... At Katima Mulilo the Zambezi River takes a sharp turn to the north to form the Zambia–Angola border. From Katima Mulilo a compass bearing due west demarcates the land border between the Caprivi, Zambia and Angola. The only common land border with Zambia is this ruler-straight line which the troops call the cutline. All South Africans know it simply as the border [84].

South Africa

The South African armed forces' experience of guerilla warfare remains confined to Rhodesia and Namibia. The sole cases of armed opposition inside South Africa were the abortive attacks by units of the military wings of the ANC and the PAC in 1961. These attacks, which were more of the nature of selected sabotage actions against government installations, had the declared aim of avoiding the loss of lives [85]. On 16 December 1961, UmKhonto We Sizwe, the military wing of the ANC, led by Nelson Mandela as Commander-in-Chief, initiated the first in a series of sabotage actions that continued for several weeks. Mandela, together with practically the entire leadership, was arrested and at the subsequent Rivonia trial of 1956, all the accused were sentenced to life imprisonment. The ANC cadres that managed to escape did not take military action again until 1967, when the alliance with ZAPU was formed in Rhodesia. After the defeat in the Wankie Game Reserve, no further military action by the ANC of South Africa has been reported.

Poqo, the military wing of the PAC, attacked isolated farms in South Africa in 1961 and killed some white South Africans, creating a short period of panic among the whites. In 1967, the PAC was said to have entered into military cooperation with ZANU in Rhodesia, as a counterpart to the PAC-ZAPU alliance, but no subsequent military action has taken place. There were some reports that PAC guerillas were trying to reach South Africa through Mozambique, but these efforts apparently failed, as did the earlier attempts by ANC guerillas to infiltrate into South Africa prior to the independence of Mozambique and Angola [86].

The South African regime, while it was still protected by the buffer zones of Rhodesia and the Portuguese territories, conducted a military build-up on an unprecedented scale after 1960 and concentrated on the acquisition of a counterinsurgency capability. These preparations indeed seemed to make an assault by a guerilla force from the outside improbable, at least until the transfer of independence to Angola and Mozambique.

References

1. de Andrade, M., *La Poésie Africaine d'Expression Portuguaise*, Anthologie (France, Pierre Jean Oswald, 1969) p. 12.
2. Galvão, H., *Santa Maria: My Crusade for Portugal* (London, Weidenfeld and Nicolson, 1961) Appendix 2, pp. 204–205.
3. Cabral, A., *Revolution in Guinea* (London, Stage I, 1969) p. 50.

4. Mondlane, E., *The Struggle for Mozambique* (Harmondsworth, UK, Penguin Books, 1969).
   (a) —, p. 125.
   (b) —, p. 191.
   (c) —, pp. 163–67.
5. Legum, C., *Africa Contemporary Record: Annual Survey and Documents 1973–74* (London, Rex Collings, 1974).
   (a) —, pp. A83–A85.
   (b) —, p. A89.
   (c) —, p. B517.
   (d) —, p. B498.
   (e) —, p. B393.
   (f) —, p. B544.
6. *Daily Telegraph,* UK, 5 February 1974.
7. *Times,* UK, 23 September 1974.
8. *Africa South of the Sahara 1972* (London, Europa Publications, 1972) p. 766.
9. *Star Weekly,* South Africa, 11 May 1974.
10. *Africa Bureau Fact Sheet,* UK, No. 35, April 1974.
11. *Anti-Apartheid News,* UK, September 1974, p. 5.
12. *A Survey of Race Relations in South Africa 1973* (Johannesburg, January 1974, South Africa Institute of Race Relations).
    (a) —, p. 165.
    (b) —, p. 48.
13. *Sechaba,* UK, No. 6, June 1974, p. 21.
14. Davidson, B., "The Cost of Colonialism to Portugal", quoted in *West Africa,* Nigeria, No. 2951, January 1974.
15. *World Armaments and Disarmament, SIPRI Yearbook 1974* (Stockholm, Almqvist & Wiksell, 1974, Stockholm International Peace Research Institute) pp. 206–207.
16. *International Herald Tribune,* USA, 19 March 1974.
17. *Africa,* UK, No. 35, July 1974.
18. *Implementation of the US Arms Embargo (Against Portugal and South Africa and Related Issues),* Hearings before the Subcommittee on Africa of the Committee on Foreign Affairs, House of Representatives, 93rd Congress, 1st Session, 20, 22 March; 6 April 1973, (Washington, US Government Printing Office, 1973).
    (a) —, p. 283.
    (b) —, p. 105.
    (c) —, p. 89.
19. *Guardian,* UK, 7 March 1973.
20. *La Cité,* Belgium, 11 October 1973.
21. *Der Spiegel,* FR Germany, No. 6, 1962.
22. *Expresso,* Portugal, 25 August 1973.
23. *O Seculo,* Portugal, 10 June 1973.
24. *Libération,* France, 6 February 1974.
25. *Le Monde Diplomatique,* France, No. 242, May 1974.
26. *Military Balance 1968–69* (London, International Institute of Strategic Studies (IISS)).
27. Special report from Mozambique by Kristina Bohman and Åke Malmström, *Dagens Nyheter,* Sweden, 27–28 April 1974. (Author's translation.)
28. *NATO's 15 Nations,* Belgium, October/November 1968.
29. *Portugal: An Informative Review,* Portugal, No. 34, 1973, p. 15.

30. *Almanac of World Military Power 1972,* 2nd edition (New York and London, R. R. Bowker Co., 1972).
31. *JP-4 Mensile di Aeronautica,* Italy, April 1974.
32. Report by Jean Ziegler, *Nouvel Observateur,* France, 24 March 1974.
33. *Star,* South Africa, 14 April 1973.
34. *Diário,* Mozambique, 1 October 1973.
35. *Diário de Noticias,* Portugal, 29 January 1973.
36. *Africa Report,* USA, September/October 1973.
37. *Aftonbladet,* Sweden, 26 June 1974.
38. Report by Michael Degnan, *Africa Report,* USA, September/October 1973.
39. *Diário,* Mozambique, 12 January 1973.
40. *African Development,* UK, May 1973.
41. *Wings over Africa,* South Africa, September 1973.
42. *Diário,* Mozambique, 22 February 1973.
43. *Primeiro de Janeiro,* Portugal, 2 October 1973.
44. *Military Balance 1974–75* (London, International Institute of Strategic Studies (IISS)).
45. *Facts and Reports,* Netherlands, No. 2, 19 January 1974.
46. *Expresso,* Portugal, 27 July 1973.
47. *Frankfurter Rundschau,* FR Germany, 1 March 1974.
48. *New York Times,* USA, 19 June 1974.
49. Wilkinson, A. R., "Angola and Mozambique: The Implications of Local Power", *Survival,* UK, September/October 1974.
50. *Journal d'Europe,* Belgium, 28 January 1974.
51. Marcum, J., "Three Revolutions", *African Report,* USA, November 1967.
52. Davidson, B., *The Liberation of Guiné* (Harmondsworth, UK, Penguin Books, 1969).
    (a) —, p. 102.
    (b) —, p. 88.
53. *Daily Telegraph,* UK, 26 May 1973.
54. Bruce, N., "Portugal's African Wars", *Conflict Studies,* UK, No. 34, March 1973.
55. *Observer,* UK, 21 January 1973.
56. Report by Colin Legum, *Observer,* UK, 17 July 1973.
57. *Provincia,* Angola, 22 March 1973.
58. *Le Monde,* France, 8 July 1974.
59. *International Herald Tribune,* USA, 25 May 1974.
60. *Diário de Noticias,* Portugal, 29 January 1973.
61. *L'Express,* France, 11 February 1974.
62. *Daily News,* Tanzania, 11 March 1974.
63. *Times,* UK, 10 April 1973.
64. *Guardian,* UK, 5 December 1973.
65. *Sunday Post,* Kenya, 28 July 1973.
66. *Daily News,* Tanzania, 2 March 1974, quoting FRELIMO war communiqué.
67. *Daily Telegraph,* UK, 11 February 1974.
68. *Rand Daily Mail,* South Africa, 22 February 1973.
69. Davidson, B., *In the Eye of the Storm: Angola's People* (London, Longman, 1972).
70. *Dagens Nyheter,* Sweden, 27–28 April 1974.
71. *Africa Diary,* India, No. 8, 19–25 February 1974.
72. UN documents A/AC 209/1538, A/8023, Add 3, and A/AC, 109 L 699.
73. *De Groene Amsterdamer,* Netherlands, 11 August 1973.

74. *African Times,* Rhodesia, 10 January 1974.

75. *Africa,* UK, No. 19, March 1973.

76. Report by David Martin, *Observer,* UK, 2 September 1973.

77. Grundy, K., *Guerilla Struggle in Africa—An Analysis and Preview* (New York, 1971, World Law Fund).

78. Report by A. J. Venter, *International Defence Review,* December 1970.

79. *Times,* UK, 25 April 1974.

80. *Africa,* India, No. 25, September 1973.

81. *Le Monde Diplomatique,* France, May 1973.

82. *Sunday Times,* UK, 1 July 1973.

83. *New York Times,* USA, 27 August 1974.

84. *South African Digest,* South Africa, 21 June 1974.

85. *Nelson Mandela Speaks,* South African Studies 4 (London, undated, Publicity and Information Bureau, ANC South Africa) p. 40.

86. PAC: "Mounting Black Resistance inside Azania", *Southern Africa II,* Stokke, O. and Widstrand, C., eds., the UN-OAU Conference, Oslo, 9–14 April 1973, p. 176.

87. Challiand, G., "Lutte Armée en Afrique" (Paris, François Maspero, 1967, Cahiers libres 101) p. 23.

88. Gibson, R., *African Liberation Movements: Contemporary Struggles against White Minority Rule* (UK, Oxford University Press, 1972, Institute of Race Relations).

89. Potholm, C. P. and Dale, R., eds., *Southern Africa in Perspective* (New York, The Free Press, 1972).

90. Martin, D., "Interpol Solves a Guerilla Whodunit", *Observer,* UK, 6 February 1972.

Part III. The military power of South Africa and Rhodesia

Square-bracketed references, thus [1], refer to the list of references on page 154.

From the time of the Sharpeville massacre, South Africa increased its military strength in all fields—manpower, equipment and arms production. It is now the leading military power in Sub-Saharan Africa, second only to Egypt in the entire African continent. In the context of the conflict in Southern Africa, the Republic of South Africa is usually described as the bastion of white supremacy in that area. This is certainly valid as far as military power is concerned.

Rhodesia's military establishment was generally regarded between 1965 and 1974 as being a mere auxiliary force to South Africa's in the event of a future large-scale conflict between the white-ruled states in Southern Africa and hostile external or internal forces. Rhodesia nevertheless possessed considerable military strength in a relative sense, if compared, for example, with Zambia or Tanzania.

South Africa's military expenditure between 1963 and 1973 exceeded that of all other African nations combined except Egypt. The same was true for the value of major arms imports. (See charts 6.1 and 6.2.) At present, South Africa could mobilize some 200 000 men in two weeks. In addition, it has 100 000 men in the reserves [1]. This total excludes the police force with its special paramilitary units numbering 3 000. The Rhodesian armed forces can mobilize some 50 000 reservists in addition to its 5 000 regular troops.

South Africa's Air Force contains some 400 aircraft, 80 of which are combat planes. The main striking force is made up of Mirage III fighter-bombers supplied by France. It is supplemented by some 300 light, private aircraft operated by 12 air commando squadrons. The Rhodesian Air Force also remains in adequate fighting condition, even though most of the 42 combat aircraft are outdated. Finally, South Africa possesses the sole local navy in the region, with around 30 first-line ships.

The domestic arms industry in South Africa, into which heavy financial and manpower resources have been channelled since 1960, is capable of producing modern counterinsurgency aircraft, armoured cars and virtually all types of smaller armaments needed by the armed forces. Efforts continue in the field of nuclear research. These developments have taken place in the face of an international arms embargo since 1963 and despite the

115

fact that South Africa took on the additional burden of supplying the Rhodesian armed forces after 1965.

South Africa's relatively rapid development into an independent modern military power could be seen as resulting from a fortunate combination of factors. First of all, the financial resources of the country have been more than adequate to support large-scale investments in expensive weaponry as well as related expenditures for education, training, support and maintenance. Secondly, the arms industry was one local undertaking among many in a general process of industrialization. To this was added the government's firm decision to become independent of foreign suppliers of military equipment, and indeed to transform South Africa into a great regional military power.

Nevertheless, as will be shown below, this self-sufficiency could not have been achieved without the active or passive support of those very foreign powers from whom the South African government declared its intention to become independent. Support was extended either in the form of agreements on arms sales or on the transfer of military and related technology to South Africa.

Chapter 6. The Republic of South Africa

I. *Military expenditure*

Between 1960 and 1962[1] the defence budget rose from $62 million to $168 million, reflecting the sudden increase in preparations for counterinsurgency warfare that followed the Sharpeville massacre and the intensified purchases of military equipment from abroad. Following the UN arms embargo in 1963, the military budget jumped from $165 million in 1963 to $375 million in 1964, a 56 per cent increase. A massive construction programme was undertaken to build up a domestic arms industry which would function independently of foreign suppliers. By 1972 the defence budget stood at $479.5 million, and in 1973 a record defence budget estimate of $691.6 million was announced. The latter figure represented 13 per cent of the total state budget [1]. The total military expenditure as a percentage of the GNP rose from 0.8 in 1960 to 2.3 in 1973, in spite of South Africa's substantial economic growth.[2] However, actual defence spending reached 5 per cent of the GNP in 1973 [2]. The most obvious conclusion to be drawn from this relatively low GNP share was that South Africa could well afford a substantial increase in defence spending.

An estimate of the total amount spent on armaments would have to include allocations for indigenous research and the development and production of arms. The South African White Paper on Defence, published in 1973, states that the 1969–73 capital expenditure on equipment was $774.5 million [3]. Of this sum, aircraft accounted for $274.7 million, ammunition for $123.8 million and radio, radar and electronics for $109 million. It is known that nearly 50 per cent of the defence budget in 1972 was devoted to the development and procurement of arms [4]. The share devoted to arms purchases rose from $157 million in 1971–72 to $452 million in 1974–75 [5]. It seems reasonable to assume that, considering the local production of more sophisticated weapons such as missiles and supersonic aircraft, a progressively larger share of this jointly presented budgetary allocation goes to development.

Military research and development

Exact information about the resources devoted to research and development is hard to obtain, although considerable sums are known to have gone

---

[1] All years mentioned in connection with military expenditure figures refer to *fiscal years* unless otherwise stated: for example, 1960=fiscal year 1960–61.
[2] The fact that the defence budget as a percentage of the GNP fell from 2.5 in 1969–70 to 2.3 in 1971–73, as was pointed out in South Africa's Defence White Paper in 1973 [3], illustrated the economic boom rather than any decrease in military expenditure.

117

Chart 6.1. Military expenditure: South Africa and Rhodesia, 1961–74

US $ million, at constant 1970 prices and exchange rates

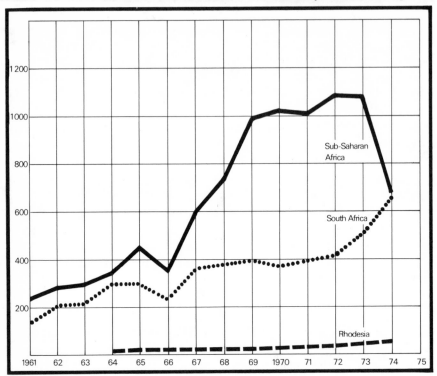

into defence research since 1962. Defence research was initially undertaken by the Council for Scientific and Industrial Research (CSIR). Its tasks were later divided up among various agencies, such as the National Institute for Rocket Research and Development and the Naval Research Institute, which were both set up in 1963. That same year, in asking Parliament to vote large sums for defence research, Defence Minister Fouche explained, "We will simply have to do our own research and make this sort of thing ourselves" [6]. In October 1966, Economic Planning Minister Haak disclosed that the CSIR would be granted over $10 million for secret defence research projects during that financial year.

Also in 1966 the Defence Research Council was established to combine the functions of the previous planning organs—the Coordinating Committee on Defence, the Defence Resources Board and the Council for Defence Research. Its tasks are to determine priorities in defence research and development, give advice on financing, investigate the results of various research projects and present recommendations on the desirability of local manufacture *versus* import of given items. The council also directs the stockpiling and control of essential supplies, such as oil, and would oversee

118

the conversion of industry in time of war. Remarkable foresight of future dangers to the supply of oil has been shown by the authorities: during the 1973 world energy crisis, which caught many other nations unprepared, it was revealed that South Africa had been preparing for just such an event as the Arab oil boycott ever since this possibility was first mentioned in 1964. Vast strategic oil reserves had been stored in unused gold mines and were said to be adequate to cover the country's needs for two years, even in the event of a total blockade. The cost of such undertakings provides grounds for speculation. As it turned out, however, no total boycott was enforced against South Africa, since Iran continued to supply most of the country's oil requirements even after 1973. Furthermore, the possession of the largest coal reserves in the southern hemisphere allows South Africa to undertake the very expensive procedure of converting coal to oil, which has been pioneered by the state-owned SASOL corporation. In 1974 it was said that enough coal had already been converted to supply 8–10 per cent of South Africa's total oil needs [7].

Other defence-related costs

The police and defence budgets are separate. In 1966 the police force was allocated $15 950 for undisclosed research. The Department of Justice also carries out research on such projects as emergency planning, for which $203 000 was granted in 1966 [8].

In 1968 the Bureau for State Security (BSS) was set up with a secret budget which did not require Treasury approval. In 1969 it became illegal to publish any information about BSS, and in 1972 this bureau acquired the status of a full government department, headed by General van den Bergh. Responsible only to the Prime Minister and exempted from parliamentary scrutiny, BSS's powers were widened by new legislation which permitted the interception of mail and the tapping of telephones. In 1973 it was estimated that South Africa spent more on the internal and external intelligence systems than the entire defence budget of Tanzania, which was $8 million that year. Some reports claim that the secret BSS budget is $64.4 million per year [9]. According to the ANC journal, *Sechaba*, the BSS budget increased from $13 million in 1973–74 to $19 million in 1974–75 [10].

II. *Manpower*

The armed forces

Prior to 1974 only white persons were called up for military service on a regular basis. The Bantus, Coloureds and Indians served in auxiliary corps in the Permanent Force, on a voluntary basis. Bantus were forbidden by law to carry arms, although there were some exceptions, especially in the army, where Bantus were employed as trackers.

The first Coloured Corps after World War II was set up in April 1963 to perform certain administrative tasks and to serve as drivers, storemen, clerks, stretcher-bearers and the like. It was reported that by 1966 over 2 000 persons had applied to the corps. Of these, 414 had been accepted, and 17 squadrons had received basic training. Beginning in April 1965 the navy admitted Coloured recruits on a permanent basis. Under the direction of white officers, they served on smaller vessels—minesweepers, for example—particularly as divers and chefs.

In January 1973 it was decided to admit Coloured youths on a voluntary basis to a military training scheme. This plan was approved by the Coloured Representatives Council and nearly 200 men were recruited for training in the Cape Corps Service Battalion. A similar service battalion for Indians was to be set up at Salisbury island.

The armed forces of South Africa, known as the South African Defence Force, comprise a small *Permanent Force,* the *Citizen Force* and a *Commando Force,* virtually all-white.

The Permanent and Citizen Forces consist of army, air force and navy units, and the Commandos have ground and air units, the latter made up of light private aircraft. The Permanent Force is responsible for the administration and training of all the armed forces in peacetime. In wartime it is absorbed into the Citizen Force. Defence capability is based on rapid mobilization of the highly trained reserves in the Citizen Force—that is, of all recruits who have completed their initial training.

The Permanent Force or the standing army (all three services) had been expanded from 7 721 members in 1961 to 18 000 by 1974. Of these, 10 000 were serving in the army, 5 500 in the air force and 3 000 in the navy. The army was organized in nine Territorial Commands, containing about 40 infantry battalions plus some airborne units. Because of the need to increase the counterinsurgency capability, the planning and conduct of COIN operations have been decentralized to these nine commands. The independent COIN force thus consists of the Commandos in the area plus specially allocated Citizen Force units. [11] The air force units were organized into strike, transport, maritime and light aircraft commands and one maintenance group. Of the regular navy staff of some 4 500 men, 420 were officers. In addition, the navy is reported to have about 9 000 trained naval reserves in the Citizen Force. In the army and navy, the regular units have been integrated with the conscripts, but in the air force they are kept separate.

In March 1974 Defence Minister Botha announced that legislation had been introduced to extend the initial training period of servicemen for the Permanent Force from 18 months to two years, with the intention of creating a larger unit of servicemen who would be prepared on all occasions to act as a deterrent force. This measure was taken in view of the deteriorating security situation in Rhodesia, Mozambique and Namibia [14].

The conscript system

There are three classes of conscripts in the *Citizen Force:* new recruits undergoing initial training, recruits who remain on active duty after completion of their initial training and recruits who remain in the reserve Citizen Force after completing both of these service periods. All of this service is compulsory during a period of 10 years, and the system has considerably increased the number of men available for mobilization in an emergency or in case of war. The draft system is now universal, which means that the size of the conscript army cannot be increased very much, unless the system is extended to the non-white population.

In 1961, the Citizen Force numbered only 2 000, but this figure rose to 16 527 by 1964 [8]. Under the compulsory draft system introduced in 1967, the number of trainees increased by 50 per cent. The annual induction figure in the 1970s was estimated to be between 25 000 and 33 000 [12]. By 1974, the Citizen Force in active duty totalled 92 000, meaning that more than 100 000 men could be mobilized at short notice, including the Permanent Force. This had been the declared goal when the compulsory system was announced in 1967 [13].

Under the current draft system, every white male citizen between the ages of 17 and 25 is liable to ten years of active duty in the military service. The minimum initial training period was increased from nine to 10 months in January 1973. Now service is 12 months irrespective of the branch or speciality [3].

After completion of the initial training programme, recruits are assigned to Citizen Force units where they undergo a continuous training of 19 days every year.

The Commando Force

The Commandos are an important complement to the Citizen Force and fulfil both home-guard, police and counterinsurgency functions. The organization is included under the nine army territorial commands. Its history dates back to the eighteenth century. Now as then, it is an all-white force, composed essentially of local residents organized for the defence of their own areas.

Originally, Commando service was entirely voluntary, but in the 1960s it was made compulsory, and the total service period was established at 16 years. According to the Defence Act of 1957, the Commandos are available to act in support of the police. Beginning in 1972, their initial training period was extended from three to nine months in order to bring their education in line with that of the Citizen Force. The training period was again lengthened in 1974, this time to 12 months, while the total service period was reduced from 16 to 10 years, also to bring it in line with compulsory service in the Citizen Force. In this way, interchange of personnel between the Citizen Force and the Commandos became possible.

In 1969 the army began to allocate national servicemen to Commando units, leading to a considerable increase in numbers and operational capacity. By 1973 the Darie Theron Combat School, established in 1968, had trained thousands of officers and lower-ranking men for the Commando organization.

The Commandos are divided into groups of five or more units. A commander with the rank of colonel is appointed for each group. All commanders are chosen from the local membership. The groups include cavalry units, leading to a considerable increase in numbers and operational capacity. In the past few years, the arms and equipment of the Commandos have been improved. By 1968, there were 205 Commando units, possessing 250 light aircraft [15]. The total number of Commandos had reached 75 000 in 1974.

The national police force

The racial composition of the police force is 50 per cent white, 45 per cent Bantu and 5 per cent Coloured or Indian. By 1974 the police numbered 33 000, including 3 000 who were employed in the special counterinsurgency units that have been established since 1965. These units are equipped with 80 Saracen armoured personnel carriers and 430 riot trucks as well as heavy infantry weapons [16]. The COIN police force has been in service since 1967 in Rhodesia and the Caprivi Strip and since 1971 in Namibia. Black policemen were generally not allowed to carry firearms until 1974. Control over the police is in the hands of the whites and is further strengthened by the 20 000-member police reserve force, which is virtually all-white.

The Police Amendment Act of 1961 set up the reserve police force, which was subsequently enlarged when some Coloureds and Indians were admitted. The government had initially envisaged recruiting 5 000 whites to the reserve to assist in performing ordinary police duties when regular policemen were required for more urgent tasks.

In 1964 the Minister of Justice stated that the strength of the police reserve was 19 663 (19 313 whites, 231 Coloureds and 110 Indians). The different racial groups serve in separate branches [8].

122

The police operate a few aircraft and a number of helicopters which are obtained from the South African Air Force when needed. (It was reported in March 1965 that the police had bought a six-seat Cessna aircraft for use by the Commissioner of Police and senior officers [17].)

In addition to normal police tasks, the South African Police fulfil a key function for national security. Motorized police patrol the South African borders, and mobile COIN units are deployed in critical areas. The Police Amendment Act No. 74 of 1965 empowers any policeman at any place within a mile of the South African border to search, without a warrant, any person, premises, vehicle or aircraft. The Minister of Justice said in the House of Assembly on 7 June 1965 that the police need these powers in order to combat the infiltration of trained saboteurs into the Republic [8].

The defence and police forces have cooperated in internal security work since the Defence Further Amendment Act No. 42 of 1961 was passed. This cooperation has been further strengthened by the Defence Amendment Act of 1963, which authorizes part-time soldiers in the Citizen Force and civilians in the Commando Force to act as policemen in time of emergency and provides for their mobilization at short notice.

Under the apartheid system, "normal" police duties are quite extensive, involving a large number of personnel for a great number of tasks. The pass system requires the daily checking of documents to control the movements of the non-white population and also calls for the constant patrolling of the Bantustan "borders" and of the segregated areas within the white zone—the compounds for miners and the black townships outside the white cities. Under the four main security laws—the Sabotage Act, the Suppression of Communism Act, the Unlawful Organizations Act and the Terrorism Act—the police force is responsible for detecting and preventing opposition to apartheid. The police network is, in fact, an elaborate system that stretches across the entire Republic and Namibia and supposedly makes underground work and infiltration on any scale impossible.

If the total number of men in the Commando organization and the police force is added to the number available for mobilization in the armed forces, the figure exceeds 300 000.

Other manpower

Additional steps that have been taken to increase the supply of trained manpower have included legislation, passed at the end of 1967, to require aliens to register for national service. Since 1969, male immigrants between the ages of 16 and 25, who have lived in the country for five years but are not citizens, have been drafted.

A civil defence training college was established for women in 1971. By the end of 1972, it had graduated 265 students and a second college was being considered.

III. *Arms procurement*

The UN embargo

The first UN embargo resolution, passed by the Security Council on 7 August 1963, calls on all states to "cease forthwith the sale and shipment of arms, ammunition of all types, and military vehicles to South Africa" [18]. Britain and France abstained. (See appendix 2.)

A second resolution, which was unanimously adopted by the Security Council on 4 December that same year, extends the embargo to cover "equipment and materials needed for the manufacture and maintenance of arms and ammunition in South Africa" [19]. Britain and France supported this resolution but reserved their right to supply equipment for "external defence".

All the traditional arms-producing countries supported these embargo resolutions and implemented them through a series of national embargoes announced in late 1963 and 1964. In a United Nations investigation of embargo compliance in 1970, all the member countries—including those listed in appendix 1 as arms suppliers to South Africa even after 1963 (see pages 205–15)—claimed that they were abiding by the embargo resolutions. Italy, for example, declared that it had "scrupulously" adhered to the restrictions, even though the South African Air Force was then in the process of equipping itself with the Impála counterinsurgency plane, produced under licence from Italy [20].

One possible conclusion, namely, that the UN embargoes were of no practical value, would require some qualification. It is obvious after examining the pattern of arms suppliers listed in appendix 1, and the development of the domestic arms industry described below, that the UN embargoes had two major results. Firstly, on the supplier's side, the UK, which had been the sole important arms supplier to South Africa during the 1950s, ceded this position to other Western countries and the area also became closed to major weapon deliveries from the United States. Secondly, the consequences for South Africa were that its armed forces had to convert to non-British equipment and its sources of arms supplies had to be diversified. The countries that took over Britain's role were notably France and Italy, but also FR Germany, Japan, Israel and several others. The transactions with France and Italy received most publicity, however, as they have involved such heavy equipment as aircraft, warships and missiles.

The new arms suppliers to South Africa became important partners in the establishment of the domestic arms industry. It is quite evident that Britain and also the United States played a role, and it would be a mistake to believe that the UN embargoes caused these two countries to abstain from all connections with South Africa's military expansion programme. The import of arms from the UK and the USA took place in spite of the embargoes, although the quantities imported diminished considerably and were limited to certain selected types of equipment.

The fact that South Africa was not left to modernize and equip its armed forces in isolation after 1963 will be explained below.

Loopholes in the UN embargoes

The first loophole arises by virtue of the fact that there is no legal standard by which to judge the enforcement of the embargo by the major arms exporting nations. The United Nations resolutions are formulated in general terms and merely prohibit the sale of "weapons" and "military technology". Member states are free to translate these generalities into the concrete rules and lists of arms that the administrations in charge of arms exports are to follow.

So, for example, on passing their national embargoes against arms exports to South Africa in 1963, all countries stated that existing contracts had to be fulfilled in accordance with normal business practice. This included the supply of spare parts for weapons already delivered—or to be delivered —under existing contracts.

In monetary terms, related equipment and spare parts account for a large part of any arms deal. For example, between 1963 and 1973, the USA sold the South African Air Force $23.3 million worth of spare parts, maintenance and testing equipment, replacement engines, overhaul and repair programmes for seven Lockheed C-130 Hercules military transport aircraft delivered before 1963 [21a]. By comparison, the basic unit price quoted for a new Hercules in 1974 was only $2.87 million. Thus, pending the termination of the various contracts, the supply of spare parts and accessories has continued, with significant consequences: without this supply, the majority of South Africa's aircraft, imported during the 1950s from Britain, Canada and the United States, would have been grounded by the end of the 1960s. In July 1970, the Canadian government finally ceased supplying spare parts, thereby giving up a source of income that brought Canada $1.2 million in 1960 alone [22].

The United States has refused to supply spare parts for certain types of equipment, notably the Sikorsky helicopters delivered in 1955. As a result, the South African Air Force switched to French Alouette helicopters in 1962.

A second loophole in the UN embargoes is the clause, upon which both Britain and France insisted in 1963, assuring South Africa of its continued access to armaments for *external* defence. Thus, according to the Simonstown Agreement of 1955, the British embargo does not cover armaments needed for naval defence. As for France, it has observed the embargo only to the extent that it has undertaken not to supply certain specified anti-guerilla weapons to South Africa. M. Debré, Minister of Defence, said in a written reply to Parliament that, according to a decision of 1962, France did *not* export light mortars, automatic weapons, low-speed attack aircraft, napalm and other weapons suitable for anti-guerilla action. But France would continue to supply heavy armaments such as warships and tanks since these were for use in "classical warfare against a modern army" [23].

Thirdly, items with a dual civilian-military use are generally not covered in the national embargoes, which explains why in principle several Western governments could not have prevented their companies from investing and participating in new, often arms-industry-related enterprises in South Africa, even if they had wished to do so. The domestic electronics industry is an example of a branch in which it may be virtually impossible for government administrative agencies to judge in advance the possible military applications of a company's products. Another example is provided by the United States, which supplied most of the light aircraft purchased by private commercial companies, flying clubs and individuals in South Africa. However, as was described in the previous section, the Commando air units are officially connected to the air force and are equipped with privately owned light aircraft. Unpublished Export Control Office figures show that between 1963 and September 1971 the United States sold 1 967 light aircraft to South Africa, including transport planes and helicopters, at a total value of $192.5 million [24]. Non-military aircraft worth $13.6 million were sold to South Africa during 1973 alone [21b].

In February 1970, the United States granted the first of what became a total of 10 licences for the export of C-130 cargo planes to SAFAIR, a charter company, which under a South African government contract flew military supplies to the South African forces in Rhodesia and Namibia [25].

A fourth loophole lies in the differences in praxis in arms-producing countries for control of the resale of armaments. The USA applies complete control in its arms exports contracts and as a rule prohibits resale to a third country, but Britain and Sweden, for example, have no such restrictions. This explains why, for instance, the Swedish Bofors cannon is still being used by both the army and the navy in South Africa.

Variations in supply policy

Over the years, the South African government also found that the manner in which embargo restrictions were interpreted depended on the attitude of the government in power. This has been especially evident in Britain and the United States.

The purchase of the British Westland Wasp naval helicopter, equipped for antisubmarine warfare, provides an illustration: four Wasps were delivered in 1964 and six more in 1966 because the British Labour government regarded these as belonging to the naval equipment covered by the Simonstown Agreement, to which Britain was a party, for the defence of the Cape Route. When the Conservative government came into power in 1971, it relaxed the arms embargo, and in February that year South Africa was allowed to place a new order with the Westland company, this time for seven Wasps. The Wasp assembly line, which had been closed down, was reopened and the first new Wasps were delivered in 1973. When Labour again took office in early 1974 only one helicopter remained to be delivered. Because the Labour government was committed to a firm anti-apartheid policy, it refused to issue an export licence for this last helicopter. The South African government reacted by threatening that the Simonstown Agreement might be revoked.

The Wasp deal received much publicity, and the anti-apartheid lobby in Britain charged the government with deliberately breaking the embargo. Although this sale involved only a very small number of helicopters, it aroused wide public interest in the *principle* involved—namely, whether any kind of cooperation with the South African regime is justifiable. It also illustrated one of the major related issues facing a leading arms-producing nation—that of keeping its domestic arms industry alive. Apprehension was expressed that political pressure to enforce the embargo would lead to domestic unemployment and labour problems. Nevertheless, on 19 March 1974, the new British Foreign Secretary, James Callaghan, announced firmly in the House of Commons that Britain would reimpose the arms embargo on South Africa.

The British aerospace industry took the unprecedented measure in 1974 of appealing directly and publicly to the Labour government to lift the embargo. The president of the Society of British Aerospace Companies, representing over 300 firms, E. R. Sisson, said in a letter to the government that export orders valued at $1.3 billion were at stake and would be granted to France within a few months' time unless the British altered their position. South Africa was said to require aircraft such as the British Nimrod, and also helicopters, aero-engines, guided weapons, radar and important port and defence installation equipment [26]. The South African contracts were said to represent "the work and livelihood of approximately 25 000 employees in industry" [27].

In a reply by Anthony Wedgwood Benn, Secretary of State for Industry, the British government firmly refused to oblige.

On 2 May 1974, the British Shipbuilders' and Repairers' National Association also expressed concern in a letter to Wedgwood Benn that the government's antagonistic attitude towards defence orders from South Africa could cause the shipbuilding industry to lose a potential market for an estimated £150 million worth of frigates and submarines over the next 5–10 years. But on 20 May the government decided to reinforce substantially its embargo on South Africa and Chile, and Prime Minister Wilson announced that the last Wasp export licence had been revoked.

In the *United States,* the Nixon administration seemed, from South Africa's point of view, to be more reasonable to deal with than either the

Johnson or the Kennedy governments had been, although no practical results followed the preliminary talks prior to Nixon's resignation in 1974.

In 1973 it was reported that the Nixon administration was considering the possible sale of a gunship plane and a long-range naval reconnaissance plane to South Africa. When the question of exporting a naval plane arose in 1965, the Johnson administration had vetoed the sale of two types to South Africa, one of which was the Breguet-Atlantic, a NATO consortium project equipped with General Electric electronic gear. Since General Electric was involved, the USA was able to prevent this sale because its re-export controls clause covers not only entire weapons but also components and spare parts. The other plane, the all-US Lockheed Orion, was reconsidered for export by Nixon in 1973 [21c].

France, which took over Britain's role after 1963 as the most important supplier of sophisticated arms to South Africa, was reported in 1974 to be considering a possible change of policy. On taking office, President Valéry Giscard d'Estaing indicated a future ban on arms sales to authoritarian regimes, in fulfillment of his electoral pledge. In South Africa, this pledge was not, however, interpreted as a threat to arms imports from France. On the contrary, during the electoral campaign, the South African press stated that Giscard d'Estaing was to be preferred to a leftist candidate such as Mitterrand [28]. Subsequent developments during 1974 pointed to an increase of contracts, involving not only military transactions but trade in general and nuclear research.

FR Germany has considerably expanded its South African connections since 1970, increasing its general trade, investments and military transactions [53].[3] Many projects related to building up the defence industry in South Africa were undertaken jointly—and without publicity—by West German and French companies in the 1960s. FR Germany is also involved in the uranium trade and in the development of nuclear technology in South Africa. This development has accelerated despite the official policy of the Bonn government, which repeatedly declared its opposition to apartheid.

For the nations supplying arms to South Africa, anti-apartheid is of secondary importance to such pragmatic interests as financial gain, domestic employment questions and access to strategic raw materials. Such considerations are hardly ever revealed during discussions of the arms embargo; but they may be inferred. One US official replied as follows when asked which criteria were used in deciding whether a military item was covered by the embargo:

The judgement that is made when we contemplate decontrolling an item is . . . a judgement made on the basis of inputs from the Department of Defense and the Department of State and their concern is *what is in the best national interest of the United States in terms of foreign policy and national security* [21d]. *(SIPRI italics.)*

---

[3] See for example *Blätter des iz3w, No. 39* [53] and *Sechaba* [32].

It appears that similar decisions based on various national interests lie behind all Western governments' approvals of export licences for military equipment destined for South Africa, and that little or no importance is attached to the issue of apartheid or of solidarity with the African population.

Arms imports

The imports of major arms[4] by South Africa from 1950 to 1974 are listed in appendix 1, page 205, and will be commented on briefly below. In addition, imports of other military equipment, of at least equal significance to the total armed strength of South Africa, are presented.

Aircraft

In 1974, the main strike force of the South African Air Force was made up of two Mirage squadrons, one a fighter-bomber squadron equipped with 20 Mirage III-Es and the other an interceptor squadron of 16 Mirage III-C fighter planes, all supplied by France during and after 1963. A new batch of 18 Mirage III-E aircraft was ordered in 1972 and delivered in 1974. From 1977, the Mirage F-1 will be licence-produced in South Africa, which will greatly improve the strike capability of the air force.

The four air force helicopter squadrons were also entirely French-equipped, with 40 Alouette III, 20 SA 330 Puma and 15 Super Frelon helicopters. An additional 12 Alouettes were assigned to the navy. The Puma, of joint Franco–British design, was delivered to South Africa in 1973. Nine Transall transport planes were purchased from France in 1969. Transall is a French–West German project: two-thirds of the plane is produced in FR Germany and the remainder in France. France paid the West German companies involved DM 66 million for this transaction.

Italy has supplied the rest of South Africa's modern aircraft. In 1969, nine Piaggio P.166 light reconnaissance planes were acquired from Italy. By 1974, 11 more had been ordered. Forty Aeritalia AM.3C multi-purpose monoplanes—highly suitable for counterinsurgency operations—were ordered in 1972. But Italy's most important contribution was its sale to South Africa in 1967 of the production licence for the M.B. 326 armed jet trainer known in the South Africa as the *Impala I*. The M.B. 326K light-strike version, the Impala II, entered production in 1974. These aircraft provide the South African Air Force with a highly modern counter-insurgency capability.

The remainder of South Africa's aircraft are fully operational but are due for replacement. Two fighter-bomber squadrons comprising 30 British

---

[4] The SIPRI arms trade registers cover only *major weapons:* aircraft, missiles, armoured vehicles and warships.

Chart 6.2. Major arms imports by Southern Africa, 1950–74

US $ million, at 1973 constant prices

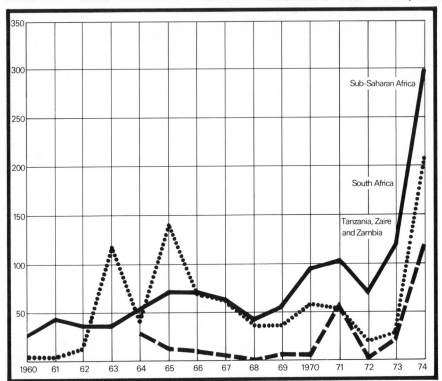

Vampires acquired in 1952–54 and 18 Canadian Sabres bought in 1956–62 need replacement. The 13 Buccaneer naval bombers in the light-bomber squadron were all grounded after accidents during a combined British–South African naval and air exercise in November 1973.

Missiles

The missile inventory by 1974 was entirely French-supplied with the exception of some 200 Sidewinder air-to-air missiles purchased in 1956 from Britain to arm the Sabre planes. All the Mirage strike planes were equipped with French missiles—notably the AS-20 and AS-30 air-to-surface and the Matra R.530 air-to-air missiles. The Mirage F-1 will carry the Matra 550 Magic short-range air-to-air missile.

The first anti-tank missile system to be deployed was the joint French–West German-designed Milan, which France began delivering in 1974. Guided by an infrared automatic system, this missile has a range of two kilometres and will greatly improve the strike capability of the army.

The first ship-to-ship missile system to be acquired by the South African

Navy was the Israeli-designed Gabriel. This deal was announced in mid-1974 and may corroborate persistent earlier reports that a military trade relationship exists between Israel and South Africa.[5] Gabriel will arm the three British-supplied antisubmarine warfare frigates.

Ground-to-air missiles, which are the foundation of any modern air defence system, have been provided by France through an ingenious arrangement: in 1964, construction of the Cactus ground-to-air missile system was begun in France according to South African specifications and with the participation of South African scientists. About 85 per cent of the cost of the research and development programme was paid for by South Africa. The existence of this programme was not revealed until 1969, when Defence Minister Botha visited France to witness a test launching of the missile, known there as the Crotale. Initial deliveries of operational systems to South Africa began in 1971. By 1973 three pre-production type batteries had been deployed on the Transvaal border, facing Mozambique.

Crotale/Cactus is an all-weather missile, transportable by air or land. It is designed to attack aircraft flying at altitudes as low as 50 metres and at speeds up to Mach 1.2. Matra was responsible for the development and manufacture of the actual missile. Thomson-CSF built the ground equipment which was initially designed to be fitted into special Hotchkiss Brandt all-terrain vehicles. Such planes as the C-130 Hercules or Transall C-160 are capable of transporting the developed version. With this missile system it is possible to track 12 different targets simultaneously and to fire 12 pairs of missiles at six targets within 11 seconds.

According to the French producers—Matra, Thomson-CSF and Hotchkiss–Brandt—France has retained the sales rights for the missile and it cannot therefore be re-exported from South Africa. But France must nonetheless secure the South African government's consent for any deal involving this defence system. Cactus was reportedly included in Defence Minister Botha's list in 1972 of possible items to be exported to "friendly countries" [29]. The question of who owns the sales rights to Cactus will probably remain unsettled, until South Africa actually delivers a Cactus system to another country. In principle, both France and South Africa can have sales rights, but it may also be true that the missile can only be sold by France. Under its French name, Crotale, the system has aroused considerable interest among Western customers. In 1974 it appeared that Norway and the United States were about to become the first nations to buy the Crotale from France.

---

[5] The Soviet press in particular, but also other sources such as the *Daily Telegraph* and the *Sunday Telegraph,* UK, and the *Algérie-Actualités,* have claimed for many years that Israel has sold large quantities of armaments to South Africa. An article in *Krasnaya Svezda,* of 30 January 1974, said that South Africa's arms imports from Israel increased sixfold between 1969 and 1973 and that South Africa had become the largest purchaser of Israeli-made firearms, artillery and ammunition. South Africa was said to be especially interested in the Israeli-made Gabriel and Jericho missile systems.

In 1972 the North American Rockwell Corporation and Thomson-CSF signed a preliminary contract to produce the Crotale if it were adopted by the US Army. The US Army has purchased five missiles for testing, at a cost of $1.4 million [21e].

In Norway, South Africa's connection with Crotale provoked a public controversy which is still unresolved.

In 1974, when South Africa acquired Jordan's entire Tigercat ground-to-air missile system, speculation arose that the ultimate customer was Rhodesia, since South Africa was already deploying the Cactus system for its own air defence. (See page 154, the Jordanian arms deal.)

Armoured vehicles

No tanks have been acquired by South Africa since 1963 except for 41 Centurions that were included in the transfer from Jordan in 1974. It is believed, however, that these tanks are also destined to be sent to Rhodesia, since the South African Army still has about 100 tanks of this type in service, supplied by Britain in the latter half of the 1950s. Plans for domestic production have also been announced.

Light armoured vehicles, more important than tanks for counterinsurgency activities, have been provided since 1963 by France, through the sale of licence-production rights for Panhard armoured cars.

Warships

Currently, the South African Navy numbers over 30 ships, of which only six are major warships of modern design. Three of these ships are British-supplied ASW frigates and three are French-supplied submarines.

Under the current expansion programme, the South African Navy will expand to a total of 45–50 ships, excluding support and auxiliary vessels. The expansion programme began in 1971 when, under the "Project Taurus" agreement with Portugal, South Africa arranged to purchase six corvettes of the "João Coutinho"-class. This corvette was designed in FR Germany at the Blohm & Voss shipyard and the project was undertaken by the Portuguese LISNAVE yard. The price of the six corvettes, which were to be armed with French Exocet ship-to-ship missiles, was quoted at $60 million. However, in September 1974, reports from Lisbon said that this project had been abandoned. Although the South African authorities denied the rumour, the future of the project appears to be uncertain [30].

The alternative supplier of new corvettes will in all likelihood be France. In October 1973 the South African naval commander visited Paris and expressed his interest in corvettes, and the following October South Africa received a French offer to build a newly designed 750-ton corvette with four Exocet missile launchers. The expansion programme also involves the acquisition of two "Agosta"-class submarines from France, ordered in 1975.

The most modern combat ships supplied by Britain under the Simonstown

Agreement were three "Whitby"-class frigates built between 1962 and 1964. They were converted to carry one Wasp helicopter each in addition to other antisubmarine warfare equipment. Each ship carries two Swedish 40-mm Bofors anti-aircraft guns.

Three patrol boats were ordered from Spain in 1971 and are now under construction.

It was reported in late 1974 that South Africa intends to purchase missile boats from Israel if the British government should turn down a request for such ships.

Small arms

South Africa had built up an impressive domestic small arms industry by 1974, capable of supplying most of the needs of the armed forces. In addition, the army was equipped with Swedish Bofors and Swiss Oerlikon anti-aircraft guns. Since the Bofors arms are licence-produced in a number of countries, the Swedish government has no means of controlling re-export. In Switzerland, the Oerlikon company went on trial in 1970, charged with illegal arms exports to several countries including South Africa.

The source of the 105-mm and 155-mm howitzers in use with the army remains unconfirmed. Heavy mortars, some types of small arms and munitions are imported from Israel.

Communications and electronics equipment

No modern defence establishment can be operated without a wide variety of electronic and communications devices. Britain, France, FR Germany, Israel, Italy and the United States have all exported such equipment to South Africa.

In 1970 it became known that the British Labour government had authorized a $70–80 million sale of military radar equipment. The Marconi company subsequently confirmed that it had signed a contract with the South African defence authorities for military radar and other electronically operated communications equipment which would be used in establishing a transcontinental radar defence system. This is an early warning system stretching across South Africa from the Atlantic to the Indian Ocean coast, controlled from underground bunkers and intended to provide protection against a possible future air attack from the north. The British Foreign Office did not consider this sale to be a breach of the embargo since the items concerned were not defined as military goods [31]. The British Aircraft Corporation, on the other hand, had been involved in 1971 in a study of South African air defence requirements prior to the Marconi deal. The study had the code name "Project 102" and investigated the deployment of the BAC Rapier or Thunderbird missile systems as a complement to the Cactus. For political reasons, however, no missiles were actually exported. These two cases illustrate some of the problems involved in maintaining a firm embargo policy line in a supplying country.

From the United States, South Africa has acquired flight instruments, optical equipment and computers. Between 1967 and 1972 communications equipment valued at $21.7 million was purchased [21f].

The ITT company in South Africa is officially undertaking only civilian tasks. Still, in the US hearings on embargo implementations, before the House Subcommittee on Foreign Affairs in 1973, it was revealed that ITT is required to obtain South African security clearance for some of its senior technical staff. This led to the charge that "clearly, the work that ITT is doing for the South African Government is of a critically strategic nature" [21g].

FR Germany has exported large amounts of electronic and communications equipment to South Africa. During the first half of 1970 alone, Siemens AG delivered electronic apparatus worth $3 million. In 1974 it was reported that a vast communications system, known as the "Advokaat", was being installed by AEG-Telefunken and Siemens AG. The project is worth $25 million. Its centre is in Cape Town, and regional headquarters have been established in Port Elizabeth, Durban and in Walvis Bay in Namibia. The "Advokaat", which will serve the South African Navy, comprises long- and short-wave transmitters, relay stations, telephone and telex installations and computerized data processing. South African officers have been trained in FR Germany to operate the system.

Communications equipment as such is generally defined as non-military, but it is regarded as essential for the modernization of the internal security programme to control the non-white population. In future, all non-whites are to be computer-checked. The fingerprints of 10 million Bantus have already been stored.[6] (This system was originally introduced into South Africa by the British in 1902 as a means of identifying the illiterate non-white population.)

In 1970, the Messerschmitt–Bölkow–Blohm (MBB) company agreed to participate in a special project, developed according to specifications from the South African defence authorities and authorized by the German Federal Ministry of Defence, which includes the delivery of a computer and radio intelligence equipment [32]. The details of this project are not known.

Herbicides

Between 1969 and 1972 the United States exported $9.6 million worth of herbicides to South Africa [21h]. Among these were the herbicides 2,4-D and 2,4,5-T; both were used for military purposes by the US armed forces in Viet-Nam. (The United States Army banned the use of Agent Orange, which is a mixture of these two chemicals, because of its danger to human

---

[6] Information given to the author by Abdul Minty, Stockholm, 19 August 1974.

beings.) Although no reports have been made of South African use of herbicides, either as defoliants or against population centres in the Republic itself, several claims have been made that a South African civilian herbicide company has been involved in chemical warfare operations against FRE-LIMO in northern Mozambique [33].

Domestic arms production

The import of military technology can be described as a more sophisticated way of acquiring arms, with far-reaching consequences for the buyer. Military know-how is purchased, and once a particular weapon is locally produced no outside authority can stop this production. The revocation of an arms production licence may thus become little more than a paper exercise. This is the Israeli government's explanation for the continuing production of the Uzi machine-gun in South Africa.

Another long-term consequence of the import of know-how is the acquisition of an export capability. South Africa can now sell certain categories of arms abroad. In some areas local production also results in considerable financial savings. According to *Paratus,* the official defence force journal, the unit production cost of locally made fuel tanks for Centurion vehicles, for example, was only $420, compared with a unit import price of $2800.

UN embargo resolutions also cover the transfer of equipment and arms production technology to South Africa, but the legal loopholes are so numerous and varied that this trade in know-how has largely escaped the control of administrative bodies in the Western countries responsible for the implementation of the arms embargo. Highly complex trade and commercial relations are often at work when a specific arms project is begun, and all details of such agreements are usually kept secret in accordance with normal business practices. The production of French Panhard armoured cars in South Africa was not revealed, for instance, until the factory had been built and production had already begun.

Much defence-related equipment is not classified as military, even though it is highly important in the everyday functioning of the armed forces. For example, the US-controlled Dunlop South Africa, the largest vehicle- and aircraft-tyre manufacturer in the country, secured a Eurodollar loan enabling it to undertake a $14-million expansion programme in 1969. According to the company's chairman, this loan makes it possible for Dunlop to provide all the tyres South Africa needs for civilian and military use.

Another militarily important industry, Parachute Industries of Southern Africa (Pty) Ltd, was set up in 1965 with the assistance of US technicians. Equipped with US machinery, the company produces 850 parachutes per month.

One method of circumventing the embargo decisions relating to the transfer of know-how has proved to be highly successful, both for the sellers and for South Africa. This approach is to establish subsidiaries in South Africa that are partly engaged in production for the civilian market. Until 1974 this practice was followed mainly by producers of electronics, avionics and communications equipment. But the list may lengthen. In connection with the protest action undertaken by the British aerospace industry against the Labour government's export restrictions to South Africa, it is reported that some of the largest British arms-producing companies were secretly negotiating with South Africa to establish subsidiaries there.

Self-sufficiency

South Africa has made repeated claims of self-sufficiency in weapon production, but occasionally it qualifies this to apply to specific types of weapons. A close investigation of its production programmes reveals that by 1974 South Africa was practically self-sufficient in the production of ammunition, all types of firearms, bombs, mines and a range of related military equipment. It was also producing armoured cars and military vehicles. The production of military aircraft, rockets and missiles was well under way. But South Africa was heavily dependent on foreign producers for assistance in its nuclear technology and chemical weapon research programmes. Warships, aero-engines and vital instrumentation equipment still had to be imported. A few indigenous designs of weapons had been developed and produced, including several types of small arms and a mine-clearing vehicle. Research work was under way for various projects involving more sophisticated technology, such as military transport aircraft, corvettes, frigates and submarines, none of which had been developed beyond the planning stage.

Thus, it is clear that the concept of self-sufficiency in armaments production needs some more elaboration. For countries with no experience of arms production, self-sufficiency usually means creating the capacity to *produce* a given weapon, rather than the capacity to *design* and *develop* it. Production capacity, in turn, develops in stages, depending on the type of weapon involved. For example, an aircraft project usually begins with the import of entire subassemblies from the seller. The final assembly is made at the local factory. Foreign technical advisers are usually required, and local technicians are sent to the selling country for training. Subsequently, local production of components is gradually increased, first using imported raw materials, and later, ideally, domestic ones. This process is known as the *indigenization* of a weapon project, and the degree of indigenization is normally measured either as a percentage of value or of content. In South Africa 100 per cent indigenization has been achieved in most of its small arms production and in its armoured car industry, and the claim of self-sufficiency in these fields is justified. But without substantial foreign aid, this achievement could not have taken place in such a relatively short time.

136

The defence industry

The foundation of South Africa's arms industry was laid during World War II, when the country—involved in the war on the side of the Allied forces—was cut off from military supplies from Britain. With the participation of British expertise, an embryo electronics industry was established, mainly for the production of radar equipment. During the war, over 5 000 armoured vehicles were locally produced, as well as howitzers, mortars and ammunition [34]. After the war many German military scientists found employment in South Africa. But it was only after 1960 that serious plans took shape to develop a local capacity to produce the major arms needed by the defence forces. As international protests mounted against the apartheid policy of the South African government and an eventual arms embargo was foreseen, preparations for several military projects were speeded up. In 1964, the Armaments Production Board, headed by Professor H. J. Samuels, was established in order to organize the acquisition of foreign military know-how.

Progress was rapid. By 1965, despite the international embargo on the transfer of military technology to South Africa, Defence Minister Botha could announce that he had acquired 127 weapon-production licences from foreign producers. In 1968 the Armaments Development and Production Corporation (ARMSCOR) was established with a capital of $144 million, to supervise the Armaments Board factories. Four years later Professor Samuels stated that South Africa had reached the stage where a weapon boycott from outside powers could no longer prevent it from acquiring arms. He also asserted that whereas in 1965 $46.3 million was spent on the manufacture of arms, this allocation had now been trebled. Of this amount, 80 per cent was invested in South Africa, where almost 1 000 contractors and subcontractors were actively engaged in the local arms industry [35]. In a debate on the defence vote in 1974, Botha mentioned, without identifying the suppliers, that a number of new licences for arms production had been acquired.

The contracting companies to which Professor Samuels referred were all privately owned; only the major military research enterprises and the Atlas Aircraft Corporation are state-owned. No information was available about how many of these private companies were, in reality, subsidiaries of foreign concerns, as Marconi (South Africa) Ltd is, for example. A reasonable guess, based on the structure of South Africa's economy in general, would be over 70 per cent. The defence industry is completely state-controlled, via the various separate boards set up for this purpose.

The aerospace industry

In 1965, construction of the Atlas aircraft factory was begun with the advisory aid of the French firm, Sud-Aviation. The factory is situated near

Johannesburg in the Transvaal. The Atlas Aircraft Corporation of South Africa (Pty) Ltd was formed to licence-produce the Italian Aermacchi M.B. 326M jet trainer/light attack plane. In 1969 ARMSCOR took over all Atlas' shares.

Over 1 000 British aircraft workers answered advertisements in London to join the Atlas factory in 1965. Italian engineers were also brought in to help set up the production line, and manufacturing operations started in 1967. Italy delivered 16 finished aircraft, plus 10 in major component form and 40 subassemblies. The licence agreement initially called for the production of 200 aircraft, excluding those originally supplied from Italy. About 60 of these were to be equipped for light-strike duties. The initial goal was to produce 70–80 per cent of this plane, excluding the engine and instrumentation, in South Africa—where it is known as the Impala. This target had almost been reached by the end of 1973.

By 1974, the Impala was being used by the South African Air Force mainly as a trainer, replacing the old Harvard planes. It is highly suitable, however, for counterinsurgency operations, having been designed and constructed for the dual role of basic trainer and tactical attack aircraft.

The Impala attack version can be armed with several alternative underwing loads; it can carry two machine-guns and two napalm tanks, two air-to-surface missiles, or two 227-kg bombs and two rocket packs each containing six 80-mm rockets. It uses a British Rolls-Royce Bristol Viper 11 turbojet engine, produced under British licence in Italy and not subject to any clause preventing its sale to a third country. There were unconfirmed reports that Rolls-Royce sent a team to the Atlas factory to provide instruction on the operation and maintenance of the engine.

Already in 1971 Defence Minister Botha announced the production of a more advanced version of the Impala. Negotiations with Italy and the UK were completed in 1973 for licensed production of the Aermacchi M.B. 326K light-strike version, to be known as the Impala II. A first batch of six prototype planes, plus parts for 15 others packed into crates for assembly by Atlas, was delivered early in 1974. In February 1974 the first flight of a South African-assembled M.B. 326K took place. The initial 50 planes were built for the South African Air Force, which planned to acquire more than 100 in all.

The Impala II is powered by two up-rated Rolls-Royce Viper 632 turbojet engines. This engine, which has a 4 000-lb thrust, was developed in collaboration by Rolls-Royce and the Italian company Fiat, and started to come off the production line in early 1974. South Africa was one of the first states to receive it. The Viper was manufactured under a Rolls-Royce licence by Piaggio, an Italian company controlled by Fiat. Fiat, in its turn, is in partnership with the Italian government in the ownership of Aeritalia, which negotiated the Aermacchi deal with South Africa.

Although few details about the Rolls-Royce agreement are known, some bits of information have appeared. When the Rolls-Royce licence was granted to Piaggio, the British government insisted at first on inserting a clause stipulating that planes equipped with the Viper engine would not be sold to South Africa. This demand was later waived, as a result of pressure from the industry, and was eventually replaced by a clause prohibiting the Impala from being exported from South Africa to Rhodesia.

When the production goals for the two Impala versions are achieved, the South African Air Force will be adequately equipped for any military air operations that appear necessary inside the Republic and in Namibia. Furthermore, the relatively low price of the Impala makes it competitive in the arms trade market. The unit cost of the M.B. 326K in 1973 was quoted at $584 000 and the flyaway cost on the M.B. 326M at $385 000. In 1974 there were some reports that an unknown number of Impalas had been exported to Jordan, as part of the arms deal involving Jordan, South Africa and Rhodesia. (See page 154.)

The eventual production of a light military aircraft by Atlas was also announced in 1971 by Defence Minister Botha. It was expected that the Italian Aeritalia AM.3C military observation and utility aircraft would be chosen. A sales agreement was concluded in 1973 for 40 AM.3Cs, to be delivered to the South African Army Air Corps as replacements for the aged Cessna 185s, but the Aeritalia group firmly denied that any licence-production deal was involved. The acquisition of the AM.3C will fill a reconnaissance capability gap in the South African Air Force. In mid-1974, delivery of these 40 planes began. In 1975, two new aircraft projects were announced by Professor Samuels of the Armaments Production Board. According to him, the Aermacchi-Lockheed AL. 60 C5 will be licence-produced in South Africa under the name *Kudu*. The AL.60 is a US-designed light plane, produced in Italy. In addition, the Italian AM.3C plane called *Bosbok,* will also be produced.

Since 1967, the Italian Partenavia P.64B Oscar-180 light aircraft has been licence-produced in South Africa where it is known as the AFIC RSA 200 Falcon. The AFIC company was formed to undertake this project and assembly of the plane was initially carried out at the Atlas factory. After 1969, AFIC acquired new facilities at Bloemfontein. This plane is a civilian flying-club type, the military application of which is confined to Air Commando use.

The build-up of local technical skill which began with relatively unsophisticated planes thus created the basic conditions for future expansion and for the undertaking of more advanced projects. On 27 June 1971 it was announced that an agreement had been concluded between ARMSCOR and Marcel Dassault/Breguet Aviation of France for the licensed production of the Mirage F 1 fighter/interceptor aircraft in South Africa. The agreement included an assurance of French industrial and technical cooperation and a provision for the training of South African staff at the Dassault works in

France. South Africa also had the option to decide what percentage of French-made parts would be used. The licence provided for manufacture of the entire aircraft, including engines and electrical equipment. This achievement would signal a breakthrough for the South African arms industry. Initial reports claimed that the production agreement also covered the Mirage III, but this turned out not to be the case.

Under French guidance, expansion and preparation work for the Mirage project went on at the Atlas plant for more than two years. By early 1974, the preparatory stage was nearly completed, despite admitted difficulties. The initial order covered 48 planes, of which 16 were F1-CZ interceptor versions and 32 were F1-AZ ground-attack versions. The South African Air Force is expected to take up to 100 Mirage F1s, and it is considered possible that, after the first 48 have been acquired, procurement will change to the F1 International M53-engined naval version, known as the Super Mirage. This would fill the South African requirement for a sophisticated naval aircraft were it not possible to purchase the Breguet-Atlantic from the UK or the Lockheed Orion from the USA.

Delivery of the initial 48 Mirages was expected during 1974 but tooling and preparation problems in France delayed the schedule. All 16 interceptors are expected to be wholly manufactured and assembled by the parent company in France and delivered to South Africa as prototypes. The first of these was completed at the end of 1974. The 32 ground-attack fighters to follow are to incorporate an increasing proportion of components built by Atlas.

The purchase of the initial Mirages was said to be one of the main factors explaining the steep increase in estimated expenditures of the South African Air Force, whose outlays rose during 1973 from $37 million to $64.7 million. The total cost of an initial production-run of 50 Mirage planes in 1971 was judged to exceed $50 million. The first locally-built Mirage is scheduled to be finished in 1977. According to Professor Samuels of the Armaments Board, this plane is considered to be "the fighter of the future" and is to remain in local production for a long time [36].

The Mirage F1 was considered in 1974 to be as good a fighter aircraft as the US Phantom and the Soviet MiG-23. It can operate from rough runways, has a combat radius of 1 000 km and a range of 3 300 m. At high altitudes the Mirage reaches a maximum level speed of Mach 2.2. Its standard fixed armament consists of two 30-mm cannon; its externally mounted weapons for interception include the French Matra R. 530 or Super 530 radar homing or infrared homing air-to-air missiles. In addition, it carries Matra Magic infrared homing air-to-air missiles on each wingtip. For ground-attack duties, the Mirage F1 usually bears an AS.37 Martel anti-radar missile or an AS.30 air-to-surface missile, or six 600-litre napalm tanks.

With the acquisition of this aircraft, the gap between the strike capability of South Africa and that of the adjacent African states will increase markedly. The Mirage F1 is a formidable attack weapon in the African context because it, like the US F-4 Phantom, has been specifically designed as a "third world plane" or a "poor man's weapon"—that is, for large-scale counterinsurgency operations from small airfields. This jargon is not related to price, however, but to the foreseen combat conditions and performance required. The cost of the Mirage F1 was quoted at $5 million in 1974, including spares but excluding the cost of R&D [37]. This means that the production costs to South Africa are likely to exceed $5 million per aircraft at the initial stage until a large enough production run has been achieved to result in what is known as "economies of scale".

Finally, some efforts have been made in the field of indigenous research and design of military aircraft. As early as 1962, the air force was evaluating a two-seater, locally built light plane called the Aeriel II, for possible use as a trainer, spotter or police-duty aircraft. In 1969, announcement was made of the construction of a STOL (short take-off and landing) transport—the Safari—capable of carrying 12 fully armed troops. None of these projects have advanced beyond the experimental stage, however. It has been speculated that the plans announced several times by ARMSCOR officials for the construction of a light transport aircraft for military as well as civilian purposes refer in reality to the licensed production of a foreign type, quite possibly the Israel Aircraft Industries' STOL transport Arava. By 1974 there was no definite information on this point. Helicopter production had also been planned for several years but had not begun in 1974. A likely choice for licensed production would seem to be the French Alouette.

The armoured vehicle industry

No light, medium or main battle tanks have yet been produced under licence or indigenously in South Africa, and for several years there did not seem to be any immediate plans or even requirements for a new tank. According to Defence Minister Botha, "South Africa does not make tanks, but these are not of great value against guerilla groups" [38].

French Panhard armoured cars have been licence-produced since 1966, and a second generation, with an indigenous engine, has also been developed. The types in production are the 4.8-ton Panhard AML 60 and the 5.5-ton Panhard AML 90, which belong to the AML 245 family and are armed with 60-mm and 90-mm cannon, respectively. They are known in South Africa as Eland armoured cars. The licence agreements are believed to have covered 1 000 units, some 600–800 of which had been produced by 1974. The second-generation type was nearing completion in 1972 and may have entered production in 1973. Earlier, the engine had been imported from France. According to the South Africa Defence White Paper in 1973, the indigenization of the Eland armoured car had reached almost 100 per cent.

The history of the Panhard project illustrates the commercial tactics involved as well as the joint Western interest in the development of the

South African arms industry. When in 1966 the Wilson government cancelled the British agreement to supply Saladin armoured cars to South Africa, an agreement was concluded instead with the French and West German governments. FR Germany undertook the construction of a factory for armoured car production in South Africa, where the French Panhards were subsequently built under licence. In this way, France for the time being avoided publicity for supplying weapons other than for "external defence", and FR Germany was rewarded with a higher South African import quota for its automobiles.

The local production of armoured cars has been sufficient to enable South Africa to export this weapon. In 1971 a number of old Saracen armoured personnel carriers were sent to the Portuguese Army in Mozambique and Saracens were also used in Rhodesia. Malawi has purchased seven new Elands since 1971, and Rhodesia was reportedly buying Elands in late 1973.

In 1972, the Armaments Board evaluated concepts of infantry vehicles suitable for local production, and in 1973 it was reported that South Africa had developed a new mine-clearing vehicle.

The following year Botha suddenly announced during a defence vote debate that construction of tanks would soon begin. This could possibly be a French AMX tank version, to be produced under licence. This assumption is based on the fact that no third world country, in the entire period since 1945, has been able to design and develop a tank that is competitive— economically and in performance—with those produced in the industrialized countries.

The rocket and missile industry

A third military branch that South Africa has managed to develop with success within a comparatively short time is the rocket and missile industry. In this effort, both French and West German industrial and technical cooperation were essential, although in different ways.

Initial contacts in this field were established between FR Germany and South Africa in 1963 when the banker Herman Abs visited the Republic to offer, for the first time, West German participation in nuclear research, a restricted area for West German scientists under the Western European Union regulations after World War II. One result was that a West German group, Lindau und Harz, set up a rocket research centre and an ionosphere station near Tsumeb in Namibia. It was charged in 1964 that this station was working in close cooperation with the German Federal Ministry of Defence and that its projects were directly financed by the latter. The two West German companies engaged in rocket production there are Waffen und Luftrüstung AG and Herman Oberth-Gesellschaft, Bremen.

In August 1963, it was announced that South Africa was engaged in research to develop military rockets of an unspecified nature. When the Rocket Research Institute was established one year later, Professor A. J. A. LeRoux said that South Africa had been forced by events in Africa to enter the missile field. That same year the Cactus project began in France.

The value to the South African missile industry of the experience of development work gained through the Cactus project can hardly be over-estimated. In 1968 Defence Minister Botha announced that the government would build a military and scientific test range on the Zululand Bantustan coast, north of Durban—the St. Lucia missile range—in cooperation with an unspecified European company. This company, he said, had already completed several similar installations, which seems to indicate that it was a West German firm. On 17 December 1968 the first short-range rockets were successfully fired from a new missile range on Fanies Island, and in 1969 an indigenously developed air-to-air missile was launched at the St. Lucia range. In 1971 the Defence Department announced that the indigenous missile, using an automatic heat-seeking homing device, had been fired successfully from a Mirage fighter and had struck a supersonic target drone. It can reportedly be used against aircraft with speeds up to Mach 2. The missile is to be produced in quantity and has good export prospects.

In 1973 a special rocket research and development centre was set up. Known as the Propulsion Division of the National Institute for Defence Research, it works on development up to the production stage of missiles and their warheads, propellants and propulsion systems.

The shipbuilding industry

In 1974 there was still no government-owned shipyard in South Africa, and the private shipyards lacked the capacity to undertake the construction of large warships. Among the few locally built ships in the South African Navy there was, for example, a 220-ton torpedo recovery ship, built by Dorman Long (Africa) Ltd in Durban in 1969 and two naval tugs which were completed by Globe Engineering Works Ltd in Cape Town in 1961 and 1969.

However, the South African authorities are determined to achieve a domestic capability in this area. Plans for submarine construction have been under way since 1968. In 1972, the Yarrow African Maritime Consultancy—which advises the Armaments Board and is connected with the well-known British Yarrow (Shipbuilders) Ltd—announced that it had been instructed to investigate the country's potential for the construction of surface warships. Yarrow then invited applications from interested shipyards, and Premier Vorster promised that the government would subsidize up to 25 per cent of the expenditure for any ship built for defence purposes. Durban was chosen as the future construction centre, being the closest port to the country's major steelworks. In 1974 it was reported that the construction of 750-ton corvettes would begin in Durban during the following year at the latest. An offer of a French design has been received.

South Africa plans to be able to construct large frigates and submarines by 1980. These plans are certain to involve the acquisition of foreign cooperation, for the same reasons as were cited above in connection with tank production.

Small arms

During the expansion period of about six years that began in 1963, South Africa managed to develop its own domestic small arms industry. It can now produce practically all types and quantities of firearms needed by the armed forces. This achievement, which has received less attention in the outside world than such spectacular projects as the Mirage and the Cactus missile, is infinitely more significant for the regime's capacity to preserve internal security.

In the field of explosives and propellants, South Africa is so productive that it can consider exporting such items. About 100 types of ammunition are being made. Self-sufficiency has also been achieved in heavy-calibre ammunition production. Infantry ammunition is produced as well, but total indigenization had not yet been reached by 1974. In the manufacture of naval ammunition, South Africa is also approaching the stage of self-sufficiency. All pyrotechnic supplies are locally made. The full range of aerial bombs up to 1 000 lb—including smoke bombs—is also locally built.

An anti-armour mine, capable of destroying heavy vehicles, has been developed and found cheaper than imported ones. Two types of shrapnel mines and canister-shot mines have also been made for army use. Anti-personnel mines are locally produced.

The basic shoulder weapon used by the army—the R-1—is an exact copy of the FN 7.62-mm automatic assault rifle produced by the Fabrique Nationale in Belgium. This is an improved version of the FN standard NATO rifle. Initially, manufacture took place in South Africa under a Belgian licence which, according to the Belgian government, was revoked after 1963. Another NATO standard weapon, the Israeli Uzi submachine-gun, is also manufactured in South Africa. During investigations conducted by the United Nations Special Committee on Apartheid in 1971, spokesmen for the Israeli Foreign Ministry stated that the Uzi had been sublicensed to South Africa by a Belgian company which had produced the gun under licence since 1955, making it impossible for the Israeli government to prevent the resale of this item to South Africa. Since then, Israel claims to have inserted a clause in all subsequent licence agreements, prohibiting sales to third countries [39].

Whether the continued South African production of these two weapons, essential for the army, takes place with or without extended Belgian licence agreements, the fact remains that no outside embargo reinforcements are likely to stifle this industry. It has been reported, in fact, that South Africa has copied many other types of weapon from the NATO inventory and is manufacturing them locally.

The support weapons in army use are basic 60-mm and 81-mm mortars, 3.5-mm rocket launchers, and 105-mm and 155-mm howitzers. No information about local production of howitzers has been given in Botha's frequent listings of locally-made military equipment. The explanation could well be one of the following: either the army still uses old types supplied by Britain during the 1950s or there is an undiscovered foreign source of supply. If howitzers were produced locally there would seem to be no reason to conceal just this production.

In 1972 it was announced that the first 90-mm field gun to be wholly produced in South Africa had been successfully tested. In addition, the National Defence Research Institute has designed and built a machine pistol capable of firing 800 rounds a minute. Presumably this will be the standard weapon for close-combat purposes in the army, replacing revolvers and hand machine carbines. Cannon production is well advanced, and calibres in the ranges from 20-mm to 260-mm bored and 20-mm to 160-mm rifles are manufactured locally.

All the manufacture listed above is carried out in ARMSCOR factories.

Efforts are also being made to decentralize strategic industries. For example, after South Africa's first sporting rifle was developed in 1970, by Musgrave of Bloemfontein, the government took over this company within a year's time. A new $1-million factory was erected at Bloemfontein for large-scale production of sporting firearms and, for the army, 7.62-mm rifles. This undertaking was announced as part of the government's plan to decentralize strategic industries.

The British company Imperial Chemical Industries, Ltd (ICI South Africa) has a 42.5 per cent interest in African Explosives and Chemical Industries Ltd, which operates the two largest commercial explosives factories in the world. In return for an annual fee, African Explosives also runs two munitions factories in the Transvaal for the South African government. In 1971, the government took over full technical control of a third munitions plant which African Explosives at Somerset West built for it in the Cape.

Chemical weapons

Nerve gas, tear gas, other poison gases, and chemicals usable as defoliants are produced in South Africa. On 24 February 1963 a South African government spokesman stated that Britain had been supplying his country with tear gas since 1912. This was corroborated by the British Foreign Office, but it has since been stated that such export is prohibited. South Africa now produces its own tear gas, mainly in one of the three small arms factories built by African Explosives at Modderfontein [40]. In

1963, Professor LeRoux of the CSIR revealed that work was being carried out on developing the poison gases Tabun, Soman and Sarin. These gases could be sprayed from the air. One gramme of Tabun is said to be able to kill 400 people [6]. Nerve gases are produced in a chemical factory in Sasolburg, near Johannesburg. Frequent statements by the South African authorities themselves have given rise to a great deal of speculation about the existence of nerve-gas bombs or similar chemical weapons in South Africa. In particular, Botha's reference to a "secret weapon" in a speech in 1966 fomented such rumours. So far, no more substantial reports have appeared about any actual testing or deployment of such weapons, although it may be added that since many countries possess them and their construction does not call for complicated technology, it is by no means impossible for South Africa to build up such an inventory.

Defence Minister Botha informed Parliament in 1968 that South African scientists had developed a napalm bomb from local raw materials. Both napalm and CS-gas (tear gas) were produced by African Explosives and Chemical Industries at Umbogintwini in Natal.

Electronics

South Africa began producing electronic items during World War II. The electronics industry was considerably expanded after 1960. In 1972 a new lightweight transmitter-receiver communication system for Commando use was developed locally. A radio beacon for paratroopers is in production. A portable radar detection system and an advanced, and reportedly unique, system for identification of aircraft are under development, and it is claimed that some classified electronic equipment can now be locally designed and manufactured.

Foreign subsidiaries in South Africa have made a considerable contribution to the development of local production in the field of military electronics and avionics. For example, in 1968 a subsidiary of the British Marconi company was set up under the name of Marconi (South Africa) Ltd. Among the initial equipment manufactured there was the Marconi ADF 370 radio compass, for use in the Impala aircraft. International Aerado is also active, producing electronic components.

Manufacture of engines

From 1971 onwards, the South African Aeronautics Research Unit has been developing a valveless pulse-jet engine, apparently as a local venture. A South African-made engine has also replaced the French one that powers the Eland armoured cars.

Two US companies, Ford and General Motors, have erected large vehicle and engine assembly plants in South Africa. Although these plants produce civilian cars, the conclusion was reached in a recent study that "in times of emergency or war, each plant could be turned over rapidly to the production

146

of weapons and other strategic requirements for the defence of Southern Africa" [41a].

Another project may also illustrate a way of acquiring new technology. A West German-controlled diesel engine subsidiary to an international company, Deutz Magirus Southern Africa, was established in South Africa and was able by 1973 to export diesel engines to Australia and the United States. The company plans to begin exporting to FR Germany as well. It should be emphasized that while there is no connection so far between this company and any military products, diesel engines are used in military vehicles as well as ships, and the acquisition of know-how in this field is thus not irrelevant for military purposes. An entirely different aspect of this general issue of the transfer of know-how to new countries is the profit motive; this type of arrangement shows how Western companies are set up to profit from the existence of a cheap labour supply in a given country. This factor is so far not so pronounced in the South African defence industry, but will increase with the growth of arms exports from South Africa to foreign buyers.

Nuclear research

To those concerned with the threat of nuclear proliferation, the prospect of South Africa achieving nuclear-power status appears highly dangerous, and not only for the African continent. In the discussions about "near-nuclear countries", conducted among researchers and organizations involved in disarmament problems, South Africa ranked rather low as a potential nuclear power until the end of the 1960s. It appeared less likely than India, Israel or Japan to join the "nuclear club". But on 20 July 1970, Prime Minister Vorster announced the development of a new uranium-enrichment technique and declared at the same time South Africa's emergence as a "medium-class power" [42]. According to Professor LeRoux, who discussed the subject in a radio interview in 1973, the discovery of the new process has put South Africa in a position to make its own nuclear arms without outside aid. This statement, and the fact that South Africa is among those states that have not signed the 1968 Non-Proliferation Treaty (NPT), gave impetus to discussions of South Africa as a future nuclear power.

Two different opinions were put forth in these deliberations: (a) that the South African claims were pretentious and exaggerated, in view of the complicated technology required to achieve a nuclear-weapons capability, or (b) that South Africa was on the verge of becoming the first nuclear power on the African continent. Nuclear scientists and technical experts in the West generally supported the first view. Politicians, organizations and individuals engaged in anti-apartheid activities tended to hold the second view. When India, as the first of the so-called near-nuclear countries, exploded an atomic device in 1974, public debate about nuclear power in general shifted towards acceptance of the latter opinion—that South Africa would soon be next.

The South African authorities themselves appear to have great nuclear aspirations. According to Dr Louw Alberts, Vice-President of the South African Atomic Energy Board, South Africa's nuclear programme is more advanced than India's. He said that the Republic has the expertise to extract and enrich uranium and the capacity to produce a nuclear bomb. He emphasized, however, that this nuclear knowledge will only be used for peaceful purposes. The real significance of nuclear progress in South Africa, he said, was that, with one-quarter of the free world's uranium reserves, the Republic was "in a bargaining position equal to that of any Arab country with a lot of oil, in terms of the world's energy crisis" [43].

If the prediction is borne out that the number of nations possessing atomic weapons will multiply within a few years in direct relation to the spread of nuclear reactor technology, South Africa indeed fulfils most of the requirements needed to become a nuclear-weapon power. It is a leading producer of uranium. A nuclear research reactor has been in operation since 1965, providing several years' experience of nuclear technology. Cooperation has been established with leading Western nations. Finally, since South Africa has not signed the NPT, the International Atomic Energy Agency cannot inspect the South African installations.

The history of research and development in the field of nuclear technology shows a general pattern of Western cooperation with South Africa in this ostensibly civilian field. The countries involved are the United States, France and FR Germany. Pioneering efforts began in South Africa when the South African Atomic Energy Board was established as a state agency in 1949, with the exclusive right to prospect for uranium. The first uranium plant was opened in 1952 under a tripartite British–US–South African agreement. At that time, the USA and Britain were the sole purchasers of South African uranium. The first nuclear reactor was bought from the United States in the early 1960s and was installed with the aid of the US corporation, Allis Chalmers [41b], at the nuclear research station at Pelindaba in the Transvaal. Several South African nuclear scientists were sent to the US Atomic Energy Commission's National Laboratory at Oak Ridge for training. By 1965 this first reactor, Safari I, had gone critical. Safari I is a research reactor which does not produce electricity. It operates on 90 per cent enriched uranium and does not therefore produce the large quantities of plutonium that are needed in the construction of nuclear weapons. South Africa has more recently constructed a second research reactor. The discovery of a new enrichment technique, coupled with the elaborate plans to develop the nation's first nuclear power station—the Koeburg A—near Cape Town, will, however, enhance the possibilities for

South Africa to opt for a nuclear-weapon programme should the government wish to do so.

France and FR Germany eventually responded positively to repeated South African offers to share its new uranium enrichment technology with Western powers, and in June 1974 Professor LeRoux announced that still other foreign interests were involved.

In August 1973, it became known that a major West German fuel concern, STEAG, was negotiating with the South African Enrichment Corporation. The West German government was directly involved, acting through the Gesellschaft für Kernforschung MbH, which had also devised a new method of uranium enrichment.

In April 1974, STEAG and the South African Atomic Energy Board signed a contract for the establishment of a uranium enrichment plant in South Africa which would "carry out a joint feasibility study of the two uranium enrichment processes" [44]. South Africa plans to be able to meet 14 per cent of the world's needs for enriched uranium by 1980, about 6 000 tons SW/year [44].[7]

Details about South Africa's enrichment technology are strictly classified, stirring much speculation among Western nuclear scientists. STEAG probably produces enriched uranium by the jet nozzle method, and this is likely to be one of the processes that will be studied in the South African plant. The South African authorities have disclosed, however, that their technique is not based on gas diffusion. Finally, it is even speculated that the South African process is in reality identical to the West German method. It is argued that there are a certain number of known enrichment processes and that it is hard to envisage that South Africa, or any other country, could discover a new process that is totally unknown to others.

Until the local plant is in operation the nuclear power station Koeburg A will use uranium that has been enriched abroad. It will become the biggest thermal station in the southern hemisphere and is scheduled to be functioning by 1982. According to an announcement in 1974, the station will be built by a Franco–US consortium, Framatome.[8] South Africa plans to have two reactors in operation at the Cape by 1985.

Should the South African government opt for a nuclear-weapon programme, this will be a move in defiance of the declared policy of most other nations in Africa. On 9 December 1974 the UN General Assembly adopted, by 131 votes to none with no abstentions, a resolution (3261E) to consider

---

[7] SW years = Separate work per year. This is the common quantitative measure of both the degree of separation of the uranium isotopes 235 and 238, and the quantity of enriched material [45].

[8] This was part of a complex pattern of a new developing trade axis involving France, Iran, South Africa and the United States, and covering such strategic commodities as oil, uranium, mining and nuclear technology. A trade agreement was signed at the same time in Paris for the construction of five nuclear power stations in Iran. Iran announced that it would continue to supply oil to South Africa. For its part, South Africa will export coal and uranium.

and respect the continent of Africa as a nuclear-free zone. Four African countries were absent—South Africa, Gabon, Malawi and Swaziland.

This resolution was introduced by African states, and recalled a "solemn declaration on the denuclearization of Africa", made by the 1964 session of the Assembly of the OAU and endorsed by the nonaligned countries' conference in Cairo in 1964 [47].

Plate 1. Portuguese Foreign Minister Soares and FRELIMO President Machel met to discuss cease-fire: Lusaka, 1974.

Plate 2. Amilcar Cabral, the founder of the PAIGC.

Chapter 7. Rhodesia

I. *Military expenditure*

The mounting guerilla threat against Rhodesia was clearly illustrated in 1974 by the rise in that country's military allocations. In the defence vote in July 1973, total defence spending had increased to $60 million, or almost 12 per cent of the state budget, as compared with $13 million spent 10 years earlier. In November, an additional $16 million had to be voted [48]. Yet another quick rate of increase was foreseen as the modernization programmes for the armed forces proceeded. Replacements for outdated air force equipment were urgently needed. In their annual reports in July 1973, the Rhodesian Army and the Air Force stressed the problems that had arisen as a result of shortages of funds and of European manpower. Without referring to the international sanctions and their possible effects, Air Marshal Wilson demanded a vigorous expansion and development programme.

II. *Manpower*

Not surprisingly in view of the increasing need for counterinsurgency measures, the shortage of manpower, which has been a constant problem since UDI in 1965, is regarded as a key issue. The whites form less than 5 per cent of the population in Rhodesia, and the government has had to rely on black Africans in the security forces to a greater extent than is the case in South Africa. Before the current expansion programme, about one-third of the 3 500-man regular army was made up of black Africans serving in the 1 000-strong battalion called the Rhodesian African Rifles. A seasoned regiment of African troops, the Rhodesian African Rifles has been in existence since 1940. Most of them come from the Vakaranga tribe. The officers are white.

Beginning in 1972, the Rhodesian Ministry of Defence devised several measures to cope with the security situation. In December 1972, the national training service period was extended from nine to 12 months. Simultaneously, army call-up was expanded to include categories previously exempted from military service because of minor physical defects. In July 1973 the number of training centres was increased and one month later the national service intake for the 18–25 year-old age-group was also raised.

On 3 April 1974, the Rhodesian Defence Ministry announced that

Europeans between 25 and 35 years of age were to be called up for military service. High gratuities were offered to those who agreed to spend an extra year in the army after completing their national service. School-leavers were to be called up as soon as possible after their education was terminated. Men older than 25 with no previous military commitment and who had lived in Rhodesia for five years were to be called up for one month of military duties. Immigrant settlers were exempted from national service during their first five years, however, in an effort to encourage more whites to settle in Rhodesia. A second battalion of the African Rifles was set up, and a campaign to enlist young men as regulars in the army and police was launched.

The regular army was to be increased from 3 500 to 5 000 men. It is organized into two infantry battalions, one artillery battery and one engineer squadron. There are also two special air service squadrons. No information is available about the number of conscripts inducted each year.

Rhodesia's Territorial Force, which functions as a reserve corps, numbered 10 000 until 1974 and is composed of men who are assigned to territorial units for three years' part-time training after completing their military service. These units are deployed as city-based battalions and as reserve battalions in the rural districts. The Territorial Force is all-white. By early 1974 an expansion of this force to 55 000 was announced.

The Rhodesian Air Force numbers 1 200 regulars. Black Africans are allowed to serve only as ground personnel.

Finally, there is the police force—called the British South Africa Police. Since 1973 it has been rearmed and functions now partly as a paramilitary force. Eight thousand men are active in the regular force. The number of police reserves is usually reported to be 35 000, but according to Secretary-General Fothergill of the Rhodesian Front Party, it totalled 60 000 by 1973 [49].

Only about a third of the active policemen are white, but whites make up nearly the entire police reserve. However, plans are being made to increase substantially the proportion of black African police.

Thus, the total number of active and reserve security forces remains low, leaving the government with two alternatives—either to count on more South African units, whether regular police or paramilitary, or to expand the universal conscript system to include the black population.

III. *Arms procurement*

Sources of supply

The British-led economic sanctions against Rhodesia after UDI in 1965 made the country dependent on South Africa for most of its current military equipment needs. Up to 1974 occasional supplies also arrived from Europe, via the ports in Portuguese-ruled Mozambique. Most such shipments were organized by private arms dealers, frequently under rather spectacular circumstances, because secrecy had to be maintained. One such deal, although non-military, which would fulfil most requirements for a fiction novel, was the acquisition of three second-hand Boeing 730 long-range transport planes by Air Rhodesia in 1973 from a West German private charter company, via Switzerland and Portugal.

Whereas the national embargoes in force against arms transfers to South Africa still left room for the supply of certain categories of weapons, as was shown in the previous section, the mandatory sanctions passed by the United Nations in 1968 against all economic relations with Rhodesia left no legal room for any military transactions at all. In fact, no country has ventured openly to defy the sanctions, not even South Africa. Nevertheless, the main source of arms is undoubtedly South Africa. The Rhodesian armed forces must have had access to an outside source of supply; otherwise their equipment would have ceased to be operational long ago due to the lack of spares. There is also scattered evidence of evasion of sanctions. For example, a British firm, Airwork Services Ltd, was still responsible for the maintenance of the Rhodesian Air Force in 1969. Similarly, the fact that the army remains adequately equipped to conduct a counterinsurgency campaign means that small arms must be coming in, in this case most certainly from South Africa, as there is no local arms industry in Rhodesia. It is quite clear that major arms, such as aircraft, have been secretly transferred from or via South Africa to Rhodesia. In 1967, South Africa imported an unspecified number of AL.60 light utility aircraft, a US Lockheed design produced under licence in Italy, and that same year 12 of these planes turned up in Rhodesia. Apart from the AL.60, no new aircraft were acquired after 1965 (see appendix 1, page 211). The Rhodesian inventory is made up of nine British Vampires and 12 Hunters in two fighter/ground attack squadrons, and 10 Canberra bombers, all supplied before 1965. An attempt in 1974 to acquire more Hunters from Jordan failed, as will be described below.

South Africa has supplied a few Eland armoured cars and older armoured cars from its own inventory.

Although some types of small arms could have been manufactured in Rhodesia, the government has not yet considered it necessary to invest in local industries of this type. Apart from South Africa, which has the domestic capability to supply practically any type of small arms and ammunition from its own factories, other possible sources have been mentioned in unconfirmed reports. It has been claimed that a private commercial company in Salisbury is in a position to sell 130 types of munitions from all parts of the world, including weapons made by one of the leading producers, the Omnipol company of Czechoslovakia [50].

The Jordanian arms deal

In July 1974, reports of a militarily significant weapons acquisition by Rhodesia appeared in the *Guardian*. According to these British accounts, Jordan, after securing a large contract for new equipment from the USA, decided to sell its British-supplied Hawker Hunter fighter planes, its Tigercat surface-to-air missile systems and its 41 Centurion tanks, plus a large number of other weapons, to Rhodesia via South Africa. As a *quid pro quo* Jordan should have contracted to receive an unspecified number of Impala counterinsurgency planes from South Africa.

Subsequent reports claimed that President Sadat of Egypt had personally intervened to stop the negotiations for the Hunter aircraft. These planes were not, in fact, delivered to South Africa, and later in 1974 reports appeared that Honduras was trying to purchase them from Jordan. The British government reacted to the news by conducting an investigation. At a meeting on 10 July 1974 in Amman, between the British Ambassador to Jordan and the Jordanian Prime Minister, assurances were given that no contract had been signed for the aircraft. However, according to the British Foreign Office, the sale of the missiles, tanks and other equipment was not immediately denied by Jordanian authorities. Later it turned out that these weapons were already in South Africa in May 1974. The contractor was a private South African company, registered in Liechtenstein, which paid Jordan $16 million for the equipment and then resold it at a considerable profit to the South African government [51]. The contract was said to provide for the supply of spare parts during a five-year period. Several sources confirmed later on that Rhodesia had bought 120 Aden cannons, over 3 000 Sura rockets and some 400 000 rounds of 30-mm ammunition as part of the same transaction [52].

The Tigercat missile system which Jordan sold consisted of 555 combat and 162 practice missiles, plus jeeps, launchers, target room simulators, radar, film analysis gear and maintenance equipment.

The general assumption that Rhodesia is the ultimate buyer of the Tigercat system and the Centurion tanks rests on two facts: South Africa is deploying the Cactus missile and already has the Centurion tank, while Rhodesia has neither tanks nor an air defence system. Furthermore, South Africa has acted as an intermediary before.

References

1. *Armed Forces Journal,* June 1973.
2. *Neue Zürcher Zeitung,* Switzerland, 8 August 1974.
3. *White Paper on Defence and Armament Production 1973 and 1975,* Republic of South Africa, Department of Defence (W.P.E., 1973 and 1975).
4. *International Defence Review,* December 1971.
5. *Star Weekly,* South Africa, 18 July 1974.

6. Quoted in Minty, A., *South Africa's Defence Strategy* (London, 1969, The Anti-Apartheid Movement) p. 5.

7. *African Bureau Fact Sheet,* UK, No. 36, May 1974.

8. *Military and Police Forces in the Republic of South Africa* (New York, 1967, UN Unit on Apartheid, Department of Political and Security Council Affairs).

9. Patel, A. M., ed., *Africa in World Affairs* (New York, The Third Press, 1973) p. 47.

10. *Sechaba,* UK, October/November/December 1974, p. 20.

11. *White Paper on Defence and Armament Production 1975,* Republic of South Africa, Department of Defence (W.P.E. 1975).

12. *Almanac of World Military Power 1972.*

13. *Cape Times,* South Africa, 16 March 1967.

14. *Financial Times,* UK, 14 March 1974.

15. *Military Balance, 1968–69* (London, International Institute for Strategic Studies (IISS)).

16. *Military Balance, 1974–75* (London, International Institute for Strategic Studies (IISS)).

17. *Star Weekly,* South Africa, 30 March 1965.

18. UN Security Council Resolution 181, 7 August 1963.

19. UN Security Council Resolution 182, 4 December 1963.

20. UN document A/AC.115/L.285, 16 March 1971.

21. *Implementation of the US Arms Embargo (Against Portugal and South Africa and Related Issues),* Hearings before the Subcommittee on Africa of the Committee on Foreign Affairs, US House of Representatives, 93rd Congress, 1st Session, 20, 22 March, 6 April 1973 (Washington, U.S. Government Printing Office, 1973).

   (a) —, p. 144.

   (b) —, p. 330.

   (c) —, p. 9.

   (d) —, Statement by Rauer H. Meyer, Director, Office of Export Controls, p. 39.

   (e) —, p. 119.

   (f) —, p. 46.

   (g) —, Statement by Jennifer Davis, Economic Research Director, American Committee on Africa, p. 82.

   (h) —, p. 61.

22. *Times,* UK, 17 July 1970.

23. *Daily Telegraph,* UK, 11 August 1974.

24. *Africa Report,* USA, January–February 1973.

25. Report by Bruce Oudes, *Times of Zambia,* Lusaka, 6 January 1975.

26. *Guardian,* UK, 30 April 1974.

27. Letter from SBAC President Simon of 30 April 1974, quoted in *International Defense Business,* USA, 20 May 1974, p. 814.

28. *Le Monde,* France, 27 August 1974.

29. *Armed Forces Journal,* February 1972.

30. *Star Weekly,* South Africa, 21 September 1974.

31. *Legal Obligations of Her Majesty's Government Arising out of the Simonstown Agreements,* Cmnd 4859 (London, HMSO, February 1971).

32. Piliso, M., "The Bonn-Pretoria Axis", *Sechaba,* UK, Vol. 8, No. 8/9, August–September 1974, p. 5.

33. *Sunday Times,* UK, 9 July 1972.

34. Harrigan, A., "The South African Military Establishment", *Military Review,* October 1973.

35. *Milavnews News Letter,* UK, 26 April 1972.

36. *Flight International,* 17 May 1971.
37. *World Armaments and Disarmament, SIPRI Yearbook 1974* (Stockholm, Almqvist & Wiksell, 1974, Stockholm International Peace Research Institute).
38. *Times,* UK, 23 October 1970.
39. UN document A/AC.115/L.285/Add 3., 21 May 1971.
40. Report by Christopher Driver, *Guardian,* UK, 16 December 1973.
41. First, R., *et al., The South African Connection: Western Investment in Apartheid* (London, Temple Smith, 1972).
    (a) —, p. 26.
    (b) —, p. 28.
42. South Africa, Debates of the House of Assembly, 20 July 1970 (Hansard, Col. 55).
43. *Rand Daily Mail,* South Africa, 1 July 1974.
44. *Rand Daily Mail,* South Africa, 23 April 1974.
45. Spence, J. E., "Nuclear Weapons and South Africa—The Incentives and Constraints on Policy", Paper presented to the Workshop on Southern Africa", Dalhousie University, Halifax, N.S., August 1973, p. 5.
46. *Nuclear Proliferation Problems* (Stockholm, Almqvist & Wiksell, 1974, Stockholm International Peace Research Institute) p. 105.
47. *Keesing's Contemporary Archives,* 3–9 February 1975, p. 26948.
48. *Africa Bureau Fact Sheet,* No. 34, February 1974.
49. *Le Monde Diplomatique,* France, May 1973.
50. *Neue Zürcher Zeitung,* Switzerland, 17 August 1974.
51. *Guardian,* UK, 9 September and 12 September 1974.
52. *Africa,* UK, No. 39, November 1974.
53. "Südafrika BRD-Waffenlieferungen: Pressemitteilung des Deutschen Komitees für Angola, Guinea-Bissau und Mozambique e.v.", Freiburg, Informationszentrum, Dritte Welt, No. 39, November 1974.

Part IV. The changing balance of power in Southern Africa

Square-bracketed references, thus [1], *refer to the list of references on page 193.*

The wars in the Portuguese colonies ended in 1974, not as the result of any final military victory but because the colonial regime had suddenly and surprisingly fallen. Guinea-Bissau achieved independence in September 1974; in Mozambique FRELIMO was officially recognized as the future ruling party, and the country became independent in June 1975. In Angola an interim government composed of the three liberation movements was set up and the country is to become independent in November 1975.

By the end of 1974 it was evident that the displacement of the old regime in Portugal had signalled the beginning of a process of change that would affect Southern Africa as a whole. The Portuguese troops remaining in Africa would no longer represent a force allied to the white minority regimes that control Rhodesia, Namibia and South Africa. On the contrary, the sole purpose of their continuing deployment was to protect the new interim governments in Mozambique and Angola and secure their transition to independence, planned for 1975. It had also become clear that the alteration in the political map of Southern Africa would provoke changes in the future approach of foreign powers in the region.

It is always possible retrospectively to find indicators pointing out the inherent logic of almost any course of events—thus it is easy to state *after* the coup that the objective conditions for an overthrow of the Caetano regime had long been present in Portugal. Nonetheless, it is interesting to consider what those conditions were and to compare them with those in the remaining, white, minority-ruled Southern African states.

Chapter 8. Factors making for disintegration in Portugal

Before the coup, dissent was widespread within Portuguese society. Opposition to the Caetano regime was evident at various levels, but not in a united form and not for identical reasons. The catalyst for all opposition groups, however—the interminability of the wars in the African colonies —made demands for a change of policy grow more and more persistent.

The difficult economic predicament in which Portugal found itself by 1974 was a paramount factor contributing to the growing domestic opposition to the Caetano government. A collision of interests was mounting between the corporate state and those powerful sectors of the economy which represented modern capitalism and demanded liberalization and certain social reforms for the sake of economic growth. Inadequacies within the country had also produced widespread discontent among the general public. Inflation had reached an annual rate of 30 per cent. Net emigration, which averaged 70 000 per year throughout the decade, had resulted in a manpower shortage that led to a scarcity of skilled labour and crippled industry. The rate of illiteracy continued to climb, since higher education was reserved for the privileged few. Agriculture, even though it employed more than a quarter of the labour force, failed to produce enough food for the country's needs.

It was Portugal's foreign policy, however, which increasingly alienated the financial groups which had once supported the regime. The wars in Africa were considered to be detrimental to the economic interests of the state because they effectively blocked Portugal's entry into the EEC. Important corporations such as the Companhia União Fabril (CUF) and the Champalimaud group, as well as some members of the ruling circles, regarded Portugal's integration with Europe as a matter of absolute priority if the economy was to develop. They viewed the idea of an empire in Africa as an anachronism.

I. *Political opposition*

By the end of 1973 it was expected in Portugal that a change of regime would be brought about either by the rightist or the liberal political opposition. The rightist opposition centered round three persons: President Americo

Thomas, General Luz Cunha, the Commander-in-Chief in Angola, and his brother-in-law, General de Arriaga, who had returned to Portugal from Mozambique in 1973. The liberal opposition was personified primarily by General Antonio de Spinola—who had been received as a national hero upon his return from Guinea-Bissau—and also by the Chief of Staff of the armed forces, General Costa Gomes.

The position of Prime Minister Caetano in the power struggle between the two groups remains unknown. At first the liberal groups appeared to have his support. A rightist coup against him was attempted in December 1973, but failed because the armed forces, General Spinola and General Costa Gomes did not support it. In January 1974, Spinola was given a specially created post as second-in-command to Costa Gomes, and his controversial book, *Portugal and the Future,* was published in Lisbon in February. In it he challenged the rightist opposition which called for an escalation of the wars in the colonies in order to win a military victory. The fact that Spinola was allowed to publish this book was interpreted as meaning that Caetano favoured Spinola's proposed solution to Portugal's dilemma. In South Africa, for example, the publication of his book was taken as Portugal's first move towards a gradual withdrawal from Africa. Caetano was expected to retire in 1974 and be succeeded by Spinola, who would then conclude peace agreements and create some sort of federation with the African territories, as outlined in the book [1].

But instead, the rightists seemed to gain ground. In March 1974, both Spinola and Costa Gomes were suddenly dismissed, and General Luz Cunha was appointed Chief of Staff. The next move was expected to be the replacement of Prime Minister Caetano by the more rightist theoretician Adriano Moreira. General de Arriaga was expected to become Defence Minister. On 16 March an abortive attempt at insurrection by an infantry regiment—loyal to Spinola—outside Lisbon, seemed further to strengthen the rightists' position.

II. *The armed forces*

The factor that finally toppled the Caetano regime turned out to be its complete loss of the loyalty of the armed forces. This had not been foreseen by the Portuguese government or by any foreign military intelligence, nor had it been intimated in any study of Portuguese Africa. The most likely future scenario in Portuguese Africa was usually said to be another 30 years of war, although in the literature and policy statements from Socialist countries or movements, a final military victory by the progressive forces was predicted. The loyalty of the troops fighting for the Caetano regime was never questioned. In 1967, a US military handbook presented the following description of the Portuguese soldier:

Conscripts from Portugal have proved quite adaptable as soldiers in combat. They are as a rule medium or less in height by US standards and are wiry and rugged . . . They are cheerful and loyal. The higher rate of pay for service in Angola is an incentive to performance there [2].

But the conscript army as well as most of its officers turned out to be neither cheerful nor blindly loyal. Thirteen years of war in Africa had cost the Portuguese 13 000 dead and 117 000 wounded, according to government sources [3].[1] General Spinola's opinion that Portugal was fighting a war that could not be won was, in fact, much more than one man's view: it was the common opinion of the troops in Africa.

Thus, in the colonies, the coup was being planned and prepared in utmost secrecy for over a year, under the leadership of young officers unknown to the Portuguese public or to the outside world.

III. *The coup in Portugal*

On 25 April 1974, the armed forces took power in Portugal and ousted the Caetano regime, ending 48 years of authoritarian rule. The new regime, the "Junta of National Salvation", declared its principal aims to be decolonization and democratization. Younger officers from all three services led the military junta representing the majority of the conscript army. At the time of the coup they called themselves "the Captains' Movement"; the name was later changed to "the Armed Forces Movement" in order to illustrate the unanimity of commitment among the military forces. The junta appealed to General Spinola shortly before the coup to accept the post of President in the new state administration, because of his liberal image and widespread popularity at that time. Spinola was also acceptable to banking and financial circles, as he was directly linked with the Champalimaud group.[2] Pending future elections, an interim civilian government was set up, and Dr Mario Soares, the exiled leader of the Socialist party, returned to Lisbon to take up the post of Foreign Minister, followed by Alvaro Cunhal, the secretary-general of the previously outlawed Communist Party, who became a minister without portfolio. But control over this government rested in the hands of the junta. Of the seven officers who represented the Armed Forces Movement, only the generals Spinola and Costa Gomes were widely known.

---

[1] In 1973, the Opposition Democratic Party in Lisbon reported that the overseas wars had cost Portugal over 10 000 dead, 30 000 wounded and 20 000 permanently disabled [4].
[2] General Spinola had obtained the government licence for the Champalimaud Group—holding a central position in banking and insurance—to erect the national steelworks. He had also served for some years on the steel company board.

During the months that followed, as the radical profile of the military regime hardened, differences of opinion about the withdrawal from Africa arose between President Spinola and the more moderate political sector on the one hand, *versus* the Armed Forces Movement and the Communist and Socialist Parties on the other.

Initially, the new regime was viewed with apprehension and outright suspicion by the African liberation movements which held President Spinola personally responsible for the death of Amilcar Cabral and denounced Spinola's proposal for a federation between Portugal and the African colonies as a species of neo-colonialism. When, in a television speech in June 1974, President Spinola outlined his African policy and called for a referendum in the colonies on the issue of independence, with federation as the ultimate goal, the schism within the ruling bodies became apparent to all. Foreign Minister Soares threatened to resign, and the preliminary talks with the PAIGC and FRELIMO came to a halt. Samora Machel rejected the idea of a referendum as an insult and called the federation proposal outdated, declaring in a speech before the OAU: "You cannot ask a slave if he wants to be free, particularly when he has already revolted" [5].

Eventually the opinions of the Socialists and officers in the interim government prevailed. Spinola had to accept the appointment of a junta leader, Colonel Vasco Gonçalves, as Prime Minister. In July a new text of the constitutional law on decolonization was published, and soon afterwards, in a historic television speech, President Spinola declared that his government's intention was to provide for the African colonies' transition to full independence.

Spinola remained convinced, however, that the colonization process was being conducted too hastily. When prevented from staging a large demonstration by what he called "the silent majority", in order to convey his apprehension, he resigned from the presidency and was succeeded by General Costa Gomes. Spinola's departure from power aroused speculation that a countercoup—similar to the one which brought down the Allende regime in Chile—might be in the making in Portugal.

IV. *The economy*

The economy posed major problems for the new regime. After the coup, the previously prohibited trade unions reappeared and countrywide strikes occurred in which workers from various branches demanded wage increases of as much as 70–100 per cent. The military junta reacted quickly, setting minimum wage levels and approving many of the strikers' demands. As a consequence, however, the rate of inflation increased and new investments in foreign-owned industries slackened off. By September 1974 it began to appear that economic difficulties might endanger the political democratization of Portugal, as had been the case in Chile. According to Foreign Minister Soares, a campaign to sabotage the Portuguese economy was instigated from abroad shortly after the coup [6].

The external payments problem, already serious before the coup, was further aggravated by increases in the prices of oil and raw materials. In addition, the aid which Portugal was to provide to the newly independent African colonies was expected to place additional pressure on the regime.

V. *Political factors*

Of the 70-odd political parties and groups that appeared after the coup, the strongest and best-organized was the Communist Party. In the West, distress was expressed that Portugal had become the first Western European country to include a Communist in the government. Within Portugal itself, the activities of rightist and leftist extremist groups brought swift responses from the ruling officers. More than 200 persons were arrested after an incident on 28 September 1974, described by the government as a rightist coup attempt. Censorship was enforced against a "Marxist" newspaper which denounced the Communist Party and the Armed Forces Movements for cooperating with each other.

VI. *Foreign relations*

When diplomatic relations were opened with the Socialist bloc in 1974, the Soviet government declared its willingness to offer economic aid to Portugal. Relations with the West posed more of a problem, however, as the presence of a military junta plus Socialists and Communists in the same government aroused the scepticism of many Western leaders. The new Portuguese rulers found it difficult to convince the most powerful of the NATO members that, even though the regime did indeed include one Communist minister, it was not a Communist government. It also had to convince the OECD countries that it was not a military dictatorship. The West remained suspicious, and while President Costa Gomes visited Washington in October to negotiate the continued lease of the Azores base to the USA, the Portuguese press carried reports about CIA activities conducted during his absence. Junta spokesmen confirmed that the regime was concerned about possible US- or NATO-led intervention in Portugal. When Dr Soares met Dr Kissinger in Tunis on 11 November 1974, he implied that Portugal might not allow the United States to go on refuelling at the Azores base in the event of a future war in the Middle East. This was later stated emphatically and may have brought about lack of confidence on the part of the USA in the new regime.

The US administration was said to be worried about the possibility of a "domino" situation arising in Europe: if, in other words, Portugal should become Communist-dominated, France, Greece, Italy and Spain might follow suit [7].

The question of US or NATO acceptance of the new Portuguese regime is of relevance in the Southern African context prior to the actual independence of Mozambique and Angola. If the junta is overthrown in Portugal, it can be argued, temptations to intervene and protect strategic interests in Africa may grow.

As was shown in Part II, NATO support played an important role in sustaining the Salazar and Caetano regimes in Portugal up to 1974. Already in May 1974 there were signs that the NATO command was concerned with the reliability of the new Portuguese regime and was hesitant to share nuclear information with it. The Caetano regime had applied for a seat in the NATO Nuclear Planning Commission, but the meeting of this group—scheduled to start on 7 November 1974 in Rome—was postponed, as no decision had been reached as to whether or not Portugal was reliable. Eventually, in 1975, the NATO command excluded Portugal from the Nuclear Planning Commission. This move took place immediately after the first free elections in Portugal and was based on the charge that Portugal had no democratic government. Another type of scepticism regarding the new Portuguese regime was shown in the Scandinavian countries with their traditional aversion for military governments.

The Portuguese government has explained its political preferences on several occasions, emphasizing in particular its wish to maintain normal relations with the United States and to remain a NATO member. However, in December, Portugal decided to give up its claim to a seat in the NATO Nuclear Commission, thus averting a possible open controversy with NATO and the United States over this issue. During his visit to the United States, President Costa Gomes emphasized that the policy aim of his government is to create an "authentic pluralistic democracy" [8].

Chapter 9. Portuguese Africa

Guinea-Bissau became independent on 10 September 1974 and was subsequently admitted to the United Nations. The last Portuguese troops withdrew on 15 October, leaving control of the government in the hands of the PAIGC.

A number of important political questions remained, of course, to be answered. According to an agreement reached between the PAIGC and Portugal during the first talks in May, the future of the Cape Verde islands was to be negotiated separately from that of Guinea-Bissau. In November 1974 the Portuguese revealed that an interim government was shortly to be formed in Cape Verde. This government took power on 30 December 1974. Composed exclusively of PAIGC and Portuguese representatives, its principal task was to prepare for independence on 3 July 1975.

The transition to independence was expected to be more difficult in Mozambique and Angola than it had been in Guinea-Bissau. In both territories, some hoped and others feared that the white inhabitants would follow the Rhodesian example and declare unilateral independence. Dr Soares warned in April 1974 that any white separatist attempt to seize power would be quite likely to lead to intervention by South Africa and result in "another Viet-Nam" [9].

After the coup, political parties calling for a UDI appeared in both countries. There was talk of partitioning Mozambique into two states, a northern one to be ruled by FRELIMO and a southern one to be governed by whites. In Angola, too, there was widespread discussion of UDI and of the possibility of dividing the country into white- and black-ruled territories. Speculation also arose that the Cabinda enclave might secede. After the coup in Portugal, two movements appeared in support of secession. Claiming to be liberation movements and to represent 8 000 Cabindans, the Democratic Union of the People of Cabinda (UPDC) and the Front pour la Libération de l'Enclave de Cabinda (FLEC) denounced all proposals to unify Cabinda with the independent Angola of the future.

In addition to the possibilities of UDI and of secession, a third factor appeared which may complicate the transition to independence in Mozambique and Angola—namely, the rise of private mercenary armies. In Mozambique, armed units, reportedly belonging to a private army led by the once-influential businessman Jorge Jardim, clashed with FRELIMO guerillas and Portuguese troops in Beira in May 1974, after which the Portuguese government broke off diplomatic relations with Malawi, from whence

Jardim was suspected of directing operations following his escape from arrest in Lisbon.

A more serious attempt at insurrection took place on 8 September 1974 when white members of the militant FICO organization occupied the radio stations, the airport and a few other keypoints in Lourenço Marques and appealed for public support of a UDI government. Calling themselves "the Dragons of Death", the rebels were protesting against the Lusaka agreement under which the Portuguese recognized FRELIMO as the sole representative of the Mozambican people and empowered it to form an interim government jointly with Portugal. The rebels remained in control for only a few days. When no aid was offered by South Africa, Rhodesia, or any other outside power, and when Portuguese and FRELIMO troops began pouring in from the north, the action withered away.

According to a South African journal, the *Star Weekly,* the so-called Commando No. 5 mercenary force was being reorganized in Johannesburg in September 1974, under the leadership of Colonel Michel Hoare, who had fought for Tshombe in Katanga in the early 1960s. In an interview one month earlier with the US magazine *Newsweek,* Colonel Hoare had denied that he had received any proposals to form a unit for action in either Angola or Mozambique, but he nevertheless boasted that with a force of 1 000 men he could defeat FRELIMO in six to eight months, provided that he "was satisfied FRELIMO did not have the popular support of the people" [10].

Rumours persisted throughout the autumn of 1974 that mercenaries might be called in by the wealthy white community in Mozambique. In mid-October a Swiss citizen was found to be trying to recruit 500 Swedish mercenaries, with the aim of setting up a force to fight FRELIMO [11]. In November, Major Sam Cassidy, who was accused of being a mercenary force commander, said in Salisbury, after having been ordered by the authorities to leave Rhodesia, that he had 700 men ready for action in each of the Portuguese colonies. The establishment of this force of ex-Congo mercenaries had so far cost $3 million [12]. Subsequent European press reports that 1 000 mercenaries from Europe were to embark from Genoa for Mozambique on 1 December 1974 were checked by the Italian government, at the request of the Italian trade unions, but without result. By the end of 1974, no mercenary force had materialized either in Italy or Africa.

Members of an Angolan citizens' committee, formed after the race riots in Luanda, visited Lisbon in July and reported to President Spinola that white settlers and some Africans had set up, with the collaboration of DGS-personnel, a secret army of 20 000 men. The movement was called the United Angolan Resistance (RUA). Advertisements appeared in Luandan newspapers immediately after the coup in Portugal, openly calling for recruits to the RUA. MPLA President Neto claimed in Dar es Salaam on 2 October that this force had grown to 40 000 men and was being financed by private sources in South Africa [13]. The Portuguese Communist Party leader Alvaro Cunhal stated in an interview with *Le Monde* on 6 October 1974 that the white opposition in Angola was armed. The existence of a 40 000-man private army seems doubtful, but more credible reports about a 1 000-man mercenary force in southern Angola caused the new High Commissioner, Admiral Rosa Coutinho, to launch an investigation in November 1974. Despite persistent rumours, no action was taken by any mercenary force or private army in Angola during 1974.

The most complicated problem facing the Portuguese turned out to be that of establishing and manning the interim governments which would organize the transition to independence in the two territories.

I. *Mozambique*

The transition to independence

Immediately after the change of regime in Portugal, FRELIMO ceased its military activities in order to achieve the best possible bargaining position. Initial misgivings about the intentions of the new regime faded somewhat when the composition of the first interim civilian government was announced.

The first meeting between Foreign Minister Soares and Samora Machel in Lusaka on 5 June 1974 bore a closer resemblance to a celebration of victory over a common enemy than to an initial confrontation between representatives of two countries at war (see plate 1). Despite appearances, however, their differences were so great that the talks were adjourned after only one day. FRELIMO rejected the first Portuguese offers of a cease-fire, presented as a precondition for negotiations. The proposed contents of negotiations were also rejected.

In accordance with President Spinola's decolonization plan, an offer was made to the effect that the population of Mozambique hold a referendum on the issue of independence within one year and set up a coalition government where all political parties would be represented, with FRELIMO as one among the others. No actual independence was even mentioned.

FRELIMO resumed its military operations after this breakdown. In June alone there were over 400 FRELIMO attacks, and on 12 July the guerillas captured the town of Morrumbala on the Malawi border after a three-day siege. A new front was opened in the Zambézia province.

At the same time the military activity of the Portuguese troops practically ceased. As FRELIMO advanced southwards, Portuguese troops were withdrawn from several posts in Cabo Delgado, Niassa and Tete. Already in May the Portuguese High Command had reportedly requested that the Rhodesian troops operating in Tete in pursuit of ZANU retire from Mozambican territory [14]. Reports from "informed military sources" claimed that the withdrawals were made because the Portuguese troops refused to fight and demanded an end to the war after the coup [15]. Eventually it emerged that President Spinola's gradual approach to decolonization was also unacceptable to the Armed Forces Movement and the Socialists in the Portuguese government. After the consolidation of power by the military junta, described earlier, Spinola retired from active participation in the negotiations with FRELIMO.

On 20 September 1974 the new interim government took over in Mozambique. This government was composed of nine ministers, six representing FRELIMO and three the Armed Forces Movement. Joaquim Chissano, one of FRELIMO's highest ranking field commanders, became the first Prime Minister. The main points of the agreement for the transition period were that there would be a Portuguese High Commissioner to watch over this period; a Mozambican police force; acceptance by FRELIMO of financial obligations undertaken by Portugal, if deemed in the interest of the nation; establishment of a central bank with funds from Portugal, and joint defence of Mozambique's borders by Portuguese and FRELIMO troops.

The Portuguese High Commissioner to Mozambique, Victor Crespo, declared that 35 000 Portuguese troops would remain in Mozambique to guarantee its security during the period of transition, but all would leave at independence in June 1975.

Domestic policy

In his speech to the nation on 20 September 1974 when the interim government took over, Samora Machel sketched a broad outline of FRELIMO policy in various fields. He declared that the new government's goal was to establish a multiracial society and asked that the whites stay in Mozambique, saying:

There are no superior and inferior races . . . There are no minorities, there are no special rights or duties for any sector of the Mozambican people. We are all Mozambicans with the rights that work gives us, and with the identical duty of building a united, prosperous, just, harmonious, peaceful and democratic nation [16].

By the end of September, however, an estimated 30 000 whites had already left the country.

Mozambique will be a one-party state. On several occasions both Samora Machel and Prime Minister Chissano have declared their disagreement with the Western notion that democracy can only be achieved in a multiparty system. For the organization of the economy—which will be the acid test of the new administration once it has consolidated its military and political power throughout the country—Samora Machel would seem to be outlining an approach leading to a closed, self-reliant economic system on the pattern of Tanzania's. Agriculture will receive absolute priority, and the guerilla armies will be used in production as well as in mobilization and organization work. "FRELIMO's army", he has said, "is not an army of parasites; it is an army with a tradition of productive labour" [16]. At the same time, Machel warned against the dangers of "ultra-leftism" that call for extreme and unrealistic measures. This was generally taken to mean that there is no risk of any abrupt severance of economic links with South Africa immediately after independence.

The relations with South Africa and, especially, the future of the Cabora Bassa Dam project are considered by most observers to be vital to the economic survival of Mozambique. The general view held in South Africa is that the FRELIMO government will not be able to afford to cut off trade with South Africa via the port of Lourenço Marques, halt the supply of workers to the mines in South Africa, or cancel the agreement for the sale of electricity to South Africa from Cabora Bassa. According to this line of thought, FRELIMO cannot sever trade with Rhodesia either.

South Africa has offered economic aid to Mozambique, and the Finance Minister, Dr N. Diederichs, has outlined as a future possibility the creation of an Economic Community of Southern Africa. He singled out Mozambique as a vital member, referring to the "well-founded realism" of its new leaders [17].

FRELIMO spokesmen have refrained from giving details of any concrete measures planned to follow independence, merely stating that no such measures of the kind proposed by Dr Diederichs will be undertaken during the period of the interim government. An exception was made, however, for the trade with Rhodesia. Before taking over the administration, spokesmen for the interim government declared that they were committed to observing the UN sanctions against Rhodesia. In fact, the railway from Beira to Salisbury was already effectively cut off by mid-1974.

On the subject of Cabora Bassa, Mozambican opinion was expressed by the politician Dr Pereira Leite in an interview with the *Star Weekly:* South Africa, he said, would definitely be supplied with electricity from Cabora Bassa under an "ingenious solution" devised by FRELIMO to replace the present agreement. On the question of the migrant labour system, Dr Leite said he did not believe that it would end completely, but that the South African mine labour organization, Wenela, might, as a first move, be prohibited from recruiting in Mozambique [18].

Foreign policy

The foreign policy issue of most relevance in the Southern African context will obviously be FRELIMO-ruled Mozambique's relations with Rhodesia and South Africa, and, in particular, the question of allowing Rhodesian and South African liberation movements free transit through or bases on Mozambican territory. Soares declared at a press conference upon his

168

arrival in Lusaka on 5 September 1974 that the interim government will not permit foreign guerilla troops to operate from Mozambique. Earlier, on 30 August, Prime Minister Vorster warned in a major statement to Parliament that if the government of independent Mozambique should support the guerillas in such a manner, South Africa would have to defend itself. But he also declared that this situation is not expected to arise.

II. *Angola*

The difficulties that the new Portuguese regime encountered in organizing the transition to independence in Mozambique were multiplied in Angola. The three liberation movements the MPLA, the FNLA and UNITA remained disunited on virtually all major policy issues. In addition, the serious split within the MPLA provided Spinola and his supporters with opportunities to manoeuvre in a direction contrary to the intentions of the Armed Forces Movement. This disunity was a major force behind the violent riots that occurred in Luanda in November 1974 and which seemed to open up the prospects for a civil war in Angola. Indirectly, differences of opinion about the policy to be followed in Angola were among the factors leading to President Spinola's resignation in September 1974.

Eventually, it became clear to all who had a stake in the future of Angola that the Armed Forces Movement was also determined to achieve an agreement in this colony for its transition to independence at the earliest possible date. Furthermore, the Armed Forces Movement had a firm opinion about the manner in which power should be divided among the representatives of the Angolan population. Finally, it refused to alter its decision to regard only the three liberation movements as representing the Angolans. This meant that the intricate schemes, briefly outlined below, that had been designed to eliminate Dr Neto's faction of the MPLA from the scene and bring new political groupings into the government, had failed.

President Spinola's approach

When the peace agreement between Portugal and FRELIMO was concluded, under which Mozambique was to be granted independence at what President Spinola considered to be an irresponsible speed, he declared that he would take personal charge of Angola's future. Spinola was not alone in favouring a more gradual approach. The more moderate sector of the political establishment and the representatives of financial interests in Portugal, Angola and abroad, supported him. On 10 August 1974, the Portuguese representative in the United Nations outlined President Spinola's formula for Angola's transition to independence within a period of two years. First, a cease-fire should be effected with the three liberation movements, to be followed by a period of self-determination under a provisional government. The three liberation movements were regarded as separate negotiating partners and were to be represented by two members each in the 12-man provisional government. The remaining six posts would be held by tribal chiefs, representatives of white political parties and the Portuguese. After two years, the provisional government would organize a referendum on the issue of Angola's independence from or federation with Portugal.

During the period leading up to his resignation, President Spinola secretly amassed support in Africa for his policy, which seemed to have much in common with that of President Mobutu of Zaire, for whom the future status of the oil-rich Cabinda enclave has been a matter of primary interest over the years. Zaire's oil is pumped though Cabinda to the Gulf terminals off the coast, and access to the area is a vital economic concern for Zaire. Tension over this issue has arisen between Zaire and the Congo: the FNLA was militarily backed by Zaire, but the Congo supported the MPLA. In late 1973, the Zaire Army conducted a manoeuvre together with FNLA units, simulating an attack on Cabinda [19]. This led to widespread speculation that Zaire was prepared, in fact, to assist the FNLA for the purpose of bringing about Cabinda's secession from Angola.

It was felt that a future Angolan government under the influence of Dr Neto and the Socialist faction of the MPLA would be detrimental to the interests of Zaire. When the split occurred within the MPLA, President Mobutu allowed the two breakaway factions—led by Daniel Chipenda and Pinto de Andrade—to establish themselves in Zaire. An effort was made to present Chipenda's faction as the "real", reorganized MPLA with which Portugal was to negotiate. President Spinola accepted this, because he was firmly convinced that Dr Neto personified the danger of a Communist take-over in Angola.

In Zaire, where it was hoped that Dr Neto's influence had been eliminated, contact was established between the MPLA factions and the FNLA for the purpose of organizing a joint committee for the negotiations with Portugal.

President Spinola's view on the Cabinda question was that the population there should be given the right to hold a referendum on the question of secession. He regarded the newly created separatist movements in Cabinda as legitimate negotiating partners. It was evident that he had embarked on a collision course *versus* the Armed Forces Movement. Foreign Minister Soares had made it clear that his government did not regard the Cabinda separatists as representing the population and said that Portugal would not allow the territory to secede from Angola.

On 15 September 1974, a secret meeting took place on the island of Sal in Cape Verde. The participants in this meeting—about which nothing was revealed until after Spinola's resignation—were President Spinola, President Mobutu, Daniel Chipenda, Pinto de Andrade and Holden Roberto of the FNLA. Their objective was to outline a plan for Angola's future, and there is reason to assume that the possibility of an autonomous Cabinda was envisaged. After the Sal meeting, the FNLA issued a declaration that it would not oppose a separate Cabinda. A similar declaration had previously been announced by Daniel Chipenda's MPLA faction [20].

President Spinola was a military man by profession who had become a politician by chance. He failed to consider several factors which—taken together—made his Angolan venture unrealistic. First, he did not realize how strong the support that the Armed Forces Movement commanded was in Portugal. Nor did he understand that the objectives of the junta in regard to decolonization were virtually identical with those of the Portuguese left, represented in the government by the Communist Party leader Alvaro Cunhal and the Foreign Minister Mario Soares. Further, Spinola and his supporters did not count on the widespread support that Agostinho Neto commanded inside Angola and among the most influential member states of the OAU. In addition, President Nyerere of Tanzania and FRELIMO's leader Samora Machel were firm personal supporters of Neto.

Finally, Portuguese military control in Cabinda was never seriously threatened, despite several armed clashes during the summer of 1974 with the newly formed units of the Front pour la Libération de l'Enclave de Cabinda which, according to some reports, were armed by Zaire. After their defeat, members of FLEC were outlawed in Cabinda and escaped to Zaire. In the aftermath of this attempt to challenge junta policy in Cabinda, some Portuguese officers were arrested and the Governor himself was replaced. Subsequently, the OAU denied recognition to FLEC and refused to hear its delegates prior to the negotiations with Portugal which began in January 1975.

With junta control firmly reestablished, the plans to separate Cabinda from Angola were no longer feasible. It is widely believed in Angola that the impetus for FLEC and the financial resources with which it had been able to launch a successful propaganda campaign inside Cabinda were provided by some Western oil concerns. The militant faction within FLEC is still preparing for a military confrontation, however. Its force of an estimated 2 000 men receives training in Zaire.

If foreign support for this movement continues to pour in, in the form of arms and money, Cabinda, once described as the Kuwait of Angola, may well prove to be its Katanga, once the Portuguese troops have left.

The Armed Forces Movement's approach

The gradual transition to independence that President Spinola had envisaged for Angola was unacceptable to the Armed Forces Movement. After his resignation the plan was dropped. Military control in the country then rested firmly with the Armed Forces Movement. When serious race riots broke out in Luanda in July, the civilian Governor was replaced by a provisional High Commissioner, Admiral Rosa Coutinho.

After the military junta took over the planning of Angola's future, it revised Spinola's earlier plan on several important points. It recognized Agostinho Neto's MPLA as the sole negotiating partner for this movement, because the officers reasoned that any solution of the Angolan situation was unrealistic without Neto. A provisional government was set up in early 1975, and the date of independence was fixed for 11 November 1975. Prior to independence, the three movements were expected to form a workable coalition.

Ever since the coup in Portugal, forces have been at work to unite the MPLA, FNLA and UNITA into a common front in Angola. In July, the so-called Bakavu Agreement, guaranteeing the unity of the movements, was signed under the aegis of the governments of the Congo Republic, Tanzania, Zaire and Zambia, which were acting on behalf of the OAU. The OAU recognized UNITA for this purpose. The process was delayed owing to the complicated situation within the MPLA, but was continued after Dr Neto regained control of the movement. He was reelected president of the new provisional central committee of the MPLA, which was set up at the congress convened in October 1974 to reorganize the movement. Subsequently, the MPLA entered into agreements with UNITA and the FNLA, in order to be able to open negotiations with Portugal. In December 1974, the Luanda office of the MPLA announced the expulsion of Daniel Chipenda, accused of involvement in assassination plots against Dr Neto in 1972 and 1973.

A summit meeting scheduled to take place in December on the Azores or Cape Verde was cancelled. Instead, it was President Jomo Kenyatta of Kenya who managed to bring the three liberation movements together. On 5 January 1975, Agostinho Neto, Jonas Savimbi and Holden Roberto met for the first time in Mombasa, Kenya, and signed an agreement to approve in principle the proposed Portuguese scheme for decolonization. They also issued a declaration that Cabinda was to be regarded as an inseparable part of Angola. On 31 January 1975, after talks with the Portuguese had been completed, power was handed over to an interim government in Angola, led by a presidential *troika* representing the three liberation groups.

Angola's attainment of full independence in November 1975 will complete the dissolution of Portugal's African empire. Until then, Portugal will retain the responsibility for defence and foreign affairs. The armed forces of the three recognized Angolan liberation movements will each contribute manpower for a unified national army. This will operate on a joint basis with 18 000 Portuguese troops drawn from the 30 000 that are currently maintained in Angola. After independence, all Portuguese troops will be withdrawn.

Chapter 10. South Africa

I. *A new policy*

Within a matter of days after the coup, South Africa recognized the new Portuguese regime. Presumably it expected President Spinola to work out an acceptable solution to the wars in Angola and Mozambique, which it saw as an increasing threat. South African officials made no immediate comment about President Spinola's declaration that the Portuguese colonies were to become independent, and no official negative reaction was expressed when the subsequent radicalization of the Portuguese government culminated in Spinola's resignation. On the contrary, spokesmen for the South African government declared on various occasions that South Africa had no intention of interfering in the internal affairs of a neighbouring state, and, moreover, that South Africa was prepared to cooperate with African governments in Mozambique and Angola. These declarations were accompanied, however, by certain reservations. Prime Minister Vorster explicitly stated during the budget debate in September 1974, that his conditions for cooperation with future black governments in Mozambique and Angola were that these governments would show themselves to be "stable" and "capable of keeping order". If, on the other hand, they were to allow South African terrorist movements to use their territories as sanctuaries, South Africa intended to defend itself by all available means [21].

South Africa's pragmatic reaction foreshadowed the adoption of a new policy in the area. In essence, it was a policy of strategic withdrawal which at best was expected to lead to South Africa's acceptance of African governments in Rhodesia and also in Namibia where—in accordance with the decision of the United Nations and the ruling of the International Court at The Hague—South Africa had been ordered to surrender its political control. A new attitude appears similarly to be reflected in the domestic politics of the National Party government in South Africa. It remains clear, however, that South Africa intends to defend itself against internal and external threats, as has been evidenced by the number of new defence measures undertaken after the coup in Portugal.

The new approach is ultimately designed to protect the apartheid system and thus reflects no change of attitude in this respect. It merely illustrates the fact that South Africa had never actually committed itself to defending Rhodesia and Namibia at all costs. Furthermore, it shows that South Africa's own existence never depended on the continuation of a Portuguese presence in Southern Africa. Portugal's eventual withdrawal from Africa had been anticipated, and it is probable that the policy options open to South Africa had been worked out well before this occurred.

II. *International pressure*

A hardening of attitudes against South Africa could be observed after the coup—especially on the part of the OAU, which had become increasingly influential as the spokesman for black Africa in international forums. An attempt was made to expel South Africa from the United Nations during the General Assembly session in autumn 1974. On 30 September, by a vote of 125-1 and nine abstentions, the General Assembly adopted an African resolution calling upon the Security Council to review South Africa's position in the organization. This move, which the OAU considered to be a triumph for the "third force" in the UN, was strongly criticized by the leading Western powers, in particular the USA and the UK, ostensibly for reasons not directly related to South Africa.[3] Subsequently, the 15-nation Security Council voted for South Africa's immediate expulsion from the United Nations, a development which was averted only by the triple veto of France, the UK and the USA. The campaign to ostracize South Africa culminated in a General Assembly vote on 11 November to suspend South Africa from participation in the current session. Two days later, South Africa recalled its UN ambassador and announced that its financial contribution to the organization would cease.

There were several indications that the unexpectedly drastic UN action had struck South Africa a harder blow than was previously believed. In his speech to the United Nations on 24 October, South African Ambassador Botha spoke in defence of the apartheid policy and predicted that the Transkei Bantustan would soon be granted independence and would apply for UN membership. Later it has been announced that the Transkei will in effect become "independent" in 1976. He also suggested that Namibia might become self-determining even before the expiration of a previously planned 10-year period.

Speculations about a coming *détente* in Southern Africa were heard following Prime Minister Vorster's speech to the Senate on 23 October, when he said: "I believe that Southern Africa has come to the cross-roads. I think that Southern Africa has to make a choice. I think that choice lies between peace on the one hand or an escalation of strife on the other" [22]. President Kaunda of Zambia welcomed this speech as "the voice of reason

---

[3] In criticizing the move to expel South Africa from the United Nations, Western states expressed apprehension that a precedent would be established for the expulsion of a nation, at the Assembly majority's wish, thereby transforming the United Nations from a universal organization into one resembling a party that could constantly be purged of unwanted members.

for which Africa and the rest of the world have been waiting". His response was interpreted as revealing the achievement of some secret agreement between Zambia and South Africa about their future relationship. Subsequently, it became known that there had indeed been secret negotiations, but that these were related to the future of Rhodesia, which will be discussed below.

In a wide-ranging speech, delivered in his constituency on 6 November, Prime Minister Vorster asked political commentators in general to "give South Africa a chance", adding that they would be surprised to see where the country would stand after some six to 12 months. He thanked Britain, the United States and France for exercising their veto rights in the Security Council and enabling South Africa to remain a UN member. Turning to the subject of Rhodesia, he emphasized that the presence of South African police there should not be interpreted as a measure for the defence of that state:

I took the responsibility several years ago to send police to Rhodesia. I said then, and I will spell it out, the police—not the Army—did not go to Rhodesia to fight Rhodesia's war or to protect and safeguard Rhodesia. They went there to fight the terrorists on their way to South Africa on the Zambesi instead of the Limpopo [23].

Concerning Namibia, he appealed to the world to give the people there an opportunity to work out their own future. On the subject of Mozambique, Vorster said he had requested and received assurances that the new regime would not tolerate the presence of foreign military forces on its territory. Several of the National Party ministers began simultaneously and for the first time to advocate the removal of certain "petty apartheid" measures. Dr H. Muller, the Minister of Foreign Affairs, declared that world attitudes towards South Africa had hardened as a result of the collapse of Portuguese rule in Africa, endangering South Africa's position in the United Nations. The elimination of unnecessary sources of irritation between the races, he believed, could improve South Africa's international image [24].

The three Western powers' rescue of South Africa in the United Nations was interpreted by its opponents, of course, as a gesture of support for the regime. But the governments of France, the UK and the USA defended their action, claiming that it may have created an option and might influence the South African government to take certain positive steps regarding Rhodesia, Namibia and also its own domestic policies. Inside South Africa, at least, both the National Party and the liberals expressed the need to take such action as a *quid pro quo* for the confidence expressed by the three-power veto.

Both Britain and the United States have tried actively to influence the South African government to consider reforms. The British Labour government has become increasingly engaged in African affairs and demanded early in 1974 that South Africa leave Namibia. On 24 October, British Foreign Minister Callaghan declared that his government intended to review the Simonstown Naval Agreement. Angered by what he saw as South Africa's attempt to depict a visit to Cape Town by a Royal Navy force, *en route* to Singapore, as evidence of British support at the time of the United Nations debate over South Africa, he said: "If we are maintaining an agreement that is politically damaging but only militarily marginally useful, then there is no equality or benefit in the Simonstown agreement and it should be brought to an end" [25]. Reportedly, the British government was planning to announce its cancellation of the Simonstown Agreement in 1975, when the defence review is to be published.

In early November 1974, Foreign Minister Callaghan started an African tour in order to discuss the situation in Rhodesia and Namibia with African heads of state. On 4 January 1975 he met Prime Minister Vorster in South Africa, who reportedly promised a "solution this decade" to the apartheid problem.

On 7 November 1974, Barbara White of the US mission to the UN called on South Africa to announce a timetable for the self-determination of Namibia. Subsequent reports in Washington claimed that the State Department was considering the options for the USA to influence South Africa to abandon its support of Rhodesia and to leave Namibia. These reports appeared in connection with a visit to South Africa by the Assistant Secretary of State for African Affairs, Donald Easum [26].

Prospects of regional change

Apart from the changing situation in Rhodesia and Namibia, which will be discussed separately, the coming independence of Mozambique and Angola brought prospects for other regional changes that will indirectly influence South Africa's future policy course. Hitherto, Malawi and the so-called BLS countries—Botswana, Lesotho and Swaziland—have been regarded as reliable *de facto* partners of South Africa, for economic if not political reasons. The position of *Botswana,* in particular, merits attention. In an interview with the *Argus African News Service* in August 1974, President Seretse Khama declared:

There is clearly no future for white minority governments in Africa. The presence of white minority governments will sooner or later have to give way to more democratic ways of government. The only question is how the transformation will come about. I am still hopeful that the worst can be avoided. But I am afraid time is running out fast [27].

He also declared his government's rejection of the federation that some Bantustan chiefs had proposed between the BLS states and the future independent South African Bantustans.

In September, Seretse Khama announced that the railway link running from Rhodesia across Botswana to Mafeking in South Africa, which in the past had been operated by South African authorities, was to be taken over

176

by Botswana in order to strengthen the UN sanctions against Rhodesia. A new road is being built connecting Botswana with Zambia, and the prospect of Botswana's gradual detachment from its virtually complete economic dependence on South Africa has become a not-too-distant possibility. The basis of Botswana's economic development was laid when diamond and copper reserves were found there. Until these discoveries were made, Botswana was little more than a supplier of black labour for South Africa. By 1974, the government could claim considerable developmental progress after eight years of independence. The fact that President Khama was one of the African heads of state involved in the secret discussions on Rhodesia with Prime Minister Vorster illustrates Botswana's growing regional importance.

The end of Portuguese rule also brought prospects of change to Swaziland, which borders on Mozambique. In July 1974, Prince Makhosini, the Prime Minister of the Kingdom of Swaziland, visited Lusaka to take part in talks between President Nyerere of Tanzania, President Kaunda of Zambia and the FRELIMO leader Samora Machel. This contact between Swaziland and a liberation movement was unprecedented, and the Prime Minister stated that he looked forward to entering into economic cooperation with independent Mozambique. "If the declaration by Portugal becomes a reality," he said, "the independence of the Kingdom of Swaziland will be enhanced to that extent" [28].

Some 80 per cent of Swaziland's exports are transported via Lourenço Marques in Mozambique, along the one Swaziland railway link that is not controlled by South Africa.

Malawi, the former British colony of Nyasaland, was oriented towards the white south after its independence. For many years its policy towards the white-ruled states differed from that of independent Africa. President Hastings Banda supported South Africa's "dialogue policy" because Malawi's total economy depended on South Africa's support and goodwill, and also because Banda assumed that no major changes would occur in the region for a considerable time to come. But some slight indications of an eventual change in Malawi's policy have already appeared. In 1972, Dr Banda was reported to be investigating the possibilities of building a Malawian link to the Tanzam railway, indicating a rapprochement with the African states in the north. That same year, at the meeting of the OAU's Liberation Committee in Dar es Salaam, Malawi surprisingly voted in favour of the proposal that countries adjacent to those in which a struggle was under way should permit free transit of men and material destined for the battle zone. Later it became known that FRELIMO units did indeed pass through Malawian territory, but it was uncertain whether this had taken place with or without Malawi's approval.

After the coup in Portugal, further signs appeared of a reorientation towards the north. In May 1974, President Kaunda of Zambia visited

Malawi, establishing the first direct contact between these two states in many years. After that, high commissioners were exchanged for the first time between Malawi and Tanzania. It did not appear far-fetched to suppose that Malawi would in the future quietly abandon the dialogue policy with the south, and reorient its economy north.

Internal change in South Africa

For South African domestic policies, the combined effect of the approaching independence of Angola and Mozambique, and the international and regional changes outlined above, has been to strengthen both the liberal opposition and the enlightened wing (*die Verligte*) of the National Party. The common view held by these groups is illustrated by the following statement made by Lawrence Gandar, former editor of the *Rand Daily Mail,* in a speech at the University of Witwatersrand:

In today's world, the commitment to ending discrimination, solemnly made by Mr Botha in the highest councils of the community of nations, is surely irreversible and, where apartheid fails to adjust to this commitment, it is apartheid that will have to give way, as it is about to do in South West Africa, for example [29].

The regional changes in Southern Africa have also brought increasing tension between the enlightened wing and the hardliners (*die Verkrampte*) within the National Party. Intraparty considerations can safely be assumed to explain much of Prime Minister Vorster's seemingly inconsistent policy declarations regarding the future of South Africa. In the 1974 general elections, the opposition Progressive Party for the first time increased its parliamentary strength from one seat to seven. The Progressive Party is re-examining its recommendations for a qualified franchise for the non-whites, with a possible view to opt for the "one-man one-vote" solution without restrictions. This in itself should not be overrated. Apart from the utterance of reformist statements, little was achieved in 1974, with one exception: in October 1974, it was announced that the government was to repeal the Masters and Servants Act. The significance of this move becomes clear when one notes that in 1972 alone there were 22 000 convictions under this act, which lays down criminal sanctions for Bantu agricultural, mine and domestic workers who are found guilty of breaking their labour contracts or leaving their employment. In all, 24 acts and ordinances are to be repealed, in what is regarded as an unprecedented concession to enlightened opinion [30].

Other recent reforms deal exclusively with "petty apartheid". For example the municipal authorities of Pretoria have become the first in South Africa to allow non-white persons to drive white taxis. In February 1975, the Nico Malan theatre in Cape Town was opened to mixed audiences at all performances.[4]

[4] Judging from the reaction to this move in the South African Nationalist press, the impression might have been created that the apartheid system had been abolished.

178

In January 1975, Vorster held consultations with leaders of the Bantustans and of the Coloured and Indian councils. He rejected all requests for substantial change, however, and merely promised that a form of leasehold property would be considered for non-whites living in the townships.

The question of parliamentary representation for some two million Coloureds—demanded by the militant, anti-apartheid Coloured Labour Party—remained unsolved. The government proposed nothing more than a certain "cabinet status" for Coloured representatives. Sonny Leon, the Labour Party leader, predicted at a press conference on 10 November in Cape Town that the government could expect a confrontation, because the Coloured people would not be satisfied to remain second-class citizens in their own country. The Indian Representative Council has made similar demands. There is also strong pressure from the whites in South Africa to change the status of Coloureds and Indians, for what is best called "strategic considerations". In November 1974, Piet Marais, a Cape Province Member of Parliament, made a widely noted speech saying that it was "plain common sense to have the country's two million brown people and 600 000 Indians on [their] side instead of pushing them into the arms of the majority black group" [31].

Such pressure explains the definite optimism that the Coloureds in South Africa express concerning their future. In contrast to the situation in Rhodesia, however, there is as yet no united non-white front against the white regime.

The government has continued to emphasize the viability of the Bantustan scheme in its official statements despite the fact that only one Bantustan—the Transkei—ruled by Chief Kaizer Matanzima, has agreed to accept independence within a time limit of five years, in accordance with the government scheme. At a conference in mid-November 1974, the remaining eight Bantustan chiefs rejected the concept of self-governing African homelands and demanded instead that black Africans achieve rights equal to those of the whites, within one single nation. Professor Hudson Nsanwisi, chief of the small Gazankulu homeland in the Transvaal, summed up these objections when he said that to agree to the Bantustan scheme would mean that "[we] would lose our claims to South Africa's wealth and would be abandoning our claims to an economy that we have helped to build up" [32]. The Bantustan leaders favoured seeking a federal solution to the race problem, but within a single economy. In reply, Prime Minister Vorster reiterated that black Africans will have majority rule *only* in their homelands, that white South Africa will be ruled by whites, and that "one-man one-vote" representation in a single parliament will never arise in South Africa.

Confrontation would thus seem to be inevitable. Even in the Transkei, African demands had not yet been met: the Transkei's coastline and its capital, Umtata, have not been handed over to Bantu administration. There is a growing frustration among the black population, whose demands for the sharing of power are increasing.

Student unrest continued during 1974, as did the severe reprisals by the authorities. In October, around 100 African students at the University of the North demonstrated for several days against the detention of student leaders, following a pro-FRELIMO rally which had been prohibited by the authorities.

Labour unrest was an even more serious problem, and some important reforms concerning the mine workers may be forthcoming. Malawi stopped supplying mine workers to South Africa after an air disaster in 1973 when 72 Malawians were killed in a plane chartered by the South African Chamber of Mines. By October 1974 this boycott had removed some 50 000 workers from the Malawian labour force in South Africa. Lesotho, in turn, introduced new legislation requiring its workers in South Africa to send home 60 per cent of their salaries, causing most of the Lesotho labour force to stop working and demand repatriation. Violent clashes took place in a gold mine at Germiston, near Johannesburg, between 1 000 striking Mozambican miners and the mine security forces who used tear gas against them. Repatriation of miners to Malawi, Lesotho and Mozambique continued throughout the year.

On 21 October, the South African Chamber of Mines announced a programme designed to diminish the country's reliance on foreign labour—which made up 72 per cent of the work force in the gold and platinum mines in 1973 [33]. In addition to the campaign which was already under way to recruit around 50 000 workers per year from the Bantustans, starting wages for the miners were increased by one-third. This meant that wages in the mines had been tripled since May 1973. In addition, a mechanization programme was begun. In November, the government eased the regulations inhibiting the recruitment of urban Africans into the mining industry. Earlier the miners had been required to return to a Bantustan on completion of their contracts, but repatriation to the area where recruitment took place was now to be permitted.

Since January 1973 when the first mass strikes took place in Durban, domestic labour organizations have increasingly challenged the system. Over 300 other strikes have occurred since then. Although limited in scope and objectives, they illustrate an improving organization. At the end of 1974, there were 22 black unions with a total of 40 000 members. These were still not recognized by the government, but trade unionism was growing and a certain measure of cooperation with white unions and employers was reported [34].

No armed opposition to the government has taken place inside South Africa since the 1960s and no military activity by either the ANC of South Africa or the PAC was reported after the defeat of the Luthuli detachment of the ANC in Rhodesia in 1966. However, a request was placed on the agenda of the meeting of the OAU 17-nation Liberation Committee in Dar es Salaam, in late November 1974, for OAU recognition of a South African liberation movement called the Unity Movement of South Africa. The status and composition of this movement remain unknown. The Vice-President of the ANC, Oliver Tambo, said during a visit to Stockholm in February 1975, that his movement was preparing to launch an armed struggle against the Vorster regime [35].

III. *Defence measures*

In August 1974 it was announced that South Africa's defence spending over the next fiscal year was to be increased substantially, by $339.13 million, to a record total of $1 037.48 million on revenue account. The largest single increase concerned the procurement of arms for land defence, for which $201.64 million was to be apportioned. The 1975 defence budget represents about 16.7 per cent of total national spending. Defence Minister Botha emphasized in an interview after the budget presentation that the increase in defence expenditure was related to the ongoing modernization programme and was not to be interpreted as evidence of an arms build-up in South Africa [36]. For 1976, a further increase of 35 per cent was announced in March 1975.

At the opening of Parliament in Cape Town on 2 August, State President Fouche said, in apparent contradiction to the Defence Minister, that the defence of South Africa was to be strengthened considerably, both in arms and numbers of men. Prior to the budget disclosure, however, the Defence Minister had announced that the projected 10-year modernization programme would now be completed within five years.

A general appeal was issued to Western governments for sophisticated weapons, such as the British Nimrod, which had been demonstrated in Cape Town in 1973 before the Labour government came into power. In September 1974, it was reported in South Africa that the Ford administration in the USA had secretly decided to sell reconnaissance aircraft, helicopters and certain second-hand military equipment to South Africa. This decision was said to have been made because of the developments in Mozambique and Angola. The report was subsequently denied by US officials [37].

The capacity of the Simonstown naval base is to be trebled at a cost of $24 million, and its dockyard is to handle 40 to 50 ships. Salisbury island is to be developed into a naval base, and if naval activity in the Indian Ocean increases, a third base is to be built at Richard's Bay. The British government's decision to review the Simonstown Agreement, coupled with the apparent lack of reaction to this from the South African government, brought widespread speculation that France or the USA would be willing to take over the British obligations. In a statement of 7 November, the British Engineering Industries Association warned the government of the consequences for British industry that would result from cancelling the Simonstown Agreement, stating that France would profit from this [38].

The US Navy Commander-in-Chief in the Pacific, and current Director of the US Strategic Institute, Admiral John McCain, was quoted as saying that "what has happened in Angola and Mozambique makes our possession of Diego Garcia more important than ever. But it also means that we absolutely need access to Simonstown and Durban" [39].

On 14 June 1974, a change in the hitherto all-white defence organization, with possible implications for the future, was announced. In connection with a counterinsurgency exercise in the Transvaal, it was revealed by Defence Minister Botha that a new policy of recruiting Africans—previously forbidden by law from carrying firearms—had already been embarked upon. Initially, the Africans were to serve in army and police counterinsurgency units in Bantustans or on the borders of the Republic.

In 1975, a new training base for black Africans is to be built and an African corps will eventually be set up and integrated into the army. Currently, a Bantu can only advance to the rank of sergeant major. The Bantustan chiefs have repeatedly demanded the right to organize the defence of their territories, which are currently protected by white troops. However, Vorster has made it clear that white South Africa will continue to control defence and foreign policy even if the Bantustans become "independent".

In January 1975 it was disclosed that an all-Indian naval service battalion was to be formed and that Indians were to serve as captains of their own crews.

In connection with the discussion on defence between the Bantustan leaders and the South African government, the defence authorities proffered another type of argument against the present Bantustan scheme. Brigadier C. L. Viljoen, Director of Operations of the South African Army, stated that the consolidation of the homelands into single pieces of territory would be beneficial to South Africa since the existing fragmentation was unacceptable from the military point of view. Furthermore, the Bantu soldiers would have to be properly motivated for anti-terrorist operations. Efforts therefore had to be made to eliminate the political and economic disabilities imposed on them under present government policies [40].

A campaign was also launched during 1974 among white South Africans to improve their own motivation for defence. Major-General J. R. Dutton, Chief of Army Staff Operations, told the Pretoria branch of the National Council of Women that the intensity of the present war would probably escalate and that all South Africans should be prepared to meet the onslaught. He said that more than half of the problems of the Defence Force stemmed from a "lack of motivation" [41].

In mid-1974, Parliament passed a new law providing for 10-year prison sentences or $16 000 in fines for refusing to participate in military service or for advising, encouraging or instigating any other person to refuse such service.

Chapter 11. Rhodesia

There are many reasons why Rhodesia has been singled out as the country most likely to experience the full impact of the change in Southern Africa resulting from the coup in Portugal. Some reasons are economic—for example, the trade routes through Mozambique are likely to be blocked; and others are political—for instance, the fact that, in the interest of self-preservation, South Africa is withdrawing its support for the Smith regime. The independence of Mozambique and Angola also reduces Rhodesia's importance as a buffer zone and aggravates its economic situation.

I. *The economic situation*

The British attitude towards Rhodesia, which, formally, is still a British colony, has been hardening ever since the Labour government took office. British opinion became even more rigidly negative after the coup in Portugal. In May 1974 discussions were started with the new Portuguese government on the issue of economic sanctions against Rhodesia. One point that was emphasized was that the closure of traffic through Mozambique would cut off most of Rhodesia's oil supplies as well as most of its export trade.

At a press conference on 13 September, Portuguese Foreign Minister Mario Soares declared, however, that the economy of Portugal was still too weak to permit it to enforce the sanctions against Rhodesia, and that the choice in Mozambique, at least in a short-term perspective, was either to take a pragmatic approach to these issues or create economic chaos. FRELIMO, the Portuguese said, was "realistic" about this issue [42].

Nonetheless, certain developments in Mozambique during 1974 did cause a certain interruption of economic relations with Rhodesia. The railway link to the port of Beira, where 80 per cent of the port traffic was made up of Rhodesian cargo, was cut on several occasions. After negotiations began between Portugal and FRELIMO in September, it was reported that Rhodesian trade through Mozambique had been reduced by 50 per cent. Continuing strikes among the dock and transport workers in Lourenço Marques also crippled trade in this port, which usually handled a large part of Rhodesian cargo. The sole remaining railway link with South Africa was the line through Botswana, which was supervised and controlled by Botswana authorities and strictly limited to lawful cargo.

184

It can be inferred that the Rhodesian government anticipated a total blockade of traffic through Mozambique, because it accelerated its programme to complete a short new railway line from the town of Rutenga in Rhodesia to Beit Bridge on the South African border, and finished it 21 months ahead of schedule. Rhodesia's increased dependence on South Africa's goodwill was thus a fact even before the interim FRELIMO government in Mozambique had taken any formal action to implement sanctions against Rhodesia.

II. *Foreign pressure for settlement*

One of the Ford administration's policy actions affecting Southern Africa was to reverse the so-called "Byrd Amendment", which had enabled the United States to import Rhodesian chrome. Japan, denounced by the OAU as one of the major sanction-breaking nations, announced in 1974 that stronger measures were to be taken against the industry on the issue of compliance. But two countries in particular are more crucial than Japan to Rhodesia's economic and political survival—namely, Britain and South Africa.

Britain

The British government agreed to the ANC's request that it take a new initiative to solve the Rhodesian problem. The ANC's aim was to arrange a new constitutional conference on Rhodesia, in which all African nationalist leaders would participate—including the imprisoned ZANU and ZAPU leaders. Foreign Secretary Callaghan has stated on several occasions that the British government expects the independence of Portuguese Africa to have a profound impact on the transition to majority rule in Rhodesia. "Everyone not utterly blind must realize", he said, "that the situation as it is developing in Mozambique and Angola is altering the internal position in Rhodesia and will continue to do so. There will be more and more pressure on Rhodesia as the months pass by" [43]. However, strong statements about Rhodesia have been made before by British governments, and British political influence over the Rhodesian settlement issue has never proved to be of any importance. This time, however, Britain's intentions for Rhodesia may actually conform to those of South Africa, whose political influence in the region is decisive.

South Africa

The treatment that Rhodesia has received in the South African media and in statements by government officials after the coup in Portugal implies that a fundamental reappraisal of military security is in the making. It has been pointed out, for example, that the capacity of the railways and ports in South Africa is not sufficient to cope with any large increase in Rhodesian cargo. Political identification is also being questioned. At the annual trade union congress in Rhodesia, A. Grobbelar, the visiting South African Secretary-General of TUCSA, declared that is would be wise on the part of South Africa to adopt a neutral position regarding the Rhodesian problem, since Rhodesia will no longer constitute a buffer zone between South Africa and the North [44].

In December 1974, some current diplomatic moves to achieve a settlement between the Smith government and the African population in Rhodesia were revealed. Most details of this diplomatic effort await confirmation, but the broad course of events is described below.

Reportedly on the initiative of Prime Minister Vorster and of President Kaunda of Zambia—who wields considerable influence within the OAU because of his record as mediator in various regional affairs—talks involving Vorster and several African heads of state were begun in utmost secrecy in mid-1974. During September and October, M. Chona, President Kaunda's political adviser, paid several visits to South Africa to prepare for the summit meeting on Rhodesia which started in Lusaka on 6 November. The participants were the heads of state of Zambia, Tanzania and Botswana, the FRELIMO president Samora Machel, and the ZANU and ZAPU leaders N. Sithole and J. Nkomo who were paroled from prison to attend the discussions. The summit meeting was adjourned after four days but was resumed in early December, and the imprisoned nationalist leaders were again brought to it. The ANC leader, Bishop Muzorewa, was also present.

The conference sketched out a five-stage programme to end minority rule in Rhodesia by 1975. It called for the following measures, designed to achieve a settlement between Britain and Rhodesia:
(a) The unification of ZANU and ZAPU; (b) Agreement on a cease-fire; (c) The convening of a constitutional conference; (d) Raising the African representation in parliament by appointment to parity; and (e) General elections according to the principle of one-man one-vote.

It seems reasonable to assume that this initiative lay behind Prime Minister Vorster's references to coming changes in Southern Africa (see page 175).

The subsequent results were ambiguous. On 12 December 1974, Prime Minister Smith announced that an agreement had been reached for a cease-fire and for the release of all political prisoners in Rhodesia. He claimed that the ANC no longer demanded majority rule as a prerequisite for a constitutional conference. At the same time, commenting on the transition to black African rule in Mozambique, Smith said: "Let me assure you, however, that there is no possibility whatever of a similar turn of events in Rhodesia" [45].

186

On 8 December, President Kaunda announced the forthcoming merger of ZAPU, ZANU and FROLIZI with the ANC. Representatives of the three liberation movements issued a joint statement that they had agreed in principle to a plan to consolidate their leadership under a reconstituted ANC. The details would be worked out within four months at a congress where the ANC executive would be enlarged. According to this joint statement, however, all four nationalist movements agreed on the principle of continued armed struggle.

At the beginning of 1975 it was clear that no effective cease-fire had been agreed upon. The Rhodesian authorities also stopped releasing political prisoners. The Smith government further refused to accept a British chairman at the planned constitutional conference, demanded by the ANC, on the grounds that this conference would concern the internal affairs of Rhodesia. The ANC leader, the Rev. Ndabaningi Sithole was arrested on 4 March 1975, and on 18 March the acting ZANU president, Herbert Chitepo, was killed by a letter-bomb in Lusaka. The sole result of these events was the renewed escalation of guerilla attacks, and the Smith government appeared to be heading for nothing less than outright war. FRELIMO president Samora Machel told the 24th session of the OAU Liberation Committee in January 1975 that an independent Mozambique would support armed struggle in Rhodesia if the current negotiations to end the constitutional dispute should fail. This is also the official policy of the OAU [47].

Subsequent events strengthen the notion, however, that the Smith government is under constant pressure from South Africa. Sithole was released from prison, for example, and allowed to leave Rhodesia. A confidential document was also made public in Salisbury on 22 February 1975, outlining the contents of previous agreements between Smith and Vorster. According to this document, Vorster had paid a clandestine visit to Rhodesia to advise Smith to agree to a constitutional conference. In principle, the Smith government was said to have accepted the recommendation that complete primary education plus one year of further schooling should be the minimum requirement for voting rights. It is estimated that this should enfranchise some 300 000 Africans and make majority rule a possibility after a five-year transitional period.

The ANC demands, however, that the transitional period be no longer than one year and that it be explicitly modelled after the Mozambican example [46].

III. *Internal developments*

The fact that the Smith government agreed in principle to the summit talks and allowed the ZANU and ZAPU leaders to leave prison temporarily to attend them is probably best interpreted as being the result of outside pressure, rather than as an indication of a change of policy on the part of the Rhodesian government. In fact, internal political developments in Rhodesia after the coup in Portugal reflect a hardening attitude towards African aspirations. FRELIMO's rise to power in Mozambique was parallelled by increasing militancy on the part of the ANC in Rhodesia. The position of the ANC approached ZANU and ZAPU policy demands.

The Rhodesian white opposition, such as it is, comes from much the same circles as it does in South Africa. In the main it comes from the business community, which has a direct interest in seeing the country's economic life return to normal, but it also includes a few liberal politicians. This opposition failed to unite in a challenge to the ruling Rhodesian Front during the general elections in August 1974. Prime Minister Smith's party received 77 per cent of the votes in what is seen as a definite declaration of confidence by the white population.

At the annual congress of the opposition Rhodesia Party, in October 1974, its president, T. Gibbs, called for a constitutional conference to be held in Rhodesia with representatives of all political opinion in the country. He denounced Ian Smith as a racist and accused both Smith and ANC leader Bishop Muzorewa of negative actions which he said were leading to a polarization of the races. He also expressed the opposition of the business community. "Instead of allowing the tribal trust lands to be called havens for the unemployed", he declared, "they must be exposed for the depressed economic areas they are, dragging down the economy as a whole by their lack of productivity" [48]. The Rhodesia Party represents a minimal sector of the white population, however.

There are indications of a growing rightist opposition to the government, voiced by a new white organization—the Southern Africa Civilization Association—which is calling for a union with South Africa. Its spokesman is the Afrikaans-language newspaper *Die Rhodesier.*

Prime Minister Smith declared on 17 May 1974 that the situation in Mozambique had been critical before the coup, and said that the establishment of a stable government there would not affect Rhodesia [49]. Nevertheless, he paid several visits to South Africa, reportedly seeking increased military aid or even a joint defence agreement with South Africa. During one such visit he warned the South African government that while Rhodesia was merely an obstacle in the way of what he called the spread of international Communism from states north of the Zambezi, the real target would be South Africa [50]. By the end of the year, however, with the possible exception of the announcement on 2 August by Deputy Minister of Police Kruger that a volunteer corps was to be formed in South Africa to take over the tasks of the police deployed in Rhodesia, no steps towards involvement were taken [51]. In fact, Kruger's move was seen as a step towards disengagement rather than involvement: a volunteer corps represents a less official commitment than the deployment of police units and can also be easily dissolved. In spring 1975 it was announced that all regular South African units were to be withdrawn from Rhodesia.

IV. *Military developments*

Guerilla activity increased considerably during and after mid-1974. Rhodesian security authorities reported 523 engagements with ZANU on the Mozambique border in June and July alone, where an estimated 400 guerillas were operating [52]. In July, the government admitted the loss of four aircraft in the northeast and claimed that they had been brought down by SAM-7 missiles. In September, ZAPU guerillas, presumably coming from Zambia, attacked in the Gwai area, and reports were heard about armed actions by FROLIZI in the Sipolilo area [53]. Sabotage incidents also occurred in the cities; by the end of the year violence had reportedly become as common in Rhodesia as in Northern Ireland.

During the latter half of 1974, the OAU substantially increased its military aid to the Rhodesian liberation movements. It was later confirmed that ZANU had received large numbers of the SAM-7 missile through Tanzania [54].

Military allocations in 1974 rose well above the budgeted sums. Over $1 million was allocated for the installation of alarm systems on farms in the northeast, and other security measures in the same area were estimated at $29 million. Road construction work along the border with Mozambique increased by 50 per cent, at a cost of $12 million. Police expenditures rose to $35 million [55]. Even excluding public construction work, the sum of related expenditures for defence and security approached $128 million. On 29 August 1974, John Wrathall, the Minister of Finance, announced an expected $66 million budget deficit, caused by the outlays for the anti-guerilla campaign. This forced the government to raise taxes by 10 per cent.

White Rhodesians were initially assured that the call-up rate would be reduced after 1976, but meanwhile a further extension of the service period from 12 to 18 months was generally anticipated. In February 1974, the government announced plans for doubling the national service intake, and in June the call-up was extended to those with no previous military experience.

On 27 October it was announced that the Rhodesian security authorities would reestablish a special white police reserve force of 10 000 to patrol white areas in the cities, in anticipation of attacks by urban guerillas. An earlier force of this kind had been disbanded in 1964.

The removal of Africans from the war zones was further accelerated during 1974, and by the end of the year some 35 "protected" villages containing around 100 000 inhabitants had arisen [56].

The physical ability of the Rhodesian regime to increase its defence establishment is limited. Unless the conscript system is expanded to include the black population, the escalating anti-guerilla war will sooner or later mean a near-total mobilization of the whites. "The parallel with Portuguese experiences in pre-April 1974 Mozambique is close", according to a comment in the *Financial Mail* of Johannesburg [57].

Chapter 12. Namibia

I. *Prospects for change*

The changing balance of power in the region is expected to bring rapid results in Namibia. The UN Commissioner for Namibia, Sean MacBride, said at a news conference in Geneva on 2 May 1974 that the coup in Portugal would mean that Namibia would become independent within one to three years [58].

Before coming to power, the Labour Party in Britain had committed itself specifically to accept the ruling by the World Court of Justice on South Africa's illegal presence in Namibia and to cancel the uranium-supply agreement between the British Atomic Energy Authority and Rio Tinto Zinc at Rossing in Namibia [59]. After the Portuguese coup, SWAPO suggested to Britain that the Labour government act to dissolve British business connections with South African-ruled Namibia. The Labour government is actively involved in the future of Namibia. Foreign Secretary Callaghan met SWAPO representatives in Lusaka in January 1975 and told them that Great Britain will support Namibia if it seeks Commonwealth membership upon independence—which is SWAPO's declared intention.

In Namibia as in Rhodesia, however, a new South African initiative could be of more decisive influence. On 26 June 1974, South Africa officially informed the United Nations that whites and non-whites in Namibia were to open discussions about the future pattern of constitutional developments. This was generally interpreted as an attempt to avert the South African delegation's expulsion from the General Assembly. SWAPO rejected the proposal for multiracial talks.

Subsequent developments create some doubt about South African intentions for Namibia. On the one hand, there are indications that the South African government will decide to leave Namibia in the wider interests of the Republic's own security. It is a common belief in South Africa that Namibia cannot be defended once Angola becomes independent. The South African Foreign Minister, Dr Hilgard Muller, during an interview in connection with his visit to the United Nations in October 1974 elaborated on what seemed to be a new approach. "South West Africa", he said "may enter confederation with us or may become federated with us . . . If we are honest we must accept full independence, should the people of South West Africa so decide in the exercise of their right to self-determination" [60]. He reiterated his government's decision to begin multiracial talks in Namibia. By November, more details of what was now

191

described as Prime Minister Vorster's "master plan" for Namibia appeared. The first step, the severance of the parliamentary ties between South Africa and Namibia, would be followed by multiracial discussions of ways to organize elections. Such a scheme would indicate that South Africa had in fact abandoned the homelands programme in Namibia.

On the other hand, a plan for the future partition of Namibia was presented by Jannie de Wet, the South African Commissioner General for the indigenous peoples of South West Africa, who proposed that the all-white Police Zone in Namibia should be granted separate independence. This state, which would encompass two-thirds of the territory, could then seek federation with South Africa. The black homelands would be free to join the federation or to exist as independent states. Ovamboland, in particular, could seek federation with Angola.

In a speech to the South African Senate on 23 October 1974, Prime Minister Vorster expressed continued reluctance to leave Namibia. "Chaos elsewhere would be child's play," he said, "compared with what would happen if South Africa left South West Africa" [61]. He emphasized that only the ethnic representatives of tribes would be accepted at the consultative conference planned to take place in Namibia. African political parties, cutting across tribal lines would not be allowed to participate. Such a conference, which would by definition exclude SWAPO representatives, was rejected by most African homeland chiefs and, of course, by SWAPO. SWAPO announced that the South African-organized election scheduled to be held in Ovamboland in January 1975 would be boycotted, just as the previous election there had been. The boycott did not succeed, however, as 55 per cent of eligible Ovambo voters participated in the election.

The publication of de Wet's plan aroused debate in South Africa. It was asked whether this proposal corresponded in effect to Vorster's "master plan" or signified a deep difference of opinion between reformists and conservatives within the National Party. No concrete action had been taken by the end of 1974.

II. *Internal developments*

Already in May 1974 the South African authorities had begun to take stronger measures against SWAPO in Namibia. Sixty political leaders were detained at Windhoek. According to SWAPO, the authorities were seeking to establish the principle that SWAPO membership constituted a "terrorist activity", thus making it possible to ban the organization.

At the opening of the second session of the Ovamboland Legislative Council in May, J. J. Loots, the South African Minister of Planning, warned that the fall of Portuguese colonial rule in Angola could leave the door open for "terrorists and other dangerous persons" to enter Ovamboland [62].

One of the first measures taken by the new Portuguese government in Angola was to release the 60 Namibians who had been imprisoned in Luanda for being SWAPO members. SWAPO, which had been restricted to using routes through UNITA-controlled territory in Angola before the coup, now won practically unrestricted access to Angolan territory and some 600 SWAPO members were able to escape arrest in Namibia by crossing Angola into Zambia.

III. *Military developments*

During June and July 1974, as the prospects for military action by SWAPO were enhanced, guerilla activity in the Caprivi Strip increased. In August, Defence Minister Botha announced that regular troops were replacing the paramilitary police units deployed in the Caprivi Strip. He emphasized that in the future, counterinsurgency operations in Namibia would be both political and military in character [62].

Simultaneously, the Ovamboland Bantustan officials received secret instructions to begin recruiting Africans into a full-time border militia. SWAPO came into possession of this information and passed it on to the UN Namibia Commissioner, emphasizing that Africans who are recruited *must* join the militia immediately or be interned indefinitely in government camps. This requirement explained the increasing flight of refugees to Angola. It was also learned that since November 1973 tribal police units were being trained to fight.

The SWAPO president, Sam Nujoma, said in Brazzaville on 14 March 1975 that South Africa had deployed more than 30 000 soldiers in Namibia [63]. In mid-1975, it was revealed that several hundred South African troops had been deployed in Southern Angola to protect the Cunene river project [64].

References

1. *Star Weekly*, South Africa, 12 January 1974.
2. Herrick, *et al., Area Handbook for Angola*, DA PAM No. 550–59 (Washington, U.S. Government Printing Office, August 1967) p. 384.
3. *Observer*, UK, 19 May 1974.
4. *Facts and Reports*, Netherlands, 24 November 1973, quoting AFP dispatch, 22 October 1973
5. *International Herald Tribune*, USA, 14 June 1974.
6. *Daily Telegraph*, UK, 19 July 1974.
7. *International Herald Tribune*, USA, 28 October 1974.
8. *International Herald Tribune*, USA, 18 November 1974.

9. *Times*, UK, 27 April 1974.
10. *Newsweek*, 26 August 1974, p. 48.
11. *Aftonbladet*, Sweden, 18 October 1974.
12. *Guardian*, UK, 14 November 1974.
13. *Daily News*, Tanzania, 3 October 1974.
14. *Star Weekly*, South Africa, 25 May 1974.
15. *International Herald Tribune*, USA, 14 June 1974.
16. *Daily News*, Tanzania, 23 September 1974.
17. AFP Interafrican News Service, France, 26 November 1974.
18. *Star Weekly*, South Africa, 28 September 1974.
19. *Journal d'Europe*, Belgium, 28 January 1974.
20. *Facts and Reports*, Netherlands, 26 October 1974, p. 5, quoting radio report: Lisbon Home Service, 3 September 1974.
21. *Star Weekly*, South Africa, 7 September 1974.
22. *Financial Times*, UK, 30 October 1974.
23. *Times*, UK, 7 November 1974.
24. *Times*, UK, 8 November 1974.
25. *International Herald Tribune*, USA, 26 October 1974.
26. *Washington Post*, USA, 14 November 1974.
27. *Africa*, UK, No. 38, October 1974.
28. *Africa*, UK, No. 36, August 1974.
29. *Times*, UK, 16 December 1974.
30. *Times*, UK, 19 October 1974.
31. *New York Times*, USA, 19 November 1974.
32. *Times*, UK, 18 November 1974.
33. *Times*, UK, 14 October 1974.
34. *Sunday Times*, UK, 17 November 1974.
35. AFP Interafrican News Service, 11 February 1975.
36. *Interavia Air Letter No. 8080*, 29 August 1974.
37. *Rand Daily Mail*, South Africa, 17 September 1974.
38. *Financial Times*, South Africa, 17 September 1974.
39. *Sunday Times*, UK, 20 October 1974.
40. *Rhodesia Herald*, Rhodesia, 8 August 1974.
41. *Rand Daily Mail*, South Africa, 3 August 1974.
42. *Times*, UK, 14 September 1974.
43. *Times*, UK, 18 July 1974.
44. *Guardian*, UK, 2 September 1974.
45. *Guardian*, UK, 12 December 1974.
46. *International Herald Tribune*, New York, 24 February 1975, quoting "The Catholic Commission for Justice and Peace", reported by Robert Magube to the Justice and Peace Executive, 17 December 1974.
47. *Rhodesia Herald*, Rhodesia, 9 January 1975.
48. *Times*, UK, 14 October 1974.
49. *Times*, UK, 18 May 1974.
50. *Daily Telegraph*, UK, 26 August 1974.
51. *Le Monde*, France, 4 August 1974.
52. *Guardian*, UK, 12 December 1974.
53. *Africa*, UK, No. 37, September 1974.
54. *Daily Telegraph*, UK, 8 March 1975.
55. *Dagens Nyheter*, Sweden, 23 August 1974, quoting TT-AFP dispatch from Salisbury, 22 August 1974.
56. Report by David Holden, *Sunday Times*, UK, 6 October 1974.
57. *Financial Mail*, South Africa, 11 October 1974.

58. *Africa Diary,* India, No. 21, 28 May 1974, p. 6977.
59. *X-Ray,* No. 8, May 1974.
60. *International Herald Tribune,* USA, 14 October 1974.
61. *Times,* UK, 24 October 1974.
62. *Africa,* UK, No. 36, August 1974.
63. *Zambia Daily Mail,* Zambia, 15 March 1975.
64. *Financial Times,* UK, 23 August 1975.

Part V. Summary and conclusions

The following topics of primary interest for this study were listed in the introduction: (a) the nature of the conflict determinants in the area, (b) whether a common pattern of conflict escalation exists in the region of Southern Africa, (c) the need for an assessment to be made of the implications of Portugal's withdrawal from Africa for the survival of the white minority regimes in South Africa and Rhodesia, and (d) the prospects of a major war between the white-ruled states and the members of the OAU, and the likelihood of foreign involvement in such a war.

An examination of the first two items involves judgement based on current and historical facts concerning the conflict in Southern Africa. The last two questions call for an element of prediction.

1. The discussion on conflict determinants in chapter 1 of this study essentially leads to the conclusion that the ultimate cause of tension in Southern Africa has been the conditions imposed on the black population by the minority white ruling class. This was true in Portuguese Africa and is equally applicable to Rhodesia, South Africa and South African-ruled Namibia. The rapid decolonization of the rest of Africa that began in the 1950s fomented a "revolution of rising expectations" in Portuguese Africa, resulting in an initial backlash, which ultimately led to the outbreak of wars of liberation in these countries.

The accusations that have been made that the African nationalists' demands have been inspired and even directed by foreign Communist powers lack any basis in reality. Little evidence exists to support such arguments as are put forward by the regimes in South Africa and Rhodesia. Their real purpose seems to be to present the issue in terms of "Communist threat" in order to gain moral and military support from the so-called "free world" to perpetuate the existing system.

2. Despite unique conditions prevailing in each of the countries concerned, there is an overall common pattern of conflict escalation. In Portuguese Africa, the increasingly brutal measures undertaken to suppress all manifestations of African nationalism made reformism impossible in effect. The outlawing of nationalistic organizations in Rhodesia, Namibia and South Africa and the legislative measures undertaken to bar black African aspirations to share political power might also usher revolution into these countries. The colonial Portuguese regime's unresponsiveness to African nationalist demands led to armed warfare as the sole means of realizing these demands. The pattern is being repeated—as yet on a smaller scale—in both Rhodesia, Namibia and South Africa.

197

The most influential factor for the outcome of African nationalism may well be the emergence of a unified nationalist movement under a strong leadership. This type of movement has as yet emerged only in Guinea-Bissau and Mozambique. The prospects for the establishment of unified nationalist African movements in Angola, Namibia, Rhodesia and South Africa are uncertain. Continued and increased repression of the Africans may well engender such united fronts, however. The merger of the previously mutually hostile Rhodesian liberation movements could be a first development in this direction. In Angola, on the other hand, continuing intermovement conflicts may still trigger a civil war prior to or after the country's transition to independence. In Namibia, the National Convention that was intended to function as an umbrella organization for the separate nationalist movements, has collapsed, and SWAPO's claim to represent the entire population is still being challenged. In South Africa, there is as yet no cohesive organization unifying the entire non-white opposition.

In this context, the role played by outside supporters of the black nationalist movements must be taken into account. The provision of military supplies, foreign training and access to bases in friendly countries was of crucial importance to the liberation movements in Angola, Guinea-Bissau and Mozambique. Furthermore, the prerequisite for military aid from the OAU has become the establishment of either a united front or a unitary movement representative of the entire black population. The merger in 1975 of the previously mutually hostile Rhodesian nationalist movements is one example of the result of outside pressure for unification. It was often stated in the past that the bilateral military aid to the nationalists had been of much greater importance than that channelled via the OAU. However, bilateral aid—such as was given to the two main competing movements in Angola —may also serve to perpetuate disunity among the movements.

3. Portugal's withdrawal from Africa leaves South Africa, South African-ruled Namibia and Rhodesia as the only white-ruled states on the continent. The conclusion reached here regarding the future of these states is that the attainment of independence by the former Portuguese colonies will also lead to the independence of Namibia and to black majority rule in Rhodesia. The Republic of South Africa provides a special case, however, as it still remains the most decisive power factor in the region and still has the possibility of choosing alternative policy courses. The main effect of the defeat of white supremacy in the rest of the region, however, has been to make it unlikely that the apartheid state will survive in a long-term perspective, even though the conditions in South Africa differ in important respects from those prevailing in the rest of the region. South Africa is a leading military power, in sharp contrast to the Portuguese colonial and Rhodesian regimes. This fact must obviously be taken into account by any movement or outside power planning military action against South Africa. Also, in contrast to both the colonial Portuguese and the present-day Rhodesian regimes, South

Africa is becoming a leading economic power in the region, with no financial obstacles to a large-scale military build-up in sight.

Within less than a year after the coup in Portugal, Guinea-Bissau had become independent, and the formal organization of the transition to independence for Angola and Mozambique had been achieved, heightening the expectations of the black populations in the remaining white-ruled nations.

In addition, the African nationalist organizations have become increasingly militant since the coup in Portugal. This changing mood was most noticeable in the ANC in Rhodesia.

In early 1975 ZANU reportedly received a large number of SAM-7 missiles through Tanzania and deployed a unit of 100 guerillas specially trained for anti-aircraft operations with this missile. Although military aid to the South African nationalist movements has been negligible in the past, the OAU stated in its January 1975 Dar es Salaam declaration that this matter will receive new attention.

The role played by the OAU in the struggle against white supremacy on the continent should not be underrated, both because of the military aid given by this organization, and because such aid is accompanied by strong pressures for unification. After 1973, the OAU concentrated its military aid to the liberation movements in Portuguese Africa. From 1975, the Rhodesian and Namibian liberation movements will be given priority if peaceful negotiations fail to achieve majority rule.

An optimistic assessment of the effects of the Portuguese settlement in the rest of Southern Africa would be to envisage a peaceful solution to both the Rhodesian and the Namibian situations. It is hoped that Prime Minister Vorster's initiatives during the autumn of 1974 will lead to a settlement based on majority rule in Rhodesia, and to South Africa's withdrawal from Namibia in accordance with the United Nations' plan for that country. Sean MacBride, the UN Commissioner for Namibia, provides an example of this optimism when estimating that Namibia's transition to independence will take place within the next three years as a direct result of the fall of the Portuguese colonial empire.

However, even if the South African government were prepared to accept black rule in Rhodesia and Namibia, this would hardly be evidence of a new policy. The Nationalist government in South Africa has always accepted black governments, except in South Africa itself, as illustrated by its continuous efforts to open up a "dialogue" with black Africa. Even the prospect of independence in Mozambique and Angola did not arouse any negative reaction; instead, a prompt offer of economic cooperation with the FRELIMO government was made. In fact, the survival of the apartheid Republic may be deemed to be best guaranteed by a settlement of both the Rhodesian and Namibian issues. In this way, international criticism of South Africa—for supporting the Ian Smith regime and for defying the

United Nations in Namibia—could be allayed. In addition, economic cooperation with the future independent states of Mozambique, Angola and Namibia is probably seen as advantageous in that its very effect would be to strengthen the present regime in South Africa. Thus, the short-term implications of the change of regime in Portugal for white-ruled Southern Africa may actually be the independence of Namibia and black majority rule in Rhodesia. South Africa's reward for acceptance of this situation would presumably be the neutralization of both these countries. Vorster has already stated that the South African regime will not accept the establishment of guerilla bases in Mozambique, and this will probably apply equally to these two territories.

If this is assumed to be a realistic assessment of South Africa's future policy, the changes in the region would not affect South Africa's apartheid policies at all, but would, in fact, guarantee their continuation.

There are alternatives, of course. The Ian Smith government in Rhodesia may prove to be insensitive to any pressure from South Africa, and guerilla warfare may escalate considerably. Even so, South Africa could abstain from involvement and merely await the course of events. Or, it could intervene and use its military power for the first time in a larger conflict situation. Such a course of action would obviously result, however, in more severe international condemnation of South Africa than at present. It could also adversely affect the rate of foreign investment in South Africa, since any country at war is automatically regarded as insecure for the growth of capital. Business confidence is a vital commodity which is easily lost. In early 1975, for example, it was reported that all the US oil companies engaged in oil-prospecting in Namibia had left the country.

In the case of Namibia, the optimal solution for South Africa may lie in the construction of some sort of federal state that will retain close economic and political links with the Republic. It has been mentioned in this context that the military threat from SWAPO might possibly be neutralized by such drastic measures as ceding the whole of Ovamboland to independent Angola.

4. Since it is concluded that the Republic of South Africa will not be able to continue to exist as the sole white-ruled state on the African continent, the main issue for the future is how apartheid will be abolished—by peaceful means or violent, that is, through a civil war or a major war involving other African states or even non-African powers.

The inherent force in African nationalism was consistently underrated by the Portuguese colonial authorities, just as it is now underrated by the ruling powers and the white population in general in Rhodesia, Namibia and South Africa. In fact, the average white person in South Africa appears ignorant of any complaints from the black population and has little knowledge of their living conditions. There is a widespread tendency to dismiss the possibility of the Africans better organizing themselves, and to fall back instead on the timeworn arguments of the primitiveness and mutual hostility of the separate tribes within the country.

Instead of educating all inhabitants to become South Africans, the South African government holds fast to its professedly unique concept of nation-building: in black Africa, it is held, ancient tribalism must be perpetuated, because the forced unification of the many separate African tribes has only brought about disasters, such as the Congo uprising and the Biafran War. The South African solution is said to provide the remedy: the eternal separation of all groups in their reserves. According to Vorster, the crash-development programme to improve living conditions in the reserves proves that South Africa is changing radically.

However, no official statement can alter the fact that the Bantustan scheme itself is inconsistent with real reform, since it is impossible for these poor enclaves to support economically the 17 million black Africans in South Africa. The fact that the Bantustan chiefs—hitherto regarded as the stooges of the white minority government—are becoming more militant, signals a greater opposition to the government's policy, under which black aspirations for complete equality with the whites can never be fulfilled.

It is not unlikely that, in the not too distant future, the government will face broadly the same situation as Ian Smith in Rhodesia: an increasingly cohesive non-white opposition inside the country, coupled with guerilla movements from outside. Such a development might, of course, be thwarted by more substantial and timely reforms of the apartheid system than those presently conceived of. There are, however, no indications that the South African whites would be prepared voluntarily to give up any basic privileges at this stage.

A policy of reform such as that advocated, for example, by liberal politicians and industrialists might also be counterproductive; it might trigger off stronger action by black South Africans for the total abolition of apartheid. Thus, both inertia and moderate change may be hazardous for the white government.

In the event of the non-white majority being determined to wrest their share of political and economic power, and of the whites being equally determined to reserve this for themselves, a collision is inevitable. At present, however, there is reason to believe that organized black labour may become an important factor promoting change, provided that the government does not bar such a development by means of increasingly oppressive legislation. With a continued lack of response on the part of the government, the prospects of the African opposition demanding revolutionary change will grow. In fact, this development is already incipient. The ANC of South Africa is a more radical movement than it was 10 years ago, and its underground strength inside the country is growing.

It seems unlikely that any Western government could take seriously the South African argument that the preservation of the apartheid system is vital to the survival of the "free world". The real purpose of any foreign action in a future large-scale crisis—presumably a situation of civil insurrection combined with guerilla attacks—would be the protection of financial interests. Such intervention would substantiate the claims of South Africa regarding its importance as a supplier of raw materials (especially uranium and gold) to the West.

The "domino theory", still mentioned in connection with a presumed spread of Communism in Southern Africa, could theoretically be resurrected once again as a basis for Western intervention. This theory, used in the context of Indo-China, was often couched in racial terms, conjuring up the image of helpless Asians who would be lost if left to themselves. But there is reason to conclude that the "domino theory" reflects not only a notion of racial superiority but also big-power arrogance towards smaller nations. This is illustrated by the expectation in the USA that if Portugal becomes Socialist, other West European countries will follow. The Portuguese military junta is not regarded as being sufficiently democratic to be trusted within NATO—a problem which never faced the Caetano regime. Smaller countries are regarded as dominoes in a gigantic children's game, standing or falling only thanks to big-power influence. This simplistic way of thinking omits many aspects of international politics and fails to clarify matters relating to the Third World. (FRELIMO may owe part of its military advances in the past to access to modern Soviet weaponry, but it would be very difficult to show how, whether and to what extent Soviet influence in Southern Africa should have increased after FRELIMO's rise to power in Mozambique.) The arrogance that can be noted in the "domino theory" stems from the belief that purely Western— or US—solutions are the sole answers to political problems anywhere in the world.

One additional pretext for aiding South Africa might be the need to counter a perceived Soviet threat in the Indian Ocean. The South African government has repeatedly offered access to Simonstown to friendly powers.

Such foreign intervention might follow the pattern familiar in Indo-China. In a situation where the white regime considered itself directly threatened, South Africa would ask NATO and the United States for military and manpower aid. It could argue that its position closely resembles that of Indo-China, in that the Communist bloc is already intervening in the region by providing arms and training to the guerillas.

All things considered, however, it is difficult to envisage any course of events that might lead to *direct* military intervention by the Western powers, especially after the experience of Indo-China. The most important lesson from Indo-China was that not even the most modern and powerful weaponry could crush a popular uprising. Some kind of *indirect* intervention to protect the white regime is far more plausible. Such intervention is already taking place, in fact, in Angola, where foreign interests are playing an important role behind the competing nationalist movements. Such methods as using mercenaries and providing clandestine financing and arms to a given nationalist movement with the desired ideological preferences, regardless of its popular support, are well known and documented, not only in Indo-China, but also in Africa—for example, in the Congo Civil War.

The possibilities that foreign pressure might successfully influence the South African government to abolish the apartheid system are very slight, although not negligible. It remains a fact that political denunciations have not and will not have any profound consequences for the South African government so long as economic relations with Western countries remain intact. Business is, however, not an activity conducted over and above politics: the idea that multinational companies operate independently of any governmental restrictions is becoming a latter-day myth, with very little basis in reality. Rather, business and governmental interests often coincide; the politician and the company director may even be one and the same person. Moreover, one can hardly expect commercial companies to be motivated more by humanitarian interests, such as improving labour conditions, than by the desire to increase their own profits. In addition, apartheid is enforced by the law, and no foreign company in South Africa can be expected to break the law single-handedly by, for example, abolishing apartheid in one factory. On the other hand, a firmly motivated government in the West is in the position to work against economic investment in South Africa. The anti-apartheid activities of the United Nations and other international organizations, as well as the activities of individuals and groups in the fields of sports and cultural relations, certainly have some impact on South Africa, which is sensitive to any suggestion that it is not representative of Western civilization.

In the last instance, the key to the future will lie with the black population in the countries concerned. The miserable conditions under which the blacks in Southern Africa live cannot be expected to produce a revolutionary movement unless a way is found to canalize black African demands and unify and organize the separate groups. If this fails to occur, the individuals affected will remain second-class citizens dominated by the rules of apartheid. Furthermore, should African opposition to the prevailing system inside these countries exhaust itself, it will not be possible for outside parties to influence the South African government towards any relaxation of apartheid.

The possibility has also been mentioned that a certain liberalization within South Africa may neutralize black opposition and make it settle for less than complete equality with the whites. This would ultimately lead to the development of a socioeconomically differentiated society in which apartheid had given way, but in which non-whites would still remain second-class citizens even though they would possess the same political rights as whites. This alternative represents more wishful thinking on the part of the privileged class, however, than a realistic assessment of actual conditions. What is at stake is not merely the issue of changing the apartheid system, but how to change it and for the benefit of whom. It is doubtful, considering the poverty and misery imposed on the blacks, that they will be content with limited reforms designed to bolster the economy. It is far more probable that they will seek to eliminate completely the doctrine and practices of white racial supremacy.

Thus, unless substantial concessions are made by the white ruling class, it appears inevitable that South Africa will experience some major upheaval in the not too distant future. Such a conflict may easily escalate, perhaps even transforming Southern Africa into the next international battlefield.

Appendix 1

Arms imports by South Africa, Rhodesia and Portugal, 1950–74

Notes:

In the three arms import registers presented here, the order of presentation is *by supplier,* ranked according to quantitative importance. No difference is made between imported weapons, weapons acquired as military aid or gifts, and licence-produced weapons; all are listed as "imported".

Weapons: Only the four categories of so-called "major weapons" appear in the register. These are aircraft, missiles, armoured vehicles and warships. (An exception is made for Portugal, where *small arms* are entered.) The weapons categories are presented in that order, beginning with aircraft, under each supplier. The separate weapons in each category follow the chronological order of delivery. Light aircraft imported by private customers are not included.

Aircraft: For the description and designation of aircraft, the system used by *Jane's All the World's Aircraft* series is generally applied. This means that the designation of an aircraft begins with the company name: *Lockheed* C-130 Hercules. The company indicated is the present manufacturer, which is not necessarily the original producer of a given item, for example *Aérospatiale* Alouette III, not *Sud-Aviation* Alouette III. For reasons of space the companies are not indicated when the imported weapon has been made as a joint project involving more than one producing country; instead the countries are indicated, for example SA 330 Puma *(Fr/UK),* not *Aérospatiale/Westland* SA 330 Puma.

For licence-produced weapons, the local company and the local designation appear, followed by the original designation, thus: Atlas "Impala I" (Aermacchi M.B. 326). The local name for a weapon is enclosed in quotation marks; the export name is not—thus, HS 125 "Mercurius", but Lockheed C-130 Hercules.

Warships: The system of description and designation used in *Jane's Fighting Ships* series is generally applied, with the exception that "vessel" and "launch" have been replaced by "ship" and "boat" in order to be consistent. The name of the vessel, when available, follows the class.

Armoured vehicles and missiles: Description and designation follow the system used in the *Military Balance* series.

Weapons in use in 1974: This is indicated after each entry for aircraft, missiles and armoured vehicles. All warships are in service unless otherwise noted. For *missiles* there is very little information on the actual *number* imported or in service.

For *Portugal,* the 1974 inventory includes a few ships imported before 1950. These were not entered into the register for reasons of consistency.

The actual number of aircraft, missiles and armoured vehicles in service in 1974 is smaller than indicated in the registers, as weapons lost in combat are not all accounted for. As stated in the text, it is possible that the air forces of Guinea-Bissau and Mozambique were practically wiped out by April 1974. The Rhodesian Air Force has also lost some planes in anti-guerilla operations. Because of lack of confirmation of the exact numbers, these losses are not deleted from the registers.

Abbreviations and conventions

Abbreviations

AA	=Anti-aircraft (guns and cannon)
AC	=Armoured car
AAM	=Air-to-air missile
APC	=Armoured personnel carrier
ASM	=Air-to-surface missile
ASW	=Antisubmarine warfare
ATM	=Anti-tank missile
batt	=Batteries (of missiles)
COIN	=Counterinsurgency
Disp: 00 t	=Displacement, in tons standard for surface warships, tons surface for submarines
Ex-UK	=Weapon in service before being sold, refurbished
MAP	=Military Assistance Program
MDAP	=United States Mutual Defense Assistance Program
mil.	=Military
Mk	=Mark, refers to production version of a given weapon
recce	=Reconnaissance
R&D	=Research and Development
SAM	=Surface-to-air missile
SSM	=Surface-to-surface missile

Conventions

..	=Not available
( )	=Our estimate
$00 mn	=Import price paid
u.c.	=Unit cost (import price)
3+	=More than three
≈	=Approximately

206

Register 1. South Africa: major arms imports, 1950–75

The first United Nations resolution calling for an arms embargo on South Africa was passed in August 1963.

Supplier	Delivery date	Number	Designation	Comment
UK	**Aircraft**			
	1952–54	50 / 27	HS Vampire FB.5 fighter / HS Vampire T.55 trainer	Some remained in service in 1974 as trainers
	(1955)	(5)	Auster A.O.P. 9 monoplane	Not in service 1974
	(1955)	9	HS 104 Devon C Mk 1 light transport	Not in service 1974
	(1955)	2	HS 114 Heron transport	Not in service 1974
	1957	8	HS Avro 696 Shackleton Mk 3 maritime recce/bomber	7 in service 1974; due for replacement
	(1959)	1	Vickers Viscount 781 transport	In service 1974
	1962	6	BAC Canberra B(I) Mk 12 bomber	All in service 1974
	1964	6	Westland Wasp HAS.Mk 1 ASW helicopter	5 lost before 1971
	1965	3	BAC Canberra T.Mk 4 trainer	Refurbished; all in service 1974
	1965	16	HS Buccaneer S. Mk 50 strike/bomber	Remaining 10 grounded 1973; to be replaced by Mirage
	1966	4	Westland Wasp HAS.Mk 1 ASW helicopter	5 lost before 1971 of 10 supplied
	1969	4	HS 125 "Mercurius" transport	3 lost in accident 1970
	1971	3	HS 125 "Mercurius" transport	Replacement for 3 lost; 4 in service 1974
	1973–74	6	Westland Wasp HAS.Mk 1 ASW helicopter	Ordered 1971; delivery of 7th Wasp stopped by Labour government 1974; total of 11 Wasps in service 1974
	Armoured vehicles			
	(1950)	(40)	Comet medium tank	20 in service 1974
	1955–59	(168)	Centurion Mk 5 main battle tank	100 sold to Switzerland 1960–61
	(1956–60)	250	Saracen APC	All in service 1974
	(1963–64)	(60)	Ferret AC	50 in service 1974
	Warships			
	1950	1	Destroyer, "W"-class: "Jan van Riebeeck"	Displ: 2 105 t; launched 1943; modernized 1964–66
	1952	1	Destroyer, "W"-class: "Simon van der Stel"	Displ: 2 105 t; launched 1943; modernized 1962–64
	1954	1	Seaward defence ship, "Ford"-class: "Gelderland"	Displ: 120 t; ex-UK
	1955	1	Seaward defence ship, "Ford"-class: "Nautilus"	Displ: 120 t; ex-UK
	1955	1	Escort minesweeper	
	1955–59	10	Coastal minesweeper, "Ton"-class	Displ: 360 t; new; armed with Bofors AA-guns
	1956	1	ASW frigate, type 15: "Vrystaat"	Displ: 2 160 t; completed 1944; armed with Bofors AA-guns
	(1961–62)	3	Seaward defence ship, "Ford"-class	Displ: 120 t; new
	1963	2	ASW frigate, type 12, "President"-class: "President Kruger", "President Steyn"	Displ: 2 144 t; launched 1960–61, refitted 1969 and 1971 to carry 1 Wasp helicopter; ex-"Whitby"-class; armed with Bofors AA-guns
	1964	1	Frigate, "President"-class: "President Pretorius"	Displ: 2 144 t; launched 1962, ex-"Whitby"-class; armed with Bofors AA-guns
	1972	1	Survey ship, "Hecla"-class: "Protea"	Displ: 1 930 t; new; replacement for "Loch"-class frigate "Natal", sunk in 1972; carries 1 helicopter

207

Supplier	Delivery date	Number	Designation	Comment
France	**Aircraft**			
	1962	7	Aérospatiale Alouette II helicopter	6 in service 1974
	1964	16	Dassault Mirage III-C all-weather interceptor/ground attack fighter	Arms: Matra R. 530 AAM; all in service 1974
	1965–66	54	Aérospatiale Alouette III helicopter	62 in service 1974
	1965–66	20	Dassault Mirage III-E long-range fighter-bomber/intruder version	Arms: AS 20/30 ASM; all in service 1974
	1966	4	Dassault Mirage III-R recce version of III-E	All in service 1974
	1966–67	16	Aérospatiale Super Frelon multi-purpose helicopter	$ 30 mn; 15 in service 1974
	1968	16	Aérospatiale Alouette III helicopter	62 in service 1974
	1968	3	Dassault Mirage III-B trainer, 2-seater version of III-A pre-series aircraft	All in service 1974
	1969–70	9	Transall C-160 (Fr/FRG) transport	$ 33 mn; all in service 1974
	1970	3	Aérospatiale Alouette III helicopter	62 in service 1974
	1970–71	20	SA 330 Puma (Fr/UK) transport helicopter	$ 27 mn; all in service 1974
	1971	1	Dassault Mirage III, version unknown	Replacement
	1973	4	Dassault Mirage III-D trainer, 2-seater version of III-E	All in service 1974
	1974	18	Dassault Mirage III-E fighter-bomber	Follow-up order mid-1972
	(1975–)	16	Dassault Mirage F1-C all-weather interceptor	First of 1971 licence prod. agreement for possibly 100+ units; all French-built; delivery to start 1975
	. .	32	Dassault Mirage F1-A ground-attack fighter	Second of 1971 licence prod. agreement; some components to be built by Atlas; first Atlas-produced F1 to be completed in 1977
	Missiles			
	1963	(96)	Matra R.530 AAM	$ 4 mn; to arm Mirage III-C
	1965–66	(60)	Nord AS.20 and AS.30 ASM	To arm Mirage III-E
	(1966)	. .	Aérospatiale AS.11 AT missile	To arm 6 Wasp helicopters
		. .	Aérospatiale Entac AT missile	To arm Panhard APCs
	1971–73	3 batt	Matra/Thomson-CSF "Cactus" mobile SAM system	Pre-production types; deployed along border with Mozambique; produced in France to South African specifications; R&D financed to 85% by South Africa
	(1975–)	. .	Matra R.550 Magic AAM	To arm Mirage F1
	(1975)	. .	Milan (Fr/FRG) portable ATM	Ordered early 1974; South Africa one of first customers
	1977	. .	Aérospatiale AM.39 Exocet air-launched AS missile	To arm Super Frelon helicopters; order 1974
	Armoured vehicles			
	1963	. .	Panhard AML-60 and AML-90 AC	Prior to licence production
	1966–74	≈800	"Eland" AC (Panhard AML 60/90)	In service 1974; current licence production possibly up to a total of 1 000 units; incl. second generation with locally-built engine

Supplier	Delivery date	Number	Designation	Comment
	Warships			
	1970–72	3	Submarine, "Daphne" type: "Emily Hobhouse", "Johanna van der Merwe", "Maria van Riebeeck"	Displ: 850 t; $ 37.8 mn; new
		1	Submarine, "Daphne" type	Under construction 1973; unconfirmed
	1978	2	"Agosta"-class submarine	Displ: 1 200 t; u.c. $30.7 mn; order 1975
USA	**Aircraft**			
	(1950)	(5)	Lockheed P-2V Neptune maritime recce/bomber	Not in service 1974
	1955	4	Sikorsky S-51 helicopter	Not in service 1974
	(1955)	23	Douglas C-47 transport	Mil. version of DC-3; all in service 1974
	(1956)	3	Sikorsky S-55 helicopter	Not in service 1974
	(1958)	2	Sikorsky S-55 helicopter	Not in service 1974
	1962	25	Cessna 185 Skywagon multi-purpose monoplane	Assigned to Army and Citizen Force; to be replaced by AM.3C from 1975
	1963	7	Lockheed C-130B Hercules transport	All in service 1974
	1965	1	Cessna 320 Skynight multipurpose monoplane	Not in service 1974
	1966	12	Cessna 185 Skywagon multipurpose monoplane	Assigned to Army and Citizen Force; to be replaced by AM.3C from 1975
	1966	5	Douglas C-54 transport	Mil. version of DC-4; all in service 1974
		. .	Helicopters and recce aircraft	USA decided to sell in 1974, acc. to *Rand Daily Mail*, 17 September 1974
	Missiles			
	(1956)	200	AIM-9 Sidewinder AAM	To arm Sabre fighters; not in service 1974
	Armoured vehicles			
	(1957–58)	50	M-3 AC	All in service 1974
	(1973–74)	≈100	V-150 Commando APC	Unconfirmed
Italy	**Aircraft**			
	1967	12	AL.60F5 (USA/It) light-utility transport	Resold to Rhodesia same year
	1967–73	234	Atlas "Impala I" (Aermacchi M.B. 326) trainer/light-attack	Licence production; 16 delivered complete and 40 in subassembly form 1967, replacing 100 Harvard trainers supplied by UK before 1950; all in service 1974
	1969	9	Piaggio P.166S "Albatross" search and surveillance version of P.166 light transport	All in service 1974
	1974	50	Atlas "Impala II" (M.B. 326 K) light-strike version of M.B. 326	First of licence production agreement; 6 delivered complete, 15 as knocked-down parts, rest as partly-finished components; total programme may be 100+
	1974–	40	Aeritalia AM.3C general-purpose monoplane	U.c. ≈ $120 000, fully equipped; ordered 1972, delivery delayed, ex-factory; to replace Cessna 185

Supplier	Delivery date	Number	Designation	Comment
	(1975)	11	Piaggio P.166S search and surveillance version of P. 166 light transport	Ordered 1972
	(1975	. .	Atlas "Kudu" (AL.60C5) light-utility transport	Licence production)
	1975	40	Atlas "Bosbok" (Aeritalia AM.3C) general purpose monplane	Licence production; being supplied in component form for local assem order 1971
Argentina	**Aircraft**			
	. .	. .	FMA IA 58 Pucará COIN fighter	May order; first production model flew in 1974 and was inspected by a South African team
Canada	**Aircraft**			
	1956–61	40	Canadair CL-13B Sabre Mk 6 (USA/Can) fighter-interceptor	36 delivered in 1956; no information on deployment in 1974; unconfirmed report of replacement by 36 new Mirage IIIs in 1973
Denmark	**Warships**			
	1965	1	Tanker "Tafelberg"	Displ: 12 500 t; launched 1958; carries helicopters
FR Germany	**Aircraft**			
	(1958)	2	Dornier Do 27 B general-purpose monoplane	Not in service 1974
	1972	. .	MBB BO 105 helicopter	
FR Germany /Portugal	**Warships**	6	Corvette "João Coutinho"-class	Displ: 1 250 t; ordered 1970; known as Project "Taurus"; to be built in Portugal on FRG licence; missile-equipped; may have been cancelled after April 1974 change of regime in Portugal
Israel	**Missiles**			
	1974–	. .	Gabriel SS missile	Order announced mid-1974; to equip 4 ships
	Armoured vehicles			
	1962	(32)	Centurion Mk 5 main battle tank	Ex-UK; 100 in service 1974
	Warships			
	. .	. .	"SAAR"-class fast missile boat	May order if UK turns down new request for ships
Jordan	**Missiles**			
	1974	717	Tigercat SAM system	Delivery incl. 555 combat missiles, 162 practice missiles, launchers, maintenance equipment; resale to Rhodesia expected; ex-UK
	Armoured vehicles			
	1974	41	Centurion main battle tank	Resale to Rhodesia expected; ex-UK, refurbished

Register 2. Rhodesia: major arms imports, 1950–74

This register includes arms originally imported by the Central African Federation and transferred to Southern Rhodesia in 1963. When Rhodesia declared its independence from Britain in 1965 (UDI), Britain imposed economic sanctions, also covering the supply of arms to Rhodesia. In 1968, the UN Security Council in its Resolution 253 imposed comprehensive mandatory sanctions on Rhodesia, amounting to a complete international trade ban, covering also the transfer of arms.

Supplier	Delivery date	Number	Designation	Comment
UK	**Aircraft**			
	1951–54	19	Supermarine Spitfire F. 22 fighter	Not in service 1974; ex-UK
	1953–55	32	HS Vampire FB.9 fighter and T11 trainer	9 FB.9 and 15 T.55 in service 1974
	1954	13	BAC Provost T.52 trainer/recce	12 in service 1974
	1956	8	Douglas C-47 transport	Mil. version of the DC-3 transport; 4 transferred to Zambia 1964; 4 in service 1974; ex-UK
	1959	30	BAC Canberra B.2 bomber	1 squad. returned to UK in 1963; 6 in service 1974
	1959	3	BAC Canberra T.4 trainer version of B.2	All in service 1974
	(1961)	1	Beechcraft Baron B.55 trainer	In service 1974 as instrument trainer; ex-USA
	1963	12	HS Hunter FGA. 9 ground-attack fighter	All in service 1974; ex-UK
	Armoured vehicles			
	(1960)	30	Ferret AC	20 in service 1974
South Africa	**Aircraft**			
	1967	12	AL.60F5 "Trojan" (USA/It.) light-utility transport	Imported from Italy to South Africa and resold to Rhodesia; 7 in service 1974
	Armoured vehicles			
	1973	(20)	"Eland" AC	French Panhard AML 60/90 version produced under licence in South Africa; all in service 1974
France	**Aircraft**			
	1962	5	Aérospatiale Alouette III helicopter	All in service 1974
	1963	3	Aérospatiale Alouette III helicopter	All in service 1974
Venezuela	**Aircraft**			
		28	Fiat/NAA F-86K Sabre fighter	Government offered to purchase; ex-FRG; negotiations denied by Venezuelan government

Register 3. Portugal: major arms imports, 1950–74

After the Angolan uprising in 1961, a number of NATO countries, including the USA and the UK, demanded assurances from Portugal that military equipment supplied would not be used in Africa. The United Nations Security Council Resolution of 31 July 1963 requested member states to prevent the sale and supply of arms—except for NATO defence purposes—to Portugal.

Supplier	Delivery date	Number	Designation	Comment
USA	**Aircraft**			
	1951–61	40	Douglas C-47 transport	20 in service 1974, for training and general transport duties in Africa
	1951–70	≈290	NA T-6G Texan-armed COIN fighter/trainer	Procured from various sources incl. USA; 35 based in Portugal for use as trainers; rest in Africa for COIN; only 40 remained in service in 1974
	1952	8	Lockheed T-33A trainer	Gift; 13 in service 1974; based in Portugal; used for advanced training
	1952–53	≈80	Republic F-84G Thunderjet fighter/bomber	MDAP delivery; due for replacement by 1974, when 25 remained based in Portugal; rest used in Africa
	1955–57	3+	Boeing SB-176 Fortress search and rescue plane	Not in service 1974; based on the Azores
	1955–57	. .	Grumman SA-16A Albatross search and rescue plane	Not in service 1974
	1955–57	. .	Sikorsky H-19A Chickasaw search and rescue helicopter	Not in service 1974
	1956	42	Lockheed PV-2 Harpoon light bomber	MDAP delivery; ex-Netherlands; based in Angola; 10 in service 1974
	(1958)	14	Douglas HC-54 D/E search and rescue plane	All in service 1974; based on the Azores
	1958–66	65	NA F-86F Sabre fighter-interceptor	Delivered for NATO defence area; 18 in service 1974; based in Portugal
	(1958)	16	Lockheed T-33A trainer	13 in service 1974; based in Portugal
	1958	11	Douglas DC-6 A/B transport	10 in service 1974; for long-range transport duties in Africa
	1958	27	Piper L-21 Super Cub monoplane	For liaison in Africa; not all remained in service 1974
	1960–61	12	Lockheed P2V-5 Neptune maritime recce/bomber	MAP delivery; ex-Netherlands; 8 in service 1974, attached to NATO for Portugal's commitment to the organization: maritime reconnaissance
	1963–64	30	Cessna T-37C trainer	25 in service 1974; based in Portugal; 18 supplied as gift
	1965	5	Douglas C-54 transport	All in service 1974; used in Africa
	1966	7	Douglas B-26 Invader light bomber	Illegal transfer; 13 seized by US government before delivery; 6 in service 1974, based in Portugal
	1971	2	Boeing 707-320C long-range transport	In service 1974; on loan from civilian airline to air force for airlift of troops to Africa; u.c. $9.2 mn
	Armoured vehicles			
	(1955)	. .	M-16 half-track APC	In service 1974
	(1955)	. .	M-4 medium tank	In service 1974

Supplier	Delivery date	Number	Designation	Comment
	Small arms			
	1968	≃1 000	155-mm guns	
	Warships			
	1953	2	Destroyer escort	Displ: 1 700 t; loan, extended 1967; no information on status 1974
	1953–54	5	Coastal minesweeper, "Ponta Delgada"-class	Displ: 375 t; ex-USA
	1955	3	Coastal minesweeper, "Ponta Delgada"-class	Displ: 375 t; ex-USA
	1955	4	Ocean minesweeper, "S. Jorge"-class	MDAP delivery; new
	1957	2	Fast frigate, "Diogo Cao"-class	Both discarded in 1968
	1959	1	Medium landing ship, "LSM"-class	Displ: 743 t; completed 1944
	1966–68	3	Fast frigate, "Almirante Pereira da Silva"-class	Licence-built by LISNAVE; launched 1961 and 1962; armed with 2 Bofors mortars
	1972	1	Survey ship, ex-"Kellar"-class	Displ: 1 200 t; completed 1969; on loan
France	**Aircraft**			
	1957	3	Aérospatiale Alouette II helicopter	20 in service 1974; about 5 based in Africa
	1958–63	21	Aérospatiale Alouette II helicopter	20 in service 1974; about 5 based in Africa
	1960	6	N. 2502 Noratlas transport	20 in service 1974; civilian version refitted into military transport by Nord Aviation; used in Africa
	1960	4	Max Holste Broussard light plane	All in use in 1974, for liaison in Africa
	1960	(4–6)	Junker JU-52 transport	Not in service 1974; for use in Africa
	1962	6	N. 2502 Noratlas transport	20 in service 1974; used in Africa
	1963–68	54	Aérospatiale Alouette III helicopter	80 in service 1974; AS. 11 and AS. 12 missiles; 60 based in Angola
	1970–71	12	SA 330 Puma (Fr/UK) transport helicopter	11 in service 1974; based in Africa
	1970–72	62	Aérospatiale Alouette III helicopter	80 in service 1974; armed with AS. 11 and AS. 12 missiles; 60 based in Angola
	. .	. .	Aérospatiale Alouette III helicopter	On order 1974, possibly as replacement for shot-down units
	. .	. .	SA 330 Puma (Fr/UK) transport helicopter	
	Missiles			
	1963–72	(400)	AS. 11 and AS. 12 ASM	To arm the ≃130 Alouette III helicopters, purchased 1963–72
	Armoured vehicles			
	(1960–64)	. .	Panhard AML-60 AC	Used in Angola in 1961; in service 1974
	(1966–70)	(100)	Panhard AML-60 AC	First appeared in Guinea-Bissau 1966; in service 1974
	. .	. .	EBR-75 AC	In service 1974
	Warships			
	1954–55	3	Patrol boat, "Maio"-class	Displ: 366 t; built in France as US offshore procurement order under MDAP; used in Africa
	1967	1	Submarine, "Albacora"-class: "Albacora"	Displ: 869 t; new; equipped for use in tropical waters. Basically similar to French "Daphne" type

213

Supplier	Delivery date	Number	Designation	Comment
	1967	1	Frigate, "Comandante João Belo"-class: "Comandante João Belo"	Displ: 1 650 t; new; equipped for use in tropical waters
	1968	2	Frigate, "Comandante João Belo"-class	Displ: 1 650 t; new; equipped for use in tropical waters
	1968	1	Submarine, "Albacora"-class: "Barracuda"	Displ: 869 t; new; equipped for use in tropical waters; basically similar to French "Daphne" type
	1969	2	Submarine, "Albacora"-class: "Cachalote" and "Delfim"	Displ: 869 t; new; equipped for use in tropical waters; basically similar to French "Daphne" type
	1969	1	Frigate, "Comandante João Belo"-class	Displ: 1 650 t; new; equipped for use in tropical waters
FR Germany	**Aircraft**			
	1961–64	40	Dornier Do 27 A-4 lightplane/ COIN	25 in service 1974 for liaison; ex-Bundeswehr; used in Africa
	1965–66	36	Fiat G. 91 R-4 COIN fighter	All in service 1974; surplus; $10 mn; 18 based in Portugal, 18 in Mozambique and Angola
	(1966)	10	Saro Skeeter helicopter	For Army; no information on status 1974
	1966–68	40	Dornier Do 27 A-4 lightplane/ COIN	25 in service 1974 for liaison; used in Africa
	1969	20	Dornier Do 27 A-4 lightplane/ COIN	25 in service 1974 for liaison; used in Africa
	1970	15+	N. 2501 D Noratlas transport	Surplus; 20 in service 1974; used in Africa
	1970–72	(50)	Dornier Do 27 A-4 lightplane/ COIN	25 in service 1974 for liaison; used in Africa
	Armoured vehicles			
	1961–64	≈100	M-41 light tank	Surplus; purchased via Spain
	1961–68	≈1 000	M-47 Patton medium tank	Surplus; via Italian firm Oto Melara
	Small arms			
	1961	10 000	Uzi submachine-gun	NATO standard weapon; Israeli design
	Warships			
	1961–62	8	Gunboat, "Bellatrix"-class	Displ: 23 t; armed with 1 Oerlikon AA gun
	1968	5	Gunboat, "Bellatrix"-class	Displ: 23 t; armed with 1 Oerlikon AA gun; licence-built in Lisbon
	1970	3	Corvette, "João Coutinho"-class	Displ: 1 252 t; new; $ 40 mn; equipped for tropical waters; carries helicopters
UK	**Aircraft**			
	1956	15	NA Harvard T.3 trainer	Ex-UK; supplied under US MAP; not in service 1974
	1962–67	150	OGMA D.5/160 lightplane/ COIN (Auster D. 5/160)	Licence-production in Portugal; about 75 in service 1974; based in Africa
	Armoured vehicles			
	(1955)	. .	FV-1609 half-track APC	In service 1974
	(1960–61)	. .	Humber Mk IV AC	Used in Angola; in service 1974

214

Supplier	Delivery date	Number	Designation	Comment
	Warships			
	1959	1	Survey ship, "Flower"-class	Displ: 1 020 t; ex-UK frigate; used off Angola and São Tomé
	1959	2	Frigate, "Alvares Cabral"-class: "Alvares Cabral" and "Pacheco Pereira"	Displ: 1 600 t; ex-UK "Bay"-class; arrived in Angola 1960 as first units of the Portuguese African Navy
	1959	1	Patrol boat, "Antares"-class: "Antares"	Displ: 18 t; new; armed with 1 Oerlikon AA-gun; used in Africa
	1961	2	Frigate, "Alvares Cabral"-class: "D. Francisco de Almeida" and Vasco da Gama	Displ: 1 600 t; ex-UK "Bay"-class; used off Mozambique and Angola since 1962
	1962	1	Patrol boat, "Antares"-class: "Regulus"	Displ: 18 t; new; armed with 1 Oerlikon AA-gun; licence-built in Portugal; used in Africa
	1966	1	Survey ship, "Afonso de Albuquerque"	Displ: 1 600 t; ex-UK "Bay"-class frigate; completed 1949
Canada	**Aircraft**			
	1952	19	Beechcraft C-45 Expeditor transport	15 in service 1974
	1954	10	DHC Chipmunk trainer	Purchased prior to licence production
	1955–60	76	OGMA Chipmunk trainer (DHC Chipmunk)	Licence production; some in service 1974
Spain	**Aircraft**			
	. .	28	CASA C-212 Aviocar transport	On order 1974
	Warships			
	1970–71	3	Corvette, "João Coutinho"-class	Displ: 1 252 t; new; built in Spain under FRG licence; equipped for tropical waters; carries helicopters
	. .	4	Corvette, "João Roby"-class	Identical with "João Coutinho"-class; ordered in 1971; launched 1973, armed with 2 Bofors AA-guns
	Small arms			
	1961–74	50 000/ year	G-3 (CETME) automatic 7.62 mm rifle	NATO standard weapon; FRG construction of factory; licence production in Portugal
Brazil	**Aircraft**			
	. .	110	Aerotec Uirapuru COIN fighter	Ordered 1971; to be licence produced; 50 to be based in Angola, 30 in Mozambique; may have been cancelled after 1974 coup in Portugal
Italy	**Warships**			
	1957	1	Fast frigate "Pero Escobar"	Displ: 1 250 t; new; US-financed; constructed in Italy to NATO standards; arrived in Angola 1960
South Africa	**Aircraft**			
	1972	1	Douglas DC-3 Dakota transport	Gift to Portuguese armed forces in Mozambique

Source: SIPRI worksheets

Appendix 2

United Nations resolutions bearing upon problems of race conflict in South Africa

Resolution 181 (1963) of 7 August 1963 [S/5386]

The Security Council,

Having considered the question of race conflict in South Africa resulting from the policies of *apartheid* of the Government of the Republic of South Africa, as submitted by the thirty-two African member states,

Recalling its resolution 134 (1960) of 1 April 1960,

Taking into account that world public opinion has been reflected in General Assembly resolution 1761 (XVII) of 6 November 1962, and particularly in its paragraphs 4 and 8,

Noting with appreciation the interim reports adopted on 6 May and 16 July 1963 by the Special Committee on the Policies of *apartheid* of the Government of the Republic of South Africa,

Noting with concern the recent arms build-up by the Government of South Africa, some of which arms are being used in furtherance of that Government's racial policies,

Regretting that some States are indirectly providing encouragement in various ways to the Government of South Africa to perpetuate, by force, its policy of *apartheid,*

Regretting the failure of the Government of South Africa to accept the invitation of the Security Council to delegate a representative to appear before it,

Being convinced that the situation in South Africa is seriously disturbing international peace and security,

1. *Strongly deprecates* the policies of South Africa in its perpetuation of racial discrimination as being inconsistent with the principles contained in the Charter of the United Nations and contrary to its obligations as a Member of the United Nations;

2. *Calls upon* the Government of South Africa to abandon the policies of *apartheid* and discrimination, as called for in Security Council resolution 134 (1960), and to liberate all persons imprisoned, interned or subjected to other restrictions for having opposed the policy of *apartheid;*

3. *Solemnly calls upon* all States to cease forthwith the sale and shipment of arms, ammunition of all types and military vehicles to South Africa;

4. *Requests* the Secretary-General to keep the situation in South Africa under observation and to report to the Security Council by 30 October 1963.

Adopted at the 1056th meeting by 9 votes to none, with 2 abstentions (France, United Kingdom of Great Britain and Northern Ireland).

Decision

At its 1073rd meeting, on 27 November 1963, the Council decided to invite the representatives of India, Liberia, Madagascar, Tunisia and Sierra Leone to participate without vote, in the discussion of the report submitted by the Secretary-General in accordance with resolution 181 (1963) above.

Resolution 182 (1963) of 4 December 1963 [S/5471]

The Security Council,

Having considered the race conflict in South Africa resulting from the policies of *apartheid* of the Government of the Republic of South Africa,

Recalling previous resolutions of the Security Council and of the General Assembly which have dealt with the racial policies of the Government of the Republic of South Africa, and in particular Security Council resolution 181 (1963) of 7 August 1963,

Having considered the Secretary-General's report contained in document S/5438 and addenda,

Deploring the refusal of the Government of the Republic of South Africa, as confirmed in the reply of the Minister of Foreign Affairs of the Republic of South Africa to the Secretary-General received on 11 October 1963 to comply with Security Council resolution 181 (1963) and to accept the repeated recommendations of other United Nations organs,

Noting with appreciation the replies to the Secretary-General's communication to the Member States on the action taken and proposed to be taken by their Governments in the context of paragraph 3 of that resolution, and hoping that all the Member States as soon as possible will inform the Secretary-General about their willingness to carry out the provisions of that paragraph,

Taking note of the reports of the Special Committee on the Policies of *apartheid* of the Government of the Republic of South Africa,

Noting with deep satisfaction the overwhelming support for resolution 1881 (XVIII) adopted by the General Assembly on 11 October 1963,

Taking into account the serious concern of the Member States with regard to the policy of *apartheid,* as expressed in the general debate in the General Assembly as well as in the discussions in the Special Political Committee,

Being strengthened in its conviction that the situation in South Africa is seriously disturbing international peace and security, and strongly deprecating the policies of the Government of South Africa in its perpetuation of racial discrimination as being inconsistent with the principles contained in the Charter of the United Nations and with its obligations as a Member of the United Nations,

Recognizing the need to eliminate discrimination in regard to basic human rights and fundamental freedoms for all individuals within the territory of the Republic of South Africa without distinction as to race, sex, language or religion,

Expressing the firm conviction that the policies of *apartheid* and racial discrimination as practised by the Government of the Republic of South Africa are abhorrent to the conscience of mankind and that therefore a positive alternative to these policies must be found through peaceful means,

1. *Appeals* to all States to comply with the provisions of Security Council resolution 181 (1963) of 7 August 1963;

2. *Urgently requests* the Government of the Republic of South Africa to cease forthwith its continued imposition of discriminatory and repressive measures which are contrary to the principles and purposes of the Charter and which are in violation of its obligations as a Member of the United Nations and of the provisions of the Universal Declaration of Human Rights;

3. *Condemns* the non-compliance by the Government of the Republic of South Africa with the appeals contained in the above-mentioned resolutions of the General Assembly and the Security Council;

4. *Again calls upon* the Government of the Republic of South Africa to liberate all persons imprisoned, interned or subjected to other restrictions for having opposed the policy of *apartheid;*

5. *Solemnly calls upon* all States to cease forthwith the sale and shipment of equipment and materials for the manufacture and maintenance of arms and ammunition in South Africa;

6. *Requests* the Secretary-General to establish under his direction and reporting to him a small group of recognized experts to examine methods of resolving the present situation in South Africa through full, peaceful and orderly application of human rights and fundamental freedoms to all inhabitants of the territory as a whole, regardless of race, colour or creed, and to consider what part the United Nations might play in the achievement of that end;

7. *Invites* the Government of the Republic of South Africa to avail itself of the assistance of this group in order to bring about such peaceful and orderly transformation;

8. *Requests* the Secretary-General to continue to keep the situation under observation and to report to the Security Council such new developments as may occur and in any case, not later than 1 June 1964, on the implementation of the present resolution.

Adopted unanimously at the 1078th meeting.

Appendix 3

*United Nations embargo against exports
to Southern Rhodesia*

Resolution 253 (1968) of 29 May 1968

The Security Council,

Recalling and reaffirming its resolutions 216 (1965) of 12 November 1965, 217 (1965) of 20 November 1965, 221 (1966) of 9 April 1966, and 232 (1966) of 16 December 1966,

Taking note of resolution 2262 (XXII) adopted by the General Assembly on 3 November 1967,

Noting with great concern that the measures taken so far have failed to bring the rebellion in Southern Rhodesia to an end,

Reaffirming that, to the extent not superseded in this resolution, the measures provided for in resolutions 217 (1965) of 20 November 1965 and 232 (1966) of 16 December 1966, as well as those initiated by Member States in implementation of those resolutions, shall continue in effect,

Gravely concerned that the measures taken by the Security Council have not been complied with by all States and that some States, contrary to resolution 232 (1966) of the Security Council and to their obligations under Article 25 of the Charter of the United Nations, have failed to prevent trade with the illegal régime in Southern Rhodesia,

Condemning the recent inhuman executions carried out by the illegal régime in Southern Rhodesia which have flagrantly affronted the conscience of mankind and have been universally condemned,

Affirming the primary responsibility of the Government of the United Kingdom to enable the people of Southern Rhodesia to achieve self-determination and independence, and in particular their responsibility for dealing with the prevailing situation,

Recognizing the legitimacy of the struggle of the people of Southern Rhodesia to secure the enjoyment of their rights as set forth in the Charter of the United Nations and in conformity with the objectives of General Assembly resolution 1514 (XV) of 14 December 1960,

Reaffirming its determination that the present situation in Southern Rhodesia constitutes a threat to international peace and security,

Acting under Chapter VII of the Charter of the United Nations,

1. *Condemns* all measures of political repression, including arrests, detentions, trials and executions which violate fundamental freedoms and rights of the people of Southern Rhodesia, and calls upon the Government

of the United Kingdom to take all possible measures to put an end to such actions;

2. *Calls upon* the United Kingdom as the administering Power in the discharge of its responsibility to take urgently all effective measures to bring to an end the rebellion in Southern Rhodesia, and enable the people to secure the enjoyment of their rights as set forth in the Charter of the United Nations and in conformity with the objectives of General Assembly resolution 1514 (XV);

3. *Decides* that, in furtherance of the objective of ending the rebellion, all States Members of the United Nations shall prevent:

(*a*) The import into their territories of all commodities and products originating in Southern Rhodesia and exported therefrom after the date of this resolution (whether or not the commodities or products are for consumption or processing in their territories, whether or not they are imported in bond and whether or not any special legal status with respect to the import of goods is enjoyed by the port or other place where they are imported or stored);

(*b*) Any activities by their nationals or in their territories which would promote or are calculated to promote the export of any commodities or products from Southern Rhodesia; and any dealings by their nationals or in their territories in any commodities or products originating in Southern Rhodesia, and exported therefrom after the date of this resolution, including in particular any transfer of funds to Southern Rhodesia for the purposes of such activities or dealings;

(*c*) The shipment in vessels or aircraft of their registration or under charter to their nationals, or the carriage (whether or not in bond) by land transport facilities across their territories of any commodities or products originating in Southern Rhodesia and exported therefrom after the date of this resolution;

(*d*) The sale or supply by their nationals or from their territories of any commodities or products (whether or not originating in their territories, but not including supplies intended strictly for medical purposes, educational equipment and material for use in schools and other educational institutions, publications, news material and, in special humanitarian circumstances, food-stuffs) to any person or body in Southern Rhodesia, or to any other person or body for the purposes of any business carried on in or operated from Southern Rhodesia, and any activities by their nationals or in their territories which promote or are calculated to promote such sale or supply;

(*e*) The shipment in vessels or aircraft of their registration, or under charter to their nationals, or the carriage (whether or not in bond) by land transport facilities across their territories of any such commodities or products which are consigned to any person or body in Southern Rhodesia, or to any other person or body for the purposes of any business carried on in or operated from Southern Rhodesia;

4. *Decides* that all States Members of the United Nations shall not make available to the illegal régime in Southern Rhodesia or to any commercial, industrial or public utility undertaking, including tourist enterprises, in Southern Rhodesia any funds, for investment or any other financial or economic resources and shall prevent their nationals and any persons within their territories from making available to the régime or to any such undertaking any such funds or resources and from remitting any other funds to persons or bodies within Southern Rhodesia, except payments exclusively for pensions or for strictly medical, humanitarian or educational purposes or for the provision of news material and in special humanitarian circumstances, food-stuffs;

5. *Decides* that all States Members of the United Nations shall:

(*a*) Prevent the entry into their territories, save on exceptional humanitarian grounds, of any person travelling on a Southern Rhodesian passport, regardless of its date of issue, or on a purported passport issued by or on behalf of the illegal régime in Southern Rhodesia;

(*b*) Take all possible measures to prevent the entry into their territories of persons whom they have reason to believe to be ordinarily resident in Southern Rhodesia and whom they have reason to believe to have furthered or encouraged, or to be likely to further or encourage, the unlawful actions of the illegal régime in Southern Rhodesia or any activities which are calculated to evade any measure decided upon in this resolution or resolution 232 (1966) of 16 December 1966;

6. *Decides* that all States Members of the United Nations shall prevent airline companies constituted in their territories and aircraft of their registration or under charter to their nationals from operating to or from Southern Rhodesia and from linking up with any airline company constituted or aircraft registered in Southern Rhodesia;

7. *Decides* that all States Members of the United Nations shall give effect to the decisions set out in operative paragraphs 3, 4, 5 and 6 of this resolution notwithstanding any contract entered into or licence granted before the date of this resolution;

8. *Calls upon* all States Members of the United Nations or of the specialized agencies to take all possible measures to prevent activities by their nationals and persons in their territories promoting, assisting or encouraging emigration to Southern Rhodesia, with a view to stopping such emigration;

9. *Requests* all States Members of the United Nations or of the specialized agencies to take all possible further action under Article 41 of the Charter to deal with the situation in Southern Rhodesia, not excluding any of the measures provided in that Article;

10. *Emphasized* the need for the withdrawal of all consular and trade representation in Southern Rhodesia, in addition to the provisions of operative paragraph 6 of resolution 217 (1965);

11. *Calls upon* all States Members of the United Nations to carry out these decisions of the Security Council in accordance with Article 25 of the Charter of the United Nations and reminds them that failure or refusal by any one of them to do so would constitute a violation of that Article;

12. *Deplores* the attitude of States that have not complied with their obligations under Article 25 of the Charter, and censures in particular those States which have persisted in trading with the illegal régime in defiance of the resolutions of the Security Council, and which have given active assistance to the régime;

13. *Urges* all States Members of the United Nations to render moral and material assistance to the people of Southern Rhodesia in their struggle to achieve their freedom and independence;

14. *Urges,* having regard to the principles stated in Article 2 of the Charter of the United Nations, States not Members of the United Nations to act in accordance with the provisions of the present resolution;

15. *Requests* States Members of the United Nations, the United Nations Organization, the specialized agencies, and other international organizations in the United Nations system to extend assistance to Zambia as a matter of priority with a view to helping it solve such special economic problems as it may be confronted with arising from the carrying out of these decisions of the Security Council;

16. *Calls upon* all States Members of the United Nations, and in particular those with primary responsibility under the charter for the maintenance of international peace and security, to assist effectively in the implementation of the measures called for by the present resolution;

17. *Considers* that the United Kingdom as the administering Power should ensure that no settlement is reached without taking into account the views of the people of Southern Rhodesia, and in particular the political parties favouring majority rule, and that it is acceptable to the people of Southern Rhodesia as a whole;

18. *Calls upon* all States Members of the United Nations or of the specialized agencies to report to the Secretary-General by 1 August 1968 on measures taken to implement the present resolution;

19. *Requests* the Secretary-General to report to the Security Council on the progress of the implementation of this resolution, the first report to be made not later than 1 September 1968;

20. *Decides* to establish, in accordance with rule 28 of the provisional rules of procedure of the Security Council, a committee of the Security Council to undertake the following tasks and to report to it with its observations:

(*a*) To examine such reports on the implementation of the present resolution as are submitted by the Secretary-General;

(*b*) To seek from any States Members of the United Nations or of the specialized agencies such further information regarding the trade of that state (including information regarding the commodities and products exempted from the prohibition contained in operative paragraph 3 (*d*) above) or regarding any acitivities by any nationals of that State or in its territories that may constitute an evasion of the measures decided upon in this resolution as it may consider necessary for the proper discharge of its duty to report to the Security Council;

21. *Requests* the United Kingdom, as the administering Power, to give maximum assistance to the committee, and to provide the committee with any information which it may receive in order that the measures envisaged in this resolution and resolution 232 (1966) may be rendered fully effective;

22. *Calls upon* all States Members of the United Nations, or of the specialized agencies, as well as the specialized agencies themselves, to supply such further information as may be sought by the Committee in pursuance of this resolution;

23. *Decides* to maintain this item on its agenda for further action as appropriate in the light of developments.

Adopted unanimously at the 1428th meeting.

Appendix 4

Selected bibliography

Reference works and annuals

Africa South of the Sahara (London, Europa Publications Ltd., annual).

African Encyclopedia (London, Oxford University Press, 1974).

A Reference Volume on the African Continent (London, *Africa Magazine*, 1973).

A Survey of Race Relations in South Africa (Johannesburg, South African Institute of Race Relations, annual).

Legum, C. *et al.*, eds., *Africa Contemporary Record: Annual Survey and Documents 1969–1970* (London, Africa Research Ltd., 1970).

Legum, C. *et al.*, eds., *Africa Contemporary Record: Annual Survey and Documents 1973–1974* (London, Rex Collings, 1974).

Paxton, J., ed., *The Statesman's Year-Book* (London, The Macmillan Press Ltd., annual).

The Military Balance (London, International Institute for Strategic Studies [IISS], annual).

World Armaments and Disarmament: SIPRI Yearbook (Stockholm, Almqvist & Wiksell, Stockholm International Peace Research Institute, annual).

Africa Research Bulletin (Exeter, England, Africa Research Ltd., monthly).

Africa Diary (New Delhi, India, Africa Publications, weekly).

"Africa", An international business, economic and political monthly (London, *Africa Journal*).

Facts and Reports, Press cuttings on Angola, Mozambique, Guinea-Bissau, Portugal and Southern Africa (Amsterdam, The Angola Committee, biweekly).

Sechaba, Official organ of the African National Congress—South Africa (London, quarterly).

X-Ray, Current Affairs in Southern Africa (London, The Africa Bureau, monthly).

"PAIGC actualités", Information bulletin of the PAIGC (Conakry and Dakar, monthly).

Special reports

Almanac of World Military Power, 2nd ed. (New York and London, R. R. Bowker Co., 1972).

Angola: Secret Government Documents on Counter-Subversion, Annexes: *Vatican-Portuguese Documentation* (Rome, IDOC International, 1974).

Anti-Apartheid Movement, Annual Report, September 1971 – August 1972 (London, 1972).

Cunene Dam Scheme (Geneva, World Council of Churches WCC Programme to Combat Racism, 1971).

"Militär in Afrika", *Afrika Spectrum 1/1971* (Hamburg, 1971, Deutsches Institut für Afrika-Forschung).

Guerilla Warfare, South African Studies 1 (London, The Publicity and Information Bureau, African National Congress of South Africa, undated).

Nelson Mandela Speaks, South African Studies 4 (London, The Publicity and Information Bureau, African National Congress of South Africa, undated).

Forward to Freedom: Strategy, Tactics and Programme of the African National Congress of South Africa (Morogoro, Tanzania, ANC of South Africa, undated).

"Issues Before the 26th General Assembly", in *International Conciliation* No. 584, September 1971 (Carnegie Endowment for International Peace).

Critical Developments in Namibia, Hearings before the Subcommittee on Africa of the Committee on Foreign Affairs, US House of Representatives, 93rd Congress, 2nd Session, 21 February and 4 April 1974 (Washington, U.S. Government Printing Office, 1974).

Implementation of the US Arms Embargo (Against Portugal and South Africa and Related Issues), Hearings before the Subcommittee on Africa of the Committee on Foreign Affairs, US House of Representatives, 93rd Congress, 1st Session, 20, 22 March, 6 April 1973 (Washington, U.S. Government Printing Office, 1973).

US Business Involvement in Southern Africa, Hearings before the Subcommittee on Africa of the Committee on Foreign affairs, US House of Representatives, 92nd Congress, 1st Session. Part I: 4, 5, 11, 12 May; 2, 3, 15, 16, 30 June and 15 July 1971; Part II: 27 September, 12 November, 6 and 7 December 1971 (Washington, U.S. Government Printing Office, 1972).

White Paper on Defence and Armament Production 1973 (Republic of South Africa, Department of Defence [W.P.D.] 1973).

Racism and Apartheid in South Africa: South Africa and Namibia (Paris, UNESCO Press, 1974).

Arkhurst, F. S., ed., *Arms and African Development,* Proceedings of the First Pan-African Citizens' Conference (New York, Praeger, 1972, Adlai Stevenson Institute of International Affairs).

Bosgra, S. J. and van Krimpen, C., *Portugal and NATO,* (Amsterdam, Angola Committee, 1969).

Bruce, N., "Portugal's African Wars", *Conflict Studies,* No. 34 (London, March, 1973, The Institute for the Study of Conflict [ISC]).

Gutteridge, W., "The Coming Confrontation in Southern Africa", *Conflict Studies,* No. 15 (London, August 1971).

Kende, I., "Guerres locales en Asie, en Afrique et en Amérique Latine (1945–1969)", *Étude sur les pays en voie de développement,* No. 60, 1973 (Budapest, 1973, Centre pour la recherche de l'Afro-Asie de l'Académie des Sciences de Hongrie).

Minty, A. S., *South Africa's Defence Strategy* (London, The Anti-Apartheid Movement, October 1969).

Phillips, V., "The Prospects for Guerilla Warfare in South Africa", *International Relations*, Vol. IV, No. 1, Journal of the David Davies Memorial Institute of International Studies (London, May 1972).

Prasad, D. and Smythe, T., eds., *Conscription. A World Survey: Compulsory Military Service and Resistance to it* (London, War Resisters' International, 1968).

Rogers, B., *South Africa: The Bantu Homelands*, International Defence and Aid Fund Pamphlet (London, 1972).

Secka, Pap-Cheyassin O., "Southern Africa: Action for Peaceful Change", *IPA Reports*, No. 2. An occasional publication of the International Peace Academy (New York, 1972).

Singer, J. D., "The Peace Researcher and Foreign Policy Prediction", *Peace Science Society (International) Papers*, Vol. 21, 1973 (The 3rd Philadelphia Conference, November, 1972).

Stukke, O. and Widstrand, C., eds., *Southern Africa*. The UN-OAU Conference, Oslo, 9–14 April 1973, Parts I–II. (Uppsala, 1973, Scandinavian Institute of African Studies).

Vigne, R., *The Transkei—A South African Tragedy* (London, The Africa Bureau, undated).

Wilkinson, A. R., "*Insurgency in Rhodesia 1957–1973*", (London, IISS, 1973) Adelphi Paper No. 100.

United Nations documents and publications

A Principle in Torment II: The UN- and Portuguese-Administered Territories (New York, Office of Public Information, United Nations, 1970).

A Trust Betrayed: Namibia, (New York, Office of Public Information, United Nations, 1974).

Apartheid in Practice, (New York, Office of Public Information, United Nations, 1971).

Foreign Economic Interests and Decolonization, A Report (New York, Office of Public Information, United Nations, 1969).

Foreign Investment in the Republic of South Africa, Unit on Apartheid, Department of Political and Security Council Affairs, UN Document ST/PSCA/SER. A/11 (New York, United Nations, 1970).

Military and Police Forces in the Republic of South Africa, Unit on Apartheid, Department of Political and Security Council Affairs, UN Document ST/PSCA/SER.A/3, A/AC.115/L.203–204 (New York, United Nations, 1967).

Note on Developments concerning the Implementation of the Arms Embargo against South Africa, Special Committee on Apartheid, UN Document A/AC.115/L.285, 16 March 1971. Mimeographed.

Report of the Special Committee on Apartheid, General Assembly Official Records, 26th Session, Supplement No. 22, (A/8422/Rev. 1), (New York, United Nations, 1971).

Report of the Special Committee on Apartheid, General Assembly Official Records: 27th Session Supplement No. 22, (A/8722), (New York, United Nations, 1972).

Working Paper on Collaboration with the South African Regime by other Governments and Economic and Financial Interests, Special Committee on Apartheid, UN Document A/AC.115/L.290, (18 March 1971, mimeographed).

Books

Race to Power: The Struggle for Southern Africa (New York, Anchor Press, 1964, Africa Research Group).

Abshire, D. M. and Samuels, M. A., *Portuguese Africa: A Handbook* (New York, Praeger, 1969, Center for Strategic and International Studies [CSIS], Georgetown University).

Ahlsén, B., *Portugisiska Afrika: Beskrivning av ett Kolonialimperium och dess sönderfall*, SIDA pocket (Stockholm, Utbildningsförlaget, 1972).

Ahlsén, B., *Sydafrika, Namibia, Rhodesia – Minoritetsstyrda länder i södra Afrika*, SIDA pocket (Stockholm, Utbildningsförlaget, 1973).

de Andrade, M., *La Poésie Africaine d'Expression Portuguaise* (Honfleur, Pierre Jean Oswald, 1969).

de Andrade, M. and Ollivier, M., *La guerre en Angola*. Étude socio-économique (Paris, Cahiers libres 209–210, François Maspero, 1971).

Barratt, J. *et al.*, eds., *Accelerated Development in South Africa* (Pretoria, South African Institute of International Affairs; London, The Macmillan Press Ltd., 1974).

Biermann, H. H. H., ed., *The Case for South Africa*, in the public statements of Eric H. Louw, Foreign Minister of South Africa (New York, MacFadden, 1963).

Cabral, A., *Revolution in Guinea* (London, Stage I, 1969).

Červenka, Z., *Vit mark i Zimbabwe* (Uppsala, The Scandinavian Institute of African Studies, 1974).

Červenka, Z. and Wallensteen, L., eds., *Botswana, Lesotho, Swaziland. Beskrivning av tre U-länder*, SIDA pocket (Stockholm, Utbildningsförlaget, 1973).

Červenka, Z., ed., *Landlocked Countries of Africa* (Uppsala, 1973, The Scandinavian Institute of African Studies).

Chaliand, G., *Lutte armée en Afrique* (Paris, Cahiers libres 101, François Maspero, 1967).

Davidson, G., *In the Eye of the Storm: Angola's People* (London, Longman Group Ltd., 1972).

Davidson, B., *The Liberation of Guiné* (Harmondsworth, UK, Penguin Books, 1969).

First, R., *et al.*, *The South African Connection: Western Investment in Apartheid* (London, Temple Smith, 1972).

Gibson, R., *African Liberation Movements: Contemporary Struggles against White Minority Rule* (Oxford University Press, 1972, Institute of Race Relations, UK).

Grundy, K. W., *Guerilla Struggle in Africa—An Analysis and Preview* (New York, World Law Fund, 1971).

Jaffe, H., *Revolten mot rasismen: Den sydafrikanska diskrimineringen och den nationella befrielserörelsen* (Stockholm, Rabén & Sjögren, 1970). Translated from the Italian.

Larkin, B. D., *China and Africa 1949–1970: The Foreign Policy of the PRC* (Berkeley, Los Angeles, London: University of California Press, 1971).

Magnusson, Å., *Sverige–Sydafrika. En studie av en ekonomisk relation* (Uppsala, 1974, The Scandinavian Institute of African Studies).

Marcum, J., *The Angolan Revolution,* Vol. I: *The Anatomy of an Explosion (1950–1962)*, (Cambridge, Mass., The M.I.T. Press, 1969).

Martin, L., *Arms and Strategy: The World Power Structure Today* (London, McKay, 1973).

Mazrui, A. and Patel, H., eds., *Africa in World Affairs: The Next Thirty Years* (New York, The Third Press, 1973).

Mondlane, E., *The Struggle for Mozambique* (Harmondsworth, UK, Penguin Books, 1969).

Mlambo, E., *Rhodesia: The Struggle for a Birthright* (London, C. Hurst & Co. [Publishers] Ltd., 1972).

Nielsen, W. A., *The Great Powers and Africa* (London, Pall Mall Press, 1969).

Potholm, P. and Dale, R., eds., *Southern Africa in Perspective* (New York, The Free Press, 1972).

Rudebeck, L., *Guinea-Bissau: A Study of Political Mobilization* (Uppsala, 1974, Scandinavian Institute of African Studies).

de Sousa Ferreira, E., *Portuguese Colonialism from South Africa to Europe* (Freiburg, Aktion Dritte Welt, 1972).

de Spinola, A., *Le Portugal et son Avenir* (Paris, Flammarion, 1974).

Venter, H. J,, *Portugal's Guerilla War: The Campaign for Africa* (Cape Town, Malherbe, 1973).

Yost, C. W., *The Conduct and Misconduct of Foreign Affairs* (New York, Random House, 1972).

228

INDEX

France 42 ff., 55, 65 ff., 75, 85, 91, 115, 124 f., 128, 148 f., 163, 174 f., 182; arms supplies to Southern Africa 65, 86 ff., 96, 129, 131 ff., 135, 137, 139, 141, 142 ff., 148 ff., 208, 211, 213

Frente de Libertação de Moçambique (FRELIMO) 7, 9, 21 ff., 45 f., 61 ff., 75 ff., 86, 97 ff., 103 ff., 107, 135, 157, 161, 164 ff., 169, 177, 180, 184 ff., 202

Frente Nacional de Libertação de Angola (FNLA) 19 ff., 61 ff., 73, 86, 96 (fn), 97, 99, 100, 105 f., 169 ff., 172

Frente para a Libertação e Independência da Guiné Portuguesa (FLING) 7, 22

Front for the Liberation of Zimbabwe (FROLIZI) 19 f., 107, 187, 189

Front pour la Libération de l'Enclave de Cabinda (FLEC) 164, 171

Fundação de Oeiras 89

G

Gabon 150
Galvao, Henrique 73
Gambia 15
Gander, Lawrence 178
Gandhi, Mahatma 81
Germany 10, 11, 13, 34, 71, 137
Germany, DR 63
Germany, FR 85, 153; arms supplies to Southern Africa 42 f., 65 ff., 88, 90, 93, 96, 124, 128 ff., 132 ff., 142 ff., 147 ff., 210, 214
Ghana 62
Gibbs, T. 188
Giscard d'Estaing, (President) Valéry 128
Gomes, (General) Francisco da Costa 159 ff., 162 f.
Gonçalves, Vasco 161
Govêrno Revolucionário de Angola no Exilo (GRAE) 20, 99
Greece 163
Grobbelar, A. 186
Grupo Unido de Moçambique (GUMO) 23
Guerilla movements. See liberation movements
Guiné 75
Guinea 15, 32, 44, 63, 98 f., 102 (fn)
Guinea-Bissau 1, 5 f., 11, 44, 49 f., 55, 62 f., 74 f., 86, 91 ff., 95, 98 f., 103, 105, 157, 164 f.; population 14 f., 72; liberation movements in 6, 16 (fn), 22, 61 ff., 74 f., 86 ff., 97, 101 f., 164 ff., 198 f., 206. See also FLING; PAIGC
Gulf Oil 5, 43, 87, 105

H

Herero Council of Chiefs 79
Herstigte Nasionale Party 38, 84

Hoare, (Colonel) Michael 165
Homelands. See Bantustans
Honduras 154

I

IBERLANT (Nato Iberian Atlantic Area Command) 49
India 57 ff., 147 ff.
Indian National Council 29, 39, 179
Indian Ocean 3, 11, 40, 46 ff., 54 ff., 58 ff., 66 ff., 133, 181 f., 202
Indigenas 77
Indonesia 54, 58
Industrial Aid Society 82
Institute for Industrial Education 82
International Atomic Energy Agency (IAEA) 148
International Court of Justice (ICJ) 8, 173, 191
International Labour Organization (ILO) 8
Iran 50, 54 f., 59, 119, 149
Iraq 57 f.
Israel 90, 124, 131, 133, 135, 141, 144, 147, 210; arms supplies to Southern Africa 133, 135, 144
Italy 45, 65 ff., 124, 133, 138 f., 153, 163, 165, 209, 215
Ivory Coast 37

J

Japan 42 ff., 85, 89, 124, 147, 185
Jardim, Jorge 94, 164
Job reservations 34
Johnson, Lyndon 128
Jordan 132, 139, 153, 210

K

Kariba Dam 106
Katanga 165, 171
Kaunda, Kenneth 107, 174, 177, 186 f.
Kennedy, John F. 66, 87, 128
Kenya 6, 172
Kenyatta, Jomo 172
Khama, Seretse 176 f.
Kissinger, Henry 162
Kozolov 56

L

Labour legislation in Namibia 33; Rhodesia 33; South Africa 32 f.
League of Nations 10, 27
Lembede, Anton 17
Lenin, I. 21
Leon, Sonny 179
LeRoux, (Prof.) A. J. A. 143, 146 f.
Lesotho 1, 12, 17, 33, 36, 65, 83, 176, 180

232

Organization of African Unity (OAU) 7, 9,
  37, 61 f., 65, 78, 99 ff., 106 f., 150, 161,
  171 ff., 174, 185 ff., 197; Liberation
  Committee 7, 62 ff., 177, 181, 187; military
  aid to liberation movements 63, 108, 189,
  198 ff.
Organization for Economic Cooperation and
  Development (OECD) 162
Ovambo Peoples Congress 79
Ovamboland Peoples Organization 79, 192 f.
Ovambos 13, 17, 73, 79 f., 192

P

Pakistan 54, 55, 58
Pan-Africanism 62
Pan Africanist Congress of Azania (PAC) 17,
  61, 63, 81 ff., 111, 180 f.
Partido Africano da Independência da Guiné
  e Cabo Verde (PAIGC) 5, 15, 22, 49 f.,
  61 ff., 74 f., 86, 92 f., 96 ff., 100 ff., 102 f.,
  164
PAIGC State Commission of Economy and
  Finance 61, 99, 101
Patricio, Rui 88
Pearce, Commission 78
Pearce, (Lord) 78
Peet, Ray 55
People's Liberation Army of Namibia
  (PLAN) 18, 109
Pereira, Aristides 22
Pereira Leite 168
Peron, Juan 50
Persian Gulf 52 ff.
Philippines 48
Pidgiguiti massacre 74
Pinto-Bull, Benjamin 22
Polarization of forces, concept of 60
Polaroid Corporation 41, 84
Polícia Internacional et de Defensa do Estado
  (PIDE) 5, 23 (fn), 73, 75
Poqo (Pan Africanist Congress) 17, 111
Portugal 1, 5, 8, 11, 13, 14, 16 (fn), 21 ff.,
  26, 30, 32 ff., 36 ff., 40, 43 f., 46, 48 f., 52,
  62, 65, 71 ff., 85, 87, 89 ff., 100, 132, 153,
  157, 162 ff., 197, 202, 210; Armed Forces
  Movement 160 f., 167, 169, 171 ff.; arms
  imports 66, 88 f., 205 ff.; army 75 f., 86 ff.,
  91 ff., 96, 105, 157, 159 ff.; military coup
  1974 1, 9, 21, 36, 64, 78, 85, 87, 96, 108 f.,
  157 ff., 164, 173, 177, 184, 191, 199; military
  expenditure 87, 94 f.
Portuguese Communist Party 19, 160 ff.,
  165 f.
Poverty Datum Line (PDL) 31 f.
Progressive Party 36 ff., 83 f., 178

R

Reagan, Ronald 55
Rehoboth Volksparty 80
Republic of South Africa. See South
  Africa
Reserves. See Bantustans
Rhodes, Cecil 11, 71
Rhodesia 3, 10 ff., 18, 20, 23, 26, 29 ff.,
  33 ff., 38, 40, 43 ff., 64 f., 71, 78 f., 86,
  104, 107, 109 f., 121 f., 126, 142, 152, 157,
  164 f., 168, 173, 175 f., 184, 186 f., 197 f.;
  economic embargo against 8 ff., 66, 71,
  152, 176 ff., 184; arms imports 124 ff.,
  139, 151 ff., 189; military expenditure
  115 ff., 151 ff., 184 ff.; liberation move-
  ments in 6, 18 f., 61 ff., 106 ff., 151, 166 ff.,
  184 ff.; 1965 Unilateral Declaration of
  Independence 11, 19, 23, 65, 78, 106, 151 f.
Rhodesia National Party 64
Rhodesia Party 188
Rhodesian Front Party 23, 38, 64, 107, 152,
  188
Rio Tinto Zinc Corporation (RTZ) 42 f., 84,
  191
Rivonia trial 7, 16, 111
Robben Island 16
Roberto, Holden 19 f., 73, 97, 99 f., 170, 172
Romania 63, 100
Rossing Uranium Mine 13, 42 f., 191
Rwanda-Burundi 6

S

Sadat, M. A. 154
Salazar, Antonio de Oliveira 30, 75 ff., 87,
  163
Samuels, H. J. 137, 139 f.
Santos, Marcelinho dos 7, 21, 75, 104
Savimbi, Jonas 19 f., 172
Schlesinger, James 54
Senegal 15, 22, 62 f., 98, 101, 103
Senghor, Leopold 99
Settlement proposals 78
Seychelles 57
Sharpeville Massacre 6 f., 40, 81, 115, 117
Simeão, Joana 23
Simango, Uria 21
Simonstown 50 f., 125 ff., 132, 176, 181 f.,
  202
Singh, Swaran 58
Sithole, Ndabaningi 19, 186 f.
Smith, Ian 19, 23, 46, 65 f., 78 f., 107, 109,
  186 f., 199 ff.
Soares, Mario 160 ff., 164, 166 ff., 170 f., 184
Somalia 55, 57, 60, 63, 66

V

Venezuela 211
Verligte Aktion 83
Verwoerd, Hendrik 23
Viet-Nam 4, 6, 56, 58, 134, 164, 202 f.
Viljoen, C. L. 182
Vorster, J. B. 12, 23, 35 f., 39, 64, 143, 147,
   169, 173 f., 176 f., 181 f., 192, 196 f., 199 ff.

W

Wedgwood-Benn, Anthony 127
Wet, Jannie de 192
White, Barbara 176
Wilson, (Dr.) Francis 31
Wilson, (Prime Minister) H. 127, 142
Wiriyamu massacre 104, 110
World Council of Churches 8, 45
Wrathall, John 189

Y

Yemen, South 57
Yost, Charles 9

Youth League of Salisbury 18
Yugoslavia 63, 99

Z

Zaire 1, 9, 14, 20, 50, 62, 97, 99 100, 106,
   165, 170 ff.
Zambezi river 9, 13, 45, 64, 107, 108 ff.,
   166, 175, 188
Zambia 1, 3, 9, 11, 13 f., 19 f., 36, 47, 65,
   105 ff., 172, 174 f., 177, 186, 193
ZAMCO consortium 45
Zanzibar 58
Zimbabwe. *See* Rhodesia
Zimbabwe African National Liberation Army
   (ZANLA) 19, 106
Zimbabwe African People's Union (ZAPU)
   18 f., 61, 63 f., 78, 106 ff., 111, 185 ff.
Zimbabwe African National Union (ZANU)
   18 f., 61, 63, 78 f., 104, 106 ff., 166, 185 ff.,
   199
Zimbabwe Liberation Army 19, 106
Zululand 82, 143
Zumwalt, (Admiral) Elmo 54